YOUR LAND
AND MINE

YOUR LAND
AND MINE

Evolution of a Conservationist

EDGAR WAYBURN, M.D.

with ALLISON ALSUP

SIERRA CLUB BOOKS

San Francisco

The Sierra Club, founded in 1892 by John Muir, has devoted itself to the study and protection of the earth's scenic and ecological resources—mountains, wetlands, woodlands, wild shores and rivers, deserts and plains. The publishing program of the Sierra Club offers books to the public as a nonprofit educational service in the hope that they may enlarge the public's understanding of the Club's basic concerns. The point of view expressed in each book, however, does not necessarily represent that of the Club. The Sierra Club has some sixty-five chapters throughout the United States and in Canada. For information about how you may participate in its programs to preserve wilderness and the quality of life, please address inquiries to Sierra Club, 85 Second Street, San Francisco, California 94105, or visit our website at www.sierraclub.org.

Published by Sierra Club Books
85 Second Street, San Francisco, CA 94105
www.sierraclub.org/books

Produced and distributed by
University of California Press
Berkeley, California
University of California Press, Ltd.
London, England
www.ucpress.edu

SIERRA CLUB, SIERRA CLUB BOOKS, and the Sierra Club design logos are registered trademarks of the Sierra Club.

Library of Congress Cataloging-in-Publication Data

Wayburn, Edgar.
    Your land and mine : the evolution of a conservationist / by Edgar Wayburn with Allison Alsup.
        p. cm.
    ISBN 1-57805-090-1 (alk.paper)
    1. Nature conservation—United States—History—20th century. 2. Wayburn, Edgar. I. Title.
QH76.W39 2004
333.72'0973—dc22   2004041665

Printed in the United States of America on New Leaf Ecobook 50 acid-free paper, which contains a minimum of 50 percent post-consumer waste, processed chlorine free. Of the balance, 25 percent is Forest Stewardship Council certified to contain no old-growth trees and to be pulped totally chlorine free.

08 07 06 05 04

10 9 8 7 6 5 4 3 2 1

To Peggy

CONTENTS

ACKNOWLEDGMENTS

I AM INDEBTED to many individuals for these memoirs. Foremost is Allison Alsup, my collaborator, who has spent innumerable hours with me, interviewing and drafting. My able and perceptive editor, Diana Landau, has tracked the memoirs for accuracy, added necessary material, and made the book more readable. My dedicated, longtime assistant Vicky Hoover has been of inestimable help and was my collaborator for chapter 9. My gratitude goes to Mike McCloskey, former executive director of the Sierra Club, who thoroughly read the entire manuscript for content and accuracy, and to Jack Hession, the Sierra Club's man in Alaska for the past thirty years, for his comments on the Alaska chapters. I wish to thank Ann Lage, the principal interviewer for my Sierra Club Oral History at the Bancroft Library. I also wish to thank the Honorable William Alsup, who repeatedly urged me to write these memoirs. Without his continued encouragement, they would not have come into being.

My deepest gratitude goes to my wife of fifty-four years, Peggy. Companion, author, and conservationist in her own right, Peggy was so often an integral part of my environmental campaigns. Her contributions are too immense for summary. Without her, the life contained in this book would not exist. Finally, to my children: to Cynthia and Laurie, who themselves carry on conservation careers most actively, and to Bill and Diana, who carry the torch.

THE WILDER SHORE

❧

*Never doubt that a small group of committed citizens
can change the world. Indeed, it the only thing that ever has.*

—Margaret Mead

THE TRAIN PULLED into the Oakland railroad station around noon on a
very hot July 31, 1933. I had been onboard since Chicago—four days at
the height of summer—and the sun had nearly melted the cars as they
lumbered along the great expanse traversed by the Union Pacific: the baked
plains of Iowa and Nebraska, the arid hills of Wyoming, and the bleached,
crusty flats and mountains of Utah and Nevada, finally passing over the
California border via the northern Sierra Nevada.

The heat was suffocating. We passengers slid open the windows for
ventilation, but with the air came dust and dirt, a gritty film that blanketed
our clothes, skin, and hair. Washing my face and hands in the tiny bathroom sink proved futile; before long I was covered again. Sweaty and
impatient, I spent the daytime away from my berth, opting for the obser-
vation car, where the seats swiveled and the windows afforded a panoramic
view of the passing country.

I was twenty-six years old when I disembarked at Oakland that afternoon, almost six feet in my shoes, 170 pounds, and with all my belongings
in two suitcases. At the ferry terminal, I boarded the next boat for San
Francisco—the epicenter of American medicine in the West during the
1930s and the place where I would begin my career as a practicing physician.
Earlier visits—as a child with my mother, who had grown up there, and on
vacation the summer after my first year in medical school—had given me a
sense that San Francisco offered the kind of life I was seeking. I was drawn

to the city's compact urbanity surrounded by open spaces ripe for escape: cultivated orchards and fields, grassy hills, endless shoreline for wandering. Of course, I was also lured by the belief that San Francisco *was* California, and therefore, *the West*—the place people went to reinvent themselves.

As the ferry pulled into the rippled blue expanse of San Francisco Bay, I leaned against the deck rail, anxiously awaiting my first view of the city, which lay invisibly ahead, its hills and downtown shrouded by summer fog. With each passing minute, the temperature ebbed until the air felt clean and cool. The sweat dried on my back, the salt on my neck mixing with wind and spray. Even before I could see San Francisco, I could feel it, and the memory of the train's heat faded quickly. The bay looked immense and soothing, its expanse yet to be fractured by such constructions as the Golden Gate Bridge, the Bay Bridge, and Treasure Island.

My future likewise waited ahead, as imperceptible as the city behind the fog. I saw my life up to that point as a succession of eventful phases, each of which I had enjoyed more than the last. With the confidence of youth, I believed success was not a question, only a matter of time. At last, traces of the city began to surface: the heights of Telegraph and Russian Hills, the downtown cluster of square-topped ten- and twelve-story buildings, and an occasional twenty-story tower I then considered tall. The boat edged closer to the pier, the Ferry Building with its clock tower rising into the sky just beyond. And I stepped off into the rest of my life.

THERE IS MAGIC in wild places. I had recognized this quite early, but it wasn't until I moved to California that the magic took hold deeply. Responding to it, I became something more than a physician. A healer of individual lives found a second career in helping to save the planet.

As a boy in Georgia, I had my favorite spots; one was a wooded area called Shirley Hills in Macon's North Highlands district. I would cross the muddy Ocmulgee River over the Spring Street Bridge and then turn upriver for a mile—walking out of the red dust of hot Georgia summers into shady groves of pine, maple, and hickory. Nestled among the trees was a small spring: Jackson Springs, we called it. It was a restful place, quiet and cool. Sometimes I came alone, other times with friends. We didn't do much of anything really—just being there was worth the hike.

Years later, I returned to find a posh subdivision. Jackson Springs was still there, but domesticated.

I encountered wildness on a much larger scale when I settled in San Francisco. There was the vast expanse of the bay itself, the open hills rising on its north side. I particularly enjoyed taking the ferry across the water to the southern end of Marin County, then the train to Mill Valley, Corte Madera, or Larkspur—in those days small villages nestled at the foot of Mount Tamalpais, whose green slopes offered the greatest possible refuge to an urban dweller.

In 1935 I backpacked into the Sierra Nevada for the first time and again felt a new dimension of wildness unfold. The backyard of John Muir, this was true wild country: flat, broad meadows carved by glaciers of past eons; rocky pinnacles bordering peaks with summits to ascend; blue or slate-colored lakes; joyously tumbling streams. All of it fascinated me, and I returned to the High Sierra many times throughout the 1930s and early '40s. It did not occur to me then that this magnificence might someday be encroached on. To most Californians before World War II, the state's wildlands seemed nearly limitless, and I was no exception to this way of thinking. I assumed they would always be here. I was a nature enthusiast, but not yet an active conservationist.

When I returned to San Francisco in 1946 after military service, I found the Bay Area in the grip of a postwar development boom that was eating up agricultural lands and open space. There was even talk of developing the area around Mount Tamalpais. I experienced a strong sense of loss and, for the first time, the feeling that I personally had to do something about it. Soon I would coin the phrase "Wilderness begins in your own backyard."

Even so, I never imagined in the 1940s that I would devote more than the next half century of my life to saving wilderness. I did not know then that my early efforts to help expand Mount Tamalpais State Park would plant the seeds for Point Reyes National Seashore and the Golden Gate National Recreation Area, the largest federally protected area adjacent to any metropolitan area. Nor did I anticipate that I would spend nearly two decades battling to ensure the survival of the earth's tallest living species— through establishing Redwood National Park. And I never could have envisioned that I would explore the wilds of Alaska and lead the fight to protect more than 100 million acres there—some of the most magnificent landscapes on the planet.

For most of my adult life, I have straddled a career in medicine and a vocation for conservation. At ninety-six, I look back and wonder how I had the energy to do both. That I was a workaholic cannot be denied. In addition to my medical practice, I also ran an outpatient clinic, worked part time as an epidemiologist, dabbled in medical research, and was active in medical organizations. Meanwhile, I served as a director or president of the Sierra Club from 1957 to 1993. Being a husband and the father of four children brought additional responsibilities.

Over the years, I found myself spending more time on Sierra Club tasks. I transferred some of my medical practice to younger colleagues. Eventually, the scales tipped clearly in favor of conservation. Here, I felt, I could make the most difference.

I am still not quite sure how I managed it all, but I think the answer begins with my wife, Peggy. She quickly embraced the ideas of the Sierra Club and became active in several campaigns. She accompanied me on all of my vacations, forgoing fancy hotels for canvas tents or open skies, trekking over mountains, and meeting with government bureaucrats. As a writer, she developed my burgeoning ideas into lively, readable articles. After our children arrived, weekends became family forays into the country, recreation doubling as conservation research. We found the time for conservation activism because we intensely wanted to, felt we had to. We did "the work" with fervor. It became our religion.

THIS BOOK IS a series of memoirs compiled in my nineties. I have chosen to focus on my environmental campaigns, so it is not an autobiography; many parts of my life and people who have played major roles in it go unmentioned. The text has been drafted from memory, from journals kept at the time of various campaigns, from my articles and personal files, and from my portion of the Sierra Club's oral history* (which can be found in

---

*Sierra Club Oral History series: vol. 27, Edgar Wayburn; *Sierra Club Statesman and Leader of the Parks and Wilderness Movement: Gaining Protection for Alaska, the Redwoods, and Golden Gate Parklands,* © 1985 by the Regents of the University of California and the Sierra Club; vol. 39, *Global Activist and Elder Statesman of the Sierra Club: International Conservation, National Parks and Protected Areas, 1980–1992,* © 1996 by the Regents of the University of California and the Sierra Club.

the Bancroft Library at the University of California). I have mentioned names as they seemed important at the time of the event or the time of writing. Undoubtedly, I have failed to note many who should be noted.

Nor should this book be considered a comprehensive historical account of any of the conservation campaigns it describes. I hope that, as the story of an individual, these memoirs will show how one dedicated person can help save a little part of the planet. I have not carried on my activism alone, however. Throughout more than a half century of conservation work, I have met and worked with dozens of individuals who have made a difference, as Margaret Mead says—stubborn fighters who have managed to keep special places on this earth wild.

I have often been asked why I devoted my life to conservation. Such a question implies a choice; yet I never felt as though I was presented with one. For me, conservation has been a compulsion; I acted because I felt I must. Ultimately, the explanation for such life decisions lies beyond reason. Simply put, however, I feel that protecting wildness is absolutely necessary. Whenever we encroach on the natural world, we crop the boundaries of our own existence as humans, cut off our fields of solace and sensation. Vistas, textures, odors, and sounds fade and then disappear. In destroying wildness, we deny ourselves the full extent of what it means to be alive. In preserving wildness, we not only recognize our place in the chain of life, but we also invite ourselves to reach, to explore, to wonder, and to make a difference.

CHAPTER ONE

GENTLE WILDERNESS

Early Adventures in the Sierra Nevada

❦

Never before had I seen so glorious a landscape,
so boundless an affluence of sublime mountain beauty.
The most extravagant description I might give of this view
to any one who has not seen similar landscapes with his
own eyes would not so much as hint its grandeur or the
spiritual glow that covered it.

—John Muir, *My First Summer in the Sierra*

I HAD MY first view of the incomparable Yosemite Valley in August 1927, from the back seat of a Cadillac touring sedan. The car belonged to my Uncle Will, who owned a tuberculosis sanitarium in the mountains between Los Gatos and Santa Cruz, south of San Francisco, and my Aunt Maude, who was behind the wheel. It was the summer after my first year of medical school, and I was out in California staying with Will and Maude.

We had left cool, foggy San Francisco that morning, heading east. In those days Yosemite was a six-hour drive along Highway 120, which entered the valley via the old Big Oak Flat Road. Soon we were passing through the scorching hot flatlands of the Central Valley, ripe fields and fruit orchards lining each side of the highway. The somniferous air blew across my face, lulling me into a stupor.

Our anticipation rose as we began to climb the Sierra foothills, dotted with rough black oak and digger pines, their pale, gray-green needles browning under the sun's gaze. Eastward, the hills rose in a series of soft, rounded humps covered in yellow grass matted like camel hair. The exposed banks of the road that sliced through the hills revealed copper-hued soil from which tiny bundles of resilient wildflowers sprouted. We passed white-planked storefronts, abandoned shacks, and skeletal gray wooden barns leaning toward collapse—the scattered remains of boom-and-bust gold-mining towns with names like Chinese Camp and Moccasin. Along the steep, winding ascent of Priest's Grade, a variation of the current Highway 120, the Highway Department had placed barrels of water for motorists to replenish overheated or boiling radiators.

Above 3,000 feet, we entered the land of conifers: ponderosa and sugar pines, incense cedar and white fir, whose trunks and thick boughs formed a cool, shady wall. Sunlight filtered through the branches in hypnotizing flashes. Through occasional breaks in the forest loomed still larger hills, purple-hued in the distance like a western movie backdrop.

Driving down from Crane Flat, we came to a tunnel where the lay of the land suggested a falling away, and I felt that something momentous loomed just ahead. As we exited the tunnel at the viewpoint locals had come to call Oh My! Point, Yosemite Valley burst upon us in a sudden and magnificent panorama. Maude stopped the car and we got out to let our eyes feast on the vista: the granite peak of Half Dome, the Cathedral Spires, the Three Brothers, the stream of Bridal Veil Falls, each an exquisite sculpture in the gallery of nature's grandest design. Nothing on the approach had suggested a landscape of this magnitude, and nothing in my previous experience had prepared me for it. To someone accustomed to the gradual rise and fall of southern Appalachia and the rolling hills of New England, the view was stunning, nearly shocking in its full, instantaneous appearance. Overwhelmed, I was surprised to find myself weeping.

On more careful study, individual formations began to distinguish themselves: Half Dome, veined in white and striated with dark lines that fell down its face like great drips of paint; the gray buttresses of Cathedral Spires; the feathery threads of Bridal Veil, seemingly suspended in air. The valley was a composition of defined angles and shaded crevasses, all contained by steep vertical walls, its near-geometric angularity standing in contrast to everything surrounding it, its compactness only adding to its perfection.

THE SIERRA WAS my first wilderness love. It is a relationship that has spanned more than seventy years and spawned countless adventures and friendships. After that first encounter with Yosemite, my affinity expanded to take in the greater Sierra Nevada: beginning in 1935 I made at least one trip every couple of years (except during the war years) to hike, explore, and climb in John Muir's "range of light." Those trips are too numerous to detail, but the sampling in this chapter may convey a taste of what has drawn me, and others, so strongly.

Richard Kaufman, in his pictorial account of the range, has called the Sierra a "gentle wilderness." The phrase is fitting; we used to joke on Sierra Club High Trips that it never rains at night in the Sierra. For the most part, we left our tents at home, opting to sleep under the open sky. Although the Sierra can be rugged and challenging, it is this benign quality that lures aficionados back again and again. The writer David Rains Wallace put it well:

> There is probably nowhere else in the world where the "otherness"
> of nature exists in such an attractive, healthful, safe, and relatively
> undamaged form as in the great California mountains, the Sierra
> Nevada in particular. . . . The water is pure, the smells pleasant
> and appetizing. There are no large quantities of biting insects. . . .
> There is sparkling granite to sit on, clear lakes to swim in, soft
> beds of fir needles to sleep on. When [John] Muir refers to God in
> his writing . . . the divine authority sounds like a highly thoughtful
> and tasteful builder . . . confidently leaving it to his clients to keep
> the place up.

In 1939, I took my first trip with the Sierra Club, a burro trip. After the war I returned many times, both in the company of the Club and independently. I climbed Mt. Whitney twice during the High Trips of 1946 and 1949. The Sierra was also the site of my first and many subsequent ecological epiphanies. You cannot come to know and love a wild place without learning to recognize when some feature is out of its healthful natural alignment.

While I did not call myself a dedicated conservationist until the late 1940s, my Sierra experience in the years before then was molding me into one, largely without my knowledge. Had it not been for those early trips, I might not have come to appreciate wild places, nor recognized the need to preserve them. With places as with people, love must come before devotion. And to protect a place, you must ideally have not only a passion for it but a ground knowledge of its character and variations, its terrain and watersheds. The Sierra was the first wild place I really came to know well and to love well.

THE WORK ETHIC had me so tight in its grip that my first two years in San Francisco passed without a vacation. Finally in the summer of 1935, satisfied that I could take a break from my budding medical practice, I made my first backpack trip in the Sierra. My trail companion was Don Carson, a fellow doctor and a fisherman, so I bought a rod and the necessary fly-fishing paraphernalia.

We hired a packer to take some of the load, carrying the rest ourselves through the high country of Yosemite National Park, from Tuolumne Meadows to Waterwheel Falls farther downstream on the Tuolumne River. There at the falls we camped, rigging a rope between pine trees to keep our food away from the many black bears. I have never forgotten the entrancing roar and rush of the water—leaping, crashing, falling on the rocks below.

From Waterwheel Falls we backpacked through Cold and Virginia Canyons, then west to Benson Lake. Leaving Virginia Canyon, we encountered an old fisherman, his skin reddened and furrowed from countless summers in the mountains. He gave us a map, as deeply creased and well used as his face, and pointed out a lake high on the ridge above Matterhorn Canyon where he said fish were abundant and fishermen few. On his advice we hiked up the canyon, bushwhacking almost 1,000 feet up the side of the ridge to find a clear, lead-gray lake of stark beauty nestled in the talus. An hour's fishing rewarded us with only a lost lure, so we put down our reels and swam in the icy water, then basked on sun-warmed rocks. After five days, we returned to our base camp at Waterwheel Falls and then to Tuolumne Meadows, where we parted.

From Yosemite I drove north on Highway 395 to Lake Tahoe, where friends had offered to put me up in their vacation house for several days.

Most call their first sight of Tahoe's brilliant blue waters a breathtaking spectacle, but it was not so for me. To my mind, relaxing by the shore of this relatively flat, if lovely, lake could not compare with exploring Yosemite's steep, rugged terrain or experiencing the magnificent vistas from altitudes five or six thousand feet higher. The soft bed and excellent meals provided by my kind hosts suffered in comparison with the self-sufficient thrill of carrying on my back everything I needed to survive. Although I had spent ten summers in boys' camps back east, those experiences had not moved me as the Sierra landscape did. Enchanted, I vowed to return.

My NEXT CHANCE to explore the Sierra came two years later, when I returned with friends Al Cox and DeWitt Burnham and a pair of pack horses. We planned a two-week trip through Fish and Silver Creek Valleys along the Mammoth Divide, south and east of Yosemite National Park. Although we fished a good deal, I found my interest focusing elsewhere; I became more and more fascinated by the landscape and how it changed according to elevation. In camp, I devoted part of every evening to keeping a detailed log of our mileage, elevation gains and descents, tree species, and vistas sighted.

From a canyon on the Sierra's west side, our route reached the John Muir Trail, which traces the crest of the Sierra for some two hundred miles north to south. Starting from south of Silver Divide, we passed glade after glade of small and large evergreens: yellow pines and tamarack, red firs, cedar, and mountain hemlock. As we climbed to String Meadow and Silver Creek, views of the San Joaquin watershed began to appear: to the west, Cattle Mountain; the broad, jagged top of Isberg Peak twelve miles northwest; Iron Mountain and the zigzagging Granite Stairway ahead northward; and to the northeast the broad, smooth plateau of Mammoth Mountain. Behind us rose the crest of the Silver Divide; directly below lay the precipitous cliffs of Silver and Fish Creeks.

The trail followed a tortuous, thigh-pounding route 1,800 feet down the side of a cascade—a drop so vertical that the trail bottomed out into the valley less than half a linear mile from the top. As I led one of the horses down the trail, I heard a rattling sound and looked down just in time to avoid stepping on the poisonous fangs of a rattlesnake. DeWitt quickly pulled out his revolver and shot—a practice I decried; but the seemingly immortal snake survived four bullets and finally had to be clubbed with a stick to end its misery. We counted nine rattles and a button.

Fish Valley was encased by steep granite cliffs that blocked all views over the ridges; the narrow valley floor was longer than Yosemite. We camped at a spot "civilized" by earlier campers, complete with an iron sheet over the fire ring, a planked table and log bench, and fir boughs for mattresses. Regrettably, they had also left heaps of horse dung and scattered food tins. The smelly garbage had attracted mice—as DeWitt rose in the morning to dress, two jumped out of his pants side pockets and a third from the leg.

Passing above the east bank of the middle fork of the San Joaquin River, we found grassland woven with streams and rivers more numerous than I had ever seen. We rejoined the middle fork again at Rainbow Falls, whose cascade fell two hundred feet over pumiced cliffs to collect in a large pool, a myriad of prisms refracting in its mist. Two and a half miles farther on, we reached the base of Devil's Postpile, an otherworldly array of giant shafts of rust-colored basalt rising more than a hundred feet. Rare and intriguing as it was, the Postpile seemed barren after the lushness of Fish Valley.

Following the Muir Trail through Red's Meadow, we continued up the gentle contours of Mammoth Divide. Leaving DeWitt and Al below, I climbed to the top of the two Red Cones, aptly named for the fiery red stones that form them. Mount Ritter dominated a vista that included Iron Mountain, the Minarets, and Banner Peak. I rejoined Al and DeWitt, and our route reached its climax at over 11,000 feet on the cream-colored sandy loam of Mammoth Mountain.

The return journey took us over the exposed rim of the divide, high above Fish Valley. From here the stream rushing through the center of the gorge a thousand feet below looked like a still, green thread. Now Al and I made a side trip, hiking to Duck Lake—green and bare-banked—then climbing the pass beyond to 11,000 feet. Here we were embraced by a kaleidoscopic panorama of shapes and color: the vast green washes of the San Joaquin watershed; the gray granite peaks of Ritter and Isberg, the cliffs above the Silver Divide. Virginia Lake was a blue sheet to the southeast;

Red Slate Mountain, richly colored as glazed pottery, stood out against the gray background. The sense of space was exhilarating. On the far side of the pass, a thousand feet down, we spotted the resplendent gleam of Purple Lake. Hot and sweaty, Al and I ran down the mountainside and dove into the chill water.

DeWitt had remarked that he liked to stop and fish a stream or a lake because he felt that he knew it much better afterward. I felt similarly about swimming in these mountain lakes. Cold and deep, the water ten feet from the shore might be thirty feet deep, twenty feet away a thousand feet. That the water was close enough to the snowpack to cause a headache did not distract me; exploring these wells of mystery thrilled me more than anything else I knew.

Under the severe alpine sun of midday, Purple Lake seemed misnamed, its surface a resonating, deep blue; but in the fading light of dusk it took on the lustrous purple-green patina of a black pearl. Mesmerized, we returned to our camp, where we stayed for two nights. We would have stayed longer, but our spot was on the trafficked route between the pack outfits at Mammoth Lake and several heavily fished lakes. Dust kicked up by the animals' hooves coated our clothes and equipment.

As we dropped into Cascade Valley, then climbed 1,700 feet up to Silver Pass, we felt fit, our legs now lean and strong. We stopped only once on the climb. At the top we were treated to yet another magnificent vista: half a dozen peaks, all over 13,000 feet, vying for supremacy.

Gray skies and damp winds, the first of our trip, followed us southward along the main fork of Mono Creek, up to Fish Camp and beyond, as we explored the Second and Fourth Recesses. This last place was possibly the single most beautiful view we had discovered, the lake an elliptical stretch of bright and shining water, its surface diffusely rippled by the wind. Above the lake, steep and mighty snow-patched cliffs rose abruptly on three sides, while a broad canyon cleaved the southern wall and a narrow winding cascade streamed into the lake some six hundred feet below.

On the last night of our trip, the wind turned forceful, the gray sky wet. We strung our automobile cover between tree branches as a tent, weighting the edges with logs against the invading rain. Inside, we stayed warm and dry and eventually fell asleep despite the wind and rain lashing the canvas.

I JOINED THE Sierra Club in 1939, not because I was fired with conservation zeal but because I wanted to go on a burro trip. By that summer, I was hooked on the Sierra Nevada and wanted to go back out into the mountains for at least two weeks. I had never hiked with burros but had heard that the Sierra Club organized such trips and was intrigued by the prospect of joining a group of like-minded hikers.

First, however, there was the matter of getting in. In 1939, the Club was a selective organization requiring sponsorship by two members. A friend, Jerry Cramer, belonged and agreed to vouch for me; eventually he found another member who, although he didn't know me, was willing to do likewise.

Those who know the Club through its environmental activism of the last few decades may find that picture difficult to reconcile with the Sierra Club of old. The Sierra Club of the 1930s only faintly resembled the international environmental organization it would grow into. In 1939, with five chapters and about three thousand members, the Club was considered a regional organization; most of its members lived in California. Although it had engaged in a few environmental campaigns—most notably John Muir's unsuccessful fight against the damming of Hetch Hetchy Valley in Yosemite—the organization remained a club in the truest sense: an outings group for people with a common enthusiasm, the Sierra Nevada.

It was an exclusive club at that. The double sponsorship requirement created an elite cadre. As Dr. Harold Crowe, a onetime Club president from Los Angeles, expressed it, "You had to be a member of the congregation before you were allowed in the church." Members tended to be successful professionals: doctors, lawyers, businessmen, teachers, professors from the University of California and Stanford. The Club consciously cultivated such prominence, and it served the members in good stead when trying to influence U.S. Forest Service and National Park Service policy. It was a strategy that relied more on influential individual members than on their weight in numbers. Other early conservation groups, such as the Save the Redwoods League, also sprang from such patrician roots. Members in those days were likely to be politically conservative; many, including myself, were Republicans. Far from opposing the interests of big business, many Club members were land developers or hydroelectric and oil-industry engineers.

But in this they merely reflected the beliefs of the age. Before the Second World War, when California's population numbered just a few million, when cities were connected by two-lane highways, when much of Los Angeles was orange groves, most applauded the rapid development of the state's industries and public works. The west's resources seemed inexhaustible. Few Sierra Club members foresaw how their interests in the economic expansion of the west and in preserving the land they loved would collide. When the collision took shape, it sparked a debate that would long divide the Club's ranks, though it would not begin in earnest for another dozen years.

I was accepted into the Sierra Club in time to sign up for the 1939 summer burro trip. We were twenty people in all, two to a burro, plus a packer and four extra burros carrying cooking and other equipment. My burro-mate was a retired schoolteacher from Fresno. Our leaders were Milton and Roger Hildebrand, sons of Joel Hildebrand, a renowned professor of chemistry at the University of California, Berkeley, and Sierra Club president for three years. Milton and Roger couldn't have been more than twenty at the time. Slim, friendly, and already well versed in the Sierra, they were natural and capable leaders, bristling with youthful energy.

We started downriver from Tuolumne Meadows, following much the same route I had taken in 1935 with Don Carson, and continued up to Benson Lake. Concerns and complications of the city soon faded, replaced by the beauty of high meadows, emerald lakes, and a magnificent horizon of white-capped granite peaks. The trip was as much a social experience as a mountain adventure. We ate dinners around a campfire, told stories, and sang to a strummed guitar. It was a group I felt I belonged with, and I found myself making new friends.

On Labor Day weekend of 1939, friends John Lee, Jon Tibbe, and I were camping in the High Sierra. We had left San Francisco on Friday in my new blue Oldsmobile convertible and driven to the middle fork of the Stanislaus River. At Clark's Fork we turned and followed a fresh dirt road for several miles to the end. We fished all Saturday and spent Sunday climbing the nearby peaks.

Nine thousand miles away, Hitler's troops had begun their assault on Poland.

By Sunday evening (September 3), John, who had just become editor of a news sheet for Standard Oil Company of California, was anxious to regain contact with the world. He persuaded us to walk back to the car and listen to the news on the radio. It was just before nine, clear and cold. A portentous full moon had risen over the eastern ridge of the canyon; stars spilled across the sky. Gray, gauzy clouds floated overhead, their strands briefly illuminated against the moon's white glare, then melting into the blue-black horizon. Fir trees whose bark shone red in the day now rose in stark silhouette over the hills at the far end of the canyon.

On the car radio, the announcer's voice rang with urgency.. Great Britain had declared war on Germany, and just hours later German U-boats had sunk the British steamship *Athenia*—despite Hitler's promise not to attack civilian vessels. The night grew colder as we sat silent in the car, listening to the grim details of fighting and casualties. We knew the implications of Great Britain's declaration. Roosevelt was already being courted by Chamberlain and Churchill; sooner or later, the United States' entry into the conflict seemed inevitable. If it came to that, I knew I would not hesitate to go, nor would any of the men I knew. But at this moment, surrounded by the quiet beauty of the canyon night, the war hardly seemed real.

As IT TURNED out, I did indeed join the Army Air Corps in 1942. After training, I spent two years in the Southwest desert, serving as chief of a medical service, doing research in aviation medicine, and then two years in Europe serving in diverse medical capacities, including as a flight surgeon. But meanwhile I was determined to pursue my Sierra idyll—a time that grew all the more precious as my departure for war loomed.

One hot afternoon in mid-July 1941, George Grey and I set out in the Oldsmobile for a two-week pack trip into the Sierra high country—an eventful expedition that was to form the climax of my prewar Sierra adventures.

Our destination was the Kern-Kaweah watershed, whose majestic beauty many friends had praised. About an hour south of San Francisco, sailing past the apricot orchards of Morgan Hill, we were stopped by a policeman's flashing lights and promptly issued a speeding ticket. In Fresno, we met up with our trail companions, John Lee and Jim Brainerd, for dinner, and together we continued in the dark, climbing out of the Central Valley past the dry grassy foothills and, several thousand feet higher, to the alpine country and giant sequoias. At 1 A.M., we pulled into Grant Grove and tossed our sleeping bags on the same spot where John and I had camped a year earlier.

The next morning we drove for another dozen miles on a dirt road to Horse Corral Meadow, where a man named Cecil, from whom we had rented animals the year before, ran a pack station. Cecil was nowhere in sight, but three saddled mules were waiting: Kate, Elberta, and Jumbo, who had accompanied us on our last trip. Cecil had again skimped on buying new equipment: Jumbo sported the same blanket already threadbare the year before, now straining its last fibers. A search turned up nothing better, so we saddled the animals, loaded up our equipment, and set out for the John Muir Trail.

Our destination was Colby Pass, at 12,000 feet. We walked east, quickly climbing a thousand feet. At 9,000 feet we expected to arrive on a mountaintop, but instead the trail delivered us to alpine meadows laden with grasses, lazy streams, and occasional swamps thick with mosquitoes. Progress was slow, and we discovered the contours of our map to be inaccurate, its placement of streams simply wrong. After a few hours I put it away, trusting to my eyes and the trail. Behind me, John periodically issued a gruff, deep-throated cough, a symptom of his persistent summer cold. Jim was out of shape and already huffing, and George, a newcomer to the high country, complained of developing blisters on his heels from his new, untested boots. Nevertheless, we made ten miles the first day and stopped at a campsite complete with a crude log table and a bathing pond. We slept under the open sky without tent or ground cloth. True to the Sierra Club maxim, it did not rain.

We spent the next day resting and fishing, adjusting to the altitude. After only one day on the trail, a faulty pack ring had badly cut Kate's back. We unsaddled her, sprinkled antiseptic powder across the mass of lacerations, and left them to air. The next morning we began a slow descent into the sandy floors of Sugarloaf Valley, stopping to swim at Ferguson Creek, then scrambling up a rock to eat lunch sans clothes.

The valley was thick with shades of green: abundant stands of silver fir and cedar, giant Sequoias towering 150 feet in the air, yellow and tamarack pines, white-trunked aspen whose leaves rippled in even the softest breeze, and others whose names I did not know. Wildflowers bloomed more profusely than I had ever seen; the great fields were awash with white, yellow, and lavender. Still a relative newcomer to the Sierra, I reveled in new wonders that unfolded with each trip. We camped along the sandy banks of Roaring River and let its hypnotic rush of rapids lull us to sleep.

Over the next few days we alternated between hiking and fishing, gradually following the trail and river to the south into Cloud Canyon. Elberta proved to be an equine Houdini, breaking free of her tethers under cover of darkness and having to be tracked each morning. All the mules required constant repacking. John and I worked the slipping saddles, perfecting the twists and loops of our diamond hitches to no avail. Eventually, we realized our hitches were not at fault; the animals had simply lost weight. We tightened the saddle straps and continued to climb, sometimes dropping a few hundred feet but always making up the loss with the next push.

At the far end of the canyon stood 11,000-foot Glacier Ridge, its top still blanketed in snow from the winter's heavy pack, its white ridges an ominous sign. Colby Pass, our route to the Kern-Kaweah Valley, waited invisibly ahead, its crest a thousand feet higher than Glacier. The chances of climbing Colby seemed slim at best. We were disappointed but continued on, passing through Barton's Meadow, so green and dripping it verged on a swamp. Mosquitoes clouded around the sweaty crevices of our skin, and we covered ourselves in repellent to no effect: we watched the irritating pink bubbles rise along our arms. At the far end of the meadow, sixty feet above the grass and its swarms, we made camp. But here colonies of stinging red ants drove us from the ground; we slept with our backs stiff against an outcropping of granite.

We were now six days in and had heard no word on the condition of Colby Pass. Except for ourselves, the trails and camps had been vacant. The pass was still five miles distant, hidden by Glacier and Whaleback

Mountains, and as the fate of our trip hung in the balance, John and I agreed to scout ahead. If the pass was relatively clear of snow, we could continue on to the Kern-Kaweah Valley as hoped. If not, we couldn't risk taking the animals into deep drifts where they could slip or plunge knee-deep in snow.

From our camp, the trail proceeded along the other side of Roaring River. Reluctant to wade in the river's main fork, fast and full with runoff, John and I hopped streams and creekbeds—but unable to find a way around, we unlaced our boots and stepped in. Our surroundings made up for the discomfort: cascades spilled down the sides of Glacier Ridge, and pockets of enchanting wildflowers sprouted from the fields and granite crags. We paused to consult our guide and identify meadow lilies, asters, and our favorite shooting stars—a tiny clustered stem whose magenta petals flare as if exploding.

Ascending the side of Whaleback Mountain, its corniced crest rising to the clouds like the barnacled spine of a whale, we approached tree line, passing scattered whitebark pines whose short, gnarled trunks reflected the High Sierra's brief summers and twisting, buffeting winds. At 11,000 feet we came upon a narrow lake carved into the granite, nearly three-quarters of a mile long and unmarked on our map. We dubbed it New Colby Lake for its proximity to the original Colby Lake—named for Will Colby, John Muir's acolyte—which lay invisibly tucked among the recesses of the Western Divide. Then we ate lunch on the polished granite shoreline of our find.

Clumps of snow dotted the trail ahead. We stepped tentatively at first, as if the white substance were somehow alien, but quickly gained confidence and trudged to the base of the pass. A look upward confirmed what we had all but admitted: twelve hundred feet above us, at least half of the trail to the pass lay under a heavy layer of snow. We could see no footprints, no traces of trail in the white blanket. Even with the summer sun, it would be several weeks before the trail would reappear. We were sure no one had climbed the pass this year, and we knew that, laden with our animals, we would not be the first.

Still racked by cough, John waited as I scrambled over the rocks and up the last four hundred feet of snow-free trail. Suddenly I heard a voice:

"Where are you?" sounding very close. Startled, I looked around and realized it was John, whose figure I could barely make out nearly half a mile away. The pass formed a natural amphitheater whose acoustics allowed us to converse as quietly as two people at a cafe table. Finally, John said he needed to get back to camp. His cold refused to abate; he was shivering from the wind.

The journey that had taken a good four hours going up we made in just two on the return. Nearing camp, I spotted George with a towel around his neck, washing his face in a shallow pool. As we again confronted crossing the Roaring River, I decided to combine crossing with a quick dip. Beneath the water I spied a submerged sheet of rock that gradually descended along the riverbed like a sidewalk. The water looked relatively calm there compared to the rock-strewn rapids several hundred feet downstream.

Holding my clothes in a bundle over my head, I stepped into the river, feeling the icy water rise to my knees, then my waist. The shelf descended more quickly than I thought and felt slick with algae under my feet. The undercurrent proved deceptively fast. Suddenly my feet lost their hold and I was swept downstream in the frigid water. I called out to George, whose relatively calm face belied his terror. I struggled against the current but was unable to counter its force, pulled closer each second to the back-breaking rapids. My only hope, I realized, was to try to steer myself toward a rock or log.

All heat had left my body; my nerves transmitted only a series of painful shocks. George ran along the bank helplessly, crashing through the underbrush, trying to stay close to me. I managed to aim toward the last large rock before the rapids; panting, fingers numb, I pulled myself up onto it. Downstream, the rapids waited less than forty feet away, threatening to snap my arms and legs.

I tossed my bundle of clothes, soaked in the struggle, to George on the bank, no more than five yards away. He seemed so close; I thought if I could only catch my breath, I could make it to him. But once back in the water, I was dragged away again. The rapids were now frighteningly close, loud, white, and frothy where they collided with jagged rocks. George yelled for me to hold on, and I fought against the current, knowing I couldn't hold out much longer. Then George thrust out a branch from the bank. I plunged toward it, grabbed the end. Too cold and exhausted to do anything else, I just held on and tried to keep my head above water as George pulled me in hand over hand. At last I climbed out of the river and collapsed on the bank, my skin beet red.

ALTHOUGH I SUFFERED no lingering effects from my watery ordeal, we spent the next day in camp, fishing, bemoaning our lost chance to climb Colby Pass and see the Kern-Kaweah, and delaying our return to civilization. That evening as we sat around the campfire stuffing ourselves with the day's catch, a long line of boy scouts with pack horses came trudging into camp. The boys, hardly more than twelve, were led by two men. As they unloaded the animals and settled their packs, one of the leaders, a thirtyish man with a long black beard, came over and asked about Colby Pass.

"Impassable," I said, describing the results of the preceding day's hike.

The scout leader laughed, then asked to borrow our shovel.

We found the shovel in our supplies, handed it over. "Now I have two shovels and fourteen boys," the black-bearded man said. "That's twenty-eight feet and arms. We'll dig our own trail over the pass. Goodnight."

George turned red, clearly incensed. Neither of us was prepared to be outdone by this scoffing Black Bart and a pack of preadolescent boys: we resolved to climb Colby. That night we sat around the campfire making plans and sorting supplies. George and I would attempt the pass, hike into the Kern-Kaweah Valley, then try to cross back into the Kings River watershed via Forester Pass—a thousand feet higher than Colby and of whose status we knew nothing—thus making a great loop. The mules would never make it, of that we were sure. Jim and John agreed to take them and rendezvous with us in four days at the junction of East and Bubb's Creeks, to the northeast.

George and I set out at 8 A.M. feeling bold and adventurous. We had neither snowshoes nor climbing equipment. Between us, only I had a real backpack; George carried a duffel bag rigged with double straps. I had loaded my Bergen pack with the heavier items—canned food and cooking supplies—while George carried the bulkier equipment, sleeping bags and air mattresses. The scouts had already broken camp and were ahead of us, up the trail and out of sight. We found them just before noon as we pulled into New Colby Lake for a light lunch. The boys were frying up foot-long fish; Black Bart boasted of twenty-inchers. George and I ate cheese sandwiches and left before they did.

Soon we reached the base of the pass. Colby's crest lay 1,200 feet above, a small dip in the great crenellated mass of the Western Divide. Already at 11,000 feet we were above tree line, the landscape just granite, snow, and a cloudless sky. We scaled the rocks skirting the base of the pass, then confronted the snow. Lacking any sign of the trail, we attempted to make our own switchbacks, but the snow proved unreliable, holding fast in some places, soft and slushy in others. Our calves plunged through to the knee and extricating ourselves was exhausting, so finally we gave up making switchbacks, instead opting for quick scrambles up the slope. For George, new to the high county and lugging an awkward duffel bag, the climb was particularly rough. We sucked in the thin air, pulled the brims of our hats down against the blinding glare. At last, near the top, granite zigzags of trail were revealed, clear of snow.

The end push proved easier. After nearly four hours of laboring up the side of the ridge, we reached Colby Pass, a twenty-five-foot-wide strip of snow and granite straddling the Great Western Divide. A marker posted the elevation at 12,250 feet—more than 3,000 feet higher than that morning's camp, and the register revealed that we *were* the first to make the pass that year. George and I stood silent except for the sound of our breath. It was as if we were poised on a great balcony, the Sierra unfolding in majestic splendor below: Goat Mountain and the middle fork of the Kings River lay to the north; southward, the snowcapped Kaweah Peaks Ridge bowed to meet the Western Divide in a stunning arc extending eight miles from where we stood. We savored the views all the more for knowing we alone had seen them that year. Scanning the slope below, we saw no sign of Black Bart and his scouts.

Time was pressing, though, so George and I reluctantly started down the southeastern side of the pass. A thousand feet lower we came to the edge of the fabulous Kern-Kaweah Valley. Still another thousand feet below, the rapid-strewn Kern River twisted through a tree-lined meadow.

A quick look back toward the pass took in threadlike streams weaving down the mountainsides, feeding the river. Following switchbacks down to the meadow, we reached camp at Gallats Lake by seven. Exhausted after eleven hours of hiking, his shoulders raw from the unpadded straps, George crawled into his sleeping bag and did not emerge until the next morning. I heated several batches of concentrated soup, passing bowls to George. The hot broth soothed our muscles like an elixir. We passed a cold night, for once wishing that we had brought a tent.

The next day we took a more leisurely pace, walking alone, never encountering another traveler. Each bend of the trail brought a view to rival the last in magnificence and variety; I couldn't choose a favorite. We took only one picture, knowing our photographic skills could never do justice to the scene. Trail conditions, however, were terrible, forcing us to guess in many places. At Junction Meadow we forded the swollen Kern River up to our hips and began to climb northward along its bank, camping four miles above Junction Meadow where Tyndall Creek intersects the Kern. Preparing for the next day's effort, we gorged on chili, Canadian bacon, fruit, and cheese.

In the morning we continued northeast along Tyndall Creek and its meadowlands. Around noon we stopped at the ranger's hut to ask about conditions on Forester Pass but found the hut abandoned. From there we could see the pass four miles away, a small, snow-filled chink in the Kern Divide, and decided to try for it that day. The approach was a long, gradual rise from 11,000 to 12,000 feet over barren terrain marked by signs of upthrust and wearing down by glaciers over millennia. Streams flowed over the speckled granite and we passed numerous lakes, some no more than small bowls scooped into the rock below a ridgeline of daunting spires. As we moved on, the snow patches grew deeper and wider, the wind more fierce. We passed two lakes still frozen solid in summer. This laid-bare landscape seemed a virtual textbook of geological time.

Before us, a series of switchbacks cut into the sheer face. On the ascent, each turn was so steep that the next switchback seemed to be immediately overhead, the angles vertigo inspiring. George and I leaned into the mountain, hugging the cliff for fear of falling off into the thousand-foot drop. Then suddenly we were in the pass, the highest on the John Muir

Trail and even narrower than Colby, a razor slit at 13,400 feet. Again we enjoyed panoramic views far north and south, but the most riveting sight lay just north of the pass, immediately below us: a portrait of winter in snow-covered fields and frozen lakes, a place seemingly immune to summer's thaw. Despite the rush of wind, the air in my lungs felt sparse, my blood thinned. Time to go: we quickly signed our names in the register, the fourth party to make Forester Pass that year.

We began our descent to the north. Distant views were eclipsed by the shadows of Mount Stanford to the west and Junction Peak to the east. Soon dusk fell, casting an orange glow over the eastward peaks. We descended below the snow line into sloping meadows, our boots sinking into soft damp earth. Patches of willows bordered the streams. In a fit of boldness, I tried to hop across one stream, slipped, and ended up wet over my waist. Without a change of clothes, I began to chill.

As night came on, George and I walked faster to stave off the cold. His straps were cutting into his shoulders, the pain unbearable, so we stopped to shift packs and forged on—now nearly jogging down the trail, praying for an acceptable camp to shield us from the sharp winds. As the last traces of light faded from the sky, we found a patch of flat land and a massive rock. As I lay in my sleeping bag waiting this time for George to heat soup, I felt a tremendous sense of accomplishment: we had made sixteen miles that day, gaining 4,000 feet in elevation and dropping another 3,000. George and I had been the only people that year to climb both passes, making the trip from the Kings River country into the Kern River watershed and back.

The next day we descended a leisurely few miles west and north, rounding out our loop and heading toward our meeting point. Bubb's Creek was flowing high with snowmelt. After spending several days at tree line or above, we found the meadows and wildflowers lush, the trees almost tropical: Jeffrey pine, silver fir, cottonwood, aspen, and an occasional mountain hemlock. We began to encounter people: a lone fisherman, a pair of girls with donkeys, a Sierra Club burro trip led by Milton Hildebrand.

At the junction, Jim and John had left a note to meet them at Charlotte Creek, three miles north. We found their camp, with them absent, and rested all afternoon. John and Jim returned at dusk, bearing fourteen fish. We spent the next day swimming and fishing, still sleeping hard the second night back after our adventures in the high country.

In the morning, drifting in and out of sleep, I heard John snort. Opening an eye, I saw him talking with a tired-looking couple at the edge of camp. John pointed at me and the man walked over.

He leaned down. His eyes were bloodshot. "Are you the doctor?"

I said I was.

"We have an emergency." He introduced himself as Pem and explained that his friend Arthur Smith was at East Lake suffering from severe chest pains. They had started in the middle of the night and hadn't let up. Pem thought it was a heart attack—angina pectoris—and said there was no way Smith could walk out. When Pem had looked for help at the lake, Milton Hildebrand, also camped there, had sent him in my direction. Pem and his wife had then walked six miles from East Lake in the dark with a flashlight, leaving Smith up at the lake with the last member of their party.

I sent Pem on to Cedar Grove, about fourteen miles west. If Pem was correct that Smith was having heart trouble, oxygen might be necessary. My friends agreed to wait until the next morning, and if they had not heard from me by then, they would head down to Cedar Grove with all our gear and ask the rangers for help. I gave John my car keys, ate a quick breakfast, packed my equipment and the emergency medical kit I always carried, and began the climb to East Lake, 2,200 feet above. The trail was steep and badly marked. Wading through loose chaparral that threatened to give way with each step, I was amazed that Pem and his wife had made the journey by flashlight without twisting their legs and falling.

I made the journey in three hours, arriving at noon. East Lake was gorgeous and clear, framed by the magnificent Mount Brewer. At the far end, I found Smith doubled over with pain though still lucid. His campmate, George Lieberman, hovered close, clearly stressed by his inability to help his friend in any way. When asked about the prior few days, Smith said he'd been fine, even with the steep elevation gains. I touched my stethoscope to his chest; his heartbeat sounded strong and steady. But when I moved lower, touching the base of his chest and abdomen, he recoiled in agony. His abdomen felt as hard as stone. Smith wasn't suffering from angina; he had a ruptured stomach ulcer that might need surgery.

Pem had been right about one thing, though: Smith wouldn't be able to walk out. He would need to be carried. I gave him a shot of morphine to ease the pain, then surveyed the possibilities for getting him back to Cedar Grove. We would have to start with a hand carry.

There were three men available: myself, Lieberman, and Milton Hildebrand, still camped nearby. Milton was one of the finest mountaineers in the Sierra, so his presence was reassuring. Earlier he had spotted two fishermen at nearby Reflection Lake, and now he took off to look for them while Lieberman and I set about constructing a makeshift stretcher from a canvas cot, a pair of pine saplings, and aluminum fishing rod cases. Soon Milton returned with the fishermen, though one of them proved useless, himself recovering from an operation and unable to lift heavy objects.

At five o'clock, we loaded Smith onto the stretcher and set off. But within minutes, we discovered the flaws in our stretcher design. The load on our hands was staggering, the trails steep and studded with large rocks. The footing was too loose to navigate without our arms for balance, and the way too narrow for more than one man in front and another in back. We unloaded Smith, cut off the cot legs, discarded the fishing rod cases and substituted aspen saplings for the pine. Then we roped the new stretcher onto the frame of Milton's Bergen pack as a harness for the man in front and devised impromptu straps from rope and fishing line for the man in back.

We set off again, our progress painfully slow, averaging less than a mile an hour. Loose rocks tumbled down the twisted trail, at times slippery from fresh brooks and snowmelt. Smith faded in and out of consciousness. As night fell, flashlight and moonbeams became our only guides. After two miles, we met a packer sent in by Pem with oxygen, which by then we realized was unnecessary. It was now a matter of manpower and speed. We sent the rider back down, telling him to bring reinforcements and arrange for an ambulance to meet us at the end of the dirt road in Zumwalt Meadows, a good five miles closer than Cedar Grove.

We crept on over the most treacherous section of trail. Even with the shoulder straps, the weight was overwhelming, forcing us to rotate frequently. At midnight we waded knee-deep through the fast current where East Creek crossed the trail, then put down the stretcher to stop for the night and await reinforcements. Milton and the fisherman returned to their camps, quickly disappearing into the black shadows. Lieberman and I started a fire to keep Smith warm, rousing ourselves several times to keep the flames from going out. We slept little.

Morning came, but no help. Smith seemed to be holding up surprisingly well, but I felt it was crucial not to delay. At nine, I slung on my pack and started down the trail. Within minutes, a short, thin man in a sailor cap appeared, saying the ranger was close behind. The ranger soon rode up on his horse; as we walked back to Smith, the ranger explained in a Tennessee accent that he was a college student working in the park for the summer and unfamiliar with this section of the trail. He'd gotten lost, he admitted. Just eighteen or nineteen, he was wearing low shoes without heels to catch his stirrups, his socks riddled with holes.

At our bivouac, the young ranger took out his shortwave radio and threw a weighted antenna over a branch. For three hours we tried to establish contact with the ranger station at Cedar Grove but were unable to make a connection. Finally he suggested I take his horse and ride out to make arrangements. I agreed, anxious to move on. It was now twenty-four hours since I had diagnosed Smith.

At 1 P.M. I met six muscular boys from the Civilian Conservation Corps, carrying a stretcher. They reported that the packer we'd sent down had arrived at Cedar Grove at 2 A.M. and alerted the ranger there; he, in turn, had taken the message to the CCC camp. Nervous about starting in the dark, the group had waited until morning. (Having negotiated the trails myself, I understood their hesitation but wished they had come anyway.) We returned to where Lieberman and the young ranger waited with Smith. We discarded our fragile, jerry-rigged carrier, transferred Smith to the new stretcher, and started down the trail. Two of the boys proved unable to bear the weight, but the remaining four, built like workhorses, made good time. Twice at river crossings the water was so high we had to balance Smith and the stretcher along the spine of the ranger's horse. I told the ranger he could leave us, but we kept the horse.

At 4:30 a second wave of CCC boys arrived, bringing the carriers to fourteen. Satisfied that Lieberman and the boys could manage on their own, I rode ahead, wanting to arrive before the group and make sure further transportation was in place. Smith would need to be taken by ambulance to Fresno and then flown to San Francisco. The boys still had at least eight miles to travel with their burden—assuming the packer had arranged for the ambulance to be at Zumwalt Meadows. If not, they would have to go another six miles on the dirt road to Cedar Grove.

Dusk gave way to night as I rode along alone. I had not been on a horse for a long time, and my bottom grew sore from rubbing against the saddle. Slowly the trail faded to black, until I could no longer make out its outline against the grass. I let the reins fall loose, trusting the experienced horse to find its way. A half moon rose, casting silver beams on the cliffs and across the meadows. The trees stood stark and knifelike; the trailside creek murmured quietly. Such a clear, lovely night would have called for reflection had I not been exhausted and otherwise occupied. Riding on across the south fork of the Kings River and Copper Creek, I found my eyes closing and my head dropping to my chest several times, only to be bounced up by a bump in the trail.

It was nearly 10 P.M. when I arrived at Zumwalt Meadows—only to find no ambulance waiting. Both my horse and I were outraged but had little choice other than to continue on. Two miles before Cedar Grove, I found another rescue party walking by flashlight. Directing them to where the sick man waited, I went on, reaching Cedar Grove around eleven. I roused the ambulance drivers and rangers and tried to make arrangements to fly Smith out of Fresno. Telephone line problems delayed our message getting through for a couple more hours and garbled it: around midnight, Pem rushed into the station at Cedar Grove station with a doctor he'd found in Grant Grove. Apparently the message that got through said to bring a doctor and emergency operating equipment immediately.

Back up the trail, the second team stopped in exhaustion to wait for replacements. At 3:30 A.M. the third rescue party took over. I caught a couple hours of sleep at the station and then drove with Pem and a ranger in the ambulance to Zumwalt Meadows. Finally, a few minutes after five, the entire group—now inflated to twenty-five—showed up. Having gone without any real sleep for two nights, walked the entire way, and carried his friend for part of it, Lieberman was on the verge of collapse; we sent him off to sleep at the station. Smith was loaded into the ambulance, which sped away over the serpentine mountain roads at fifty miles an hour. On the way to Fresno, Pem told me that Smith was vice president of the California and Hawaiian Sugar Refining Company. He had alerted the company president of Smith's condition, and that gentleman was on his way to Fresno in person to secure the plane arrangements.

When the ambulance pulled into the Fresno airport at half past eight, I strode to the counter to inquire about the plane. The attendant just stared at me and did nothing. It took me a few seconds to realize that after two weeks in the backcountry I was filthy and bearded, boots and khakis dustier than a mountain goat. Spotting Pem, the C&H president, a Mr. Campiglia, came over and introduced himself, shaking my hand reluctantly. He seemed to have difficulty believing I was a doctor. We boarded the plane, a four-passenger Stinson. By 11 A.M.—almost forty-eight hours after I found Smith at East Lake—we wheeled him into Stanford Hospital.

The nurse on duty, one with whom I had worked numerous times, held up her hand as we approached the emergency doors.

"No family beyond this point," she said, looking dubiously at me.

"But this is my patient," I said.

She leaned closer, furrowing her brow, trying to decipher the face under the grime and sweat. "Dr. Wayburn, is that you?"

Amazingly enough, Smith's ulcer healed without an operation. Within a few days, he was ready to be released. And so ended my last trip into the High Sierra before I reported for military service midway through 1942.

CHAPTER TWO

THE HILLS OF HOME

Saving the Marin County Wildlands

🌿

We should err on the side of protecting too much,
rather than too little. The burden of proof should be on
those who would dismantle our natural legacy.

—Sylvia Earle, *Wild Earth*

AFTER FOUR YEARS of military service, I returned to San Francisco eager to reestablish my medical practice and return to the pleasures of civilian life. The place I came home to, however, was not the same one I had left. Although the Bay Area was thousands of miles from any battlefield, World War II had irrevocably altered its landscapes so quickly and drastically that I experienced culture shock on coming home.

San Francisco had been the point of embarkation for all military operations in the Pacific theater and a center for shipbuilding and other paramilitary industries—the beginning of the state's billion-dollar defense trade. Houses had to be built to accommodate the workers and their families. With all of the city's vacant lots already built on, older houses were demolished for new, larger flats; in the downtown area, four-story structures were replaced by towers twenty-five or thirty-five stories high.

Many people brought to California by the war, including thousands of servicemen and–women who had passed through, decided to settle in or near the city by the bay. The surrounding farms disappeared as tract homes displaced pastureland and artichoke fields. Developments began covering the hills. The bedroom communities across San Francisco Bay to the north in eastern Marin County, to the east beyond Oakland and Berkeley, and to the south on the Peninsula became established towns and cities. All this expansion happened in the space of a few years.

The Bay Area's wealth of open spaces had much to do with why I'd chosen to settle here, and these encroachments on the natural landscape disturbed me. As a solitary individual, I felt there was little I could do to stem the tide of development. Only to the north, in southern and western Marin, did extensive open space remain—in the shadow of Mount Tamalpais with its rugged, steep terrain and foggy coastline. This area soon became my favorite weekend escape.

Late one Sunday afternoon while hiking on Tamalpais, I paused on a cliff overlooking the Pacific to watch the setting sun dawdle on the ocean's horizon, tinting the surrounding sky a brilliant rose. At my back, a full moon crept slowly into the night. It was as if I stood on the boundary of two worlds: a place where night met day, land met sea, east met west.

These hills of home were a wilderness practically in my backyard—a place where one could always find solace from the hustle of the work week. I had always thought of the Marin hills as open space, inviolable. But I now realized I could not take for granted that they would always be there. Here was a place that deserved my attention as a conservationist—and that of the Sierra Club.

In the fall of 1947, I was elected to the executive committee of the Sierra Club's San Francisco Bay Chapter. I had run reluctantly after friends Bob Schallenberger and Jack Dearth, both members, had convinced me to put up my name. The same people had been in office year after year, they said; the Club needed new blood. At first I resisted their pleas, as work continued to occupy so much of my time, and I was already involved with the San Francisco Medical Society. But Bob and Jack argued persuasively that the Club would pursue a more aggressive conservation agenda—including campaigns to preserve open space in the Bay Area—if only some young turks could get on the local executive committee.

So now I was in a position to work more effectively through the Club's resources to help safeguard my treasured home landscapes. And though I could not have known it, I was also about to acquire a life's partner in this work of a lifetime.

Since coming back from the war I had been subletting an apartment on Taylor Street from the artist Werner Phillip and his wife, Elizabeth, who were away on an extended vacation. When they returned, an apartment just above in the same building fortuitously became available, which I leased. I soon became friendly with the Phillips, and one evening not long after I moved in, they invited me to a party celebrating Werner's fiftieth birthday.

Among Werner's talents was portraiture, and people who sat for him often attended their parties. To this one, unbeknownst to me, Elizabeth and Werner had invited three of Werner's subjects—all young, unmarried women. I was at this time nearly forty, and though I had dated a number of women, I'd never had time to devote myself seriously to a relationship; my work had been too demanding. My neighbors, however, had decided it was time for me to settle down and had ensured their plans by making sure I was the only available bachelor in the room.

I soon found myself engaged in conversation. All of the women were attractive, but one in particular caught my eye: Peggy Elliott, a slim, graceful, brown-haired copywriter who worked at the advertising agency J. Walter Thompson. Werner had recently painted Peggy's portrait, but she hadn't bought it, a decision she later regretted when the painting was sold. Peggy was stylish in a black hat, a vestige of her New York days as an assistant editor at *Vogue* magazine. The hat's broad brim veiled her features, and I found myself having to bend down to look into her fair face and blue eyes.

Lively and articulate as well as beautiful, this young woman occupied my attention for much of the evening. She was a decade younger than I. She smoked, but I was willing to overlook that. I asked her if she liked to hike.

"Oh, I love to hike," she said. Growing up, she had spent her summers on the north shore of Long Island, where she had frequently gone walking. We made a date for the next weekend.

The following Sunday I knocked on the door of Peggy's studio apartment on Nob Hill. With me were my friend and fellow hiker Bob Schallenberger and his girlfriend, Bessie Lawrence, all of us dressed for the occasion in khakis and leather boots, long-sleeved shirts, and hats. Peggy opened the door wearing a delicate white sleeveless blouse, white shorts, and white canvas sneakers—an outfit she had purchased from the City of Paris department store expressly for our date. Later she admitted that her first thought upon seeing us was, "Who *are* these people?" Her second, which good breeding fortunately forbade acting on, was to shut the door.

We drove across the Golden Gate Bridge and over the Panoramic Highway to Pantoll Meadow on Mount Tamalpais. Our destination, Stinson Beach, lay some three miles and 1,600 feet below, through groves of Douglas fir and redwood. We began our descent on the Steep Ravine Trail, which lived up to its name: so steep in places that ladders had been installed to bridge the levels. Arriving at the golden sands of Stinson, western Marin's most popular beach, we rented lockers, towels, and gray wool tank suits from the concessionaire (fifty cents a person) and went for a swim in the ocean.

There remained, of course, the matter of going back up the mountain. As Peggy would later confess, the highest elevation on Long Island was 150 feet, her former "hikes" had really been level walks, and she regularly took taxis to cross the street. She also smoked two packs of cigarettes a day. About a third of the way back up, Peggy and Bob, also a smoker, began stopping every few hundred feet to light up. I was growing apprehensive, perhaps even a bit irritated; the day was growing late and Peggy looked exhausted. I suggested they wait while I hiked ahead and drove back down the highway to a point where it met the trail. But Peggy adamantly refused. "You will not. I'm walking," she said, crushing her cigarette and stomping up the trail.

She did make it back to the car, though the next morning she was unable to get out of bed and called in sick to work. Unaware of this, I remained impressed with her for completing such a tough hike. She, for her part, was sure she never wanted to see me again. But when I called and asked her to dinner and dancing at the Mark Hopkins Hotel, she gave me a second chance. With the best orchestra in town and a skyline view of the city, the "Top of the Mark" was *the* place to go in San Francisco.

After just three weeks, we both knew the relationship was serious. It wasn't just a matter of physical attraction. Peggy was intelligent and trusting; in turn, I found myself able to confide in her in a way I'd found difficult with other women. Moreover, she showed growing enthusiasm for the outdoor pursuits and interest in my concern for preserving natural landscapes.

We were married in September 1947, five and a half months after our first meeting. It was a small affair, a civil judge performing the ceremony in Aunt Maude and Uncle Will's living room. The only other witnesses were Peggy's mother and my brother Lewis, who had flown down from Medford, Oregon. Exceedingly private, I had told few friends, and we had few in common at that point. My mother was unable to leave Georgia, as my stepfather was in the hospital; in fact, he died the day of the ceremony.

For our honeymoon, Peggy and I drove through the northern California redwoods country and up the coast of Oregon and Washington, ultimately reaching the Empress Hotel in Victoria, British Columbia. On the left side of the car, for most of the trip north, rocky cliffs gave way to the Pacific; to the right, thick stands of Douglas fir blanketed the hills. Logging in northern California and Oregon has since reduced these vast forests to scattered patches. We did not stop to camp or hike but stayed only in hotels; Peggy had insisted we leave all the camping gear at home.

The next year we bought a pretty, shingled house at 2619 Divisadero Street between Broadway and Vallejo on one of San Francisco's steepest hills. The incline is so steep that residents have to park their cars perpendicular to the curb, with the chassis at a sharp angle. To get out, a passenger on the downhill side has to climb over the driver's seat or else risk opening the passenger door and tumbling down the hill. The house faced east, and its back windows framed the bay, the Golden Gate, and across the water, the hills of Marin.

LIKE MOST PEOPLE who have lived in one place long enough to grow roots, I considered my home landscape special. But the slopes and valleys of Marin County are in fact unique, the product of climatic and topographical conditions unrepeated anywhere else in the world. Marin is coastal range country. Its soils are composed of metamorphosed rubble formed by eons of friction between two tectonic plates—the rift known as the San Andreas Fault. Its hills—actually ridges that run more or less north-south—are edged on the west by sandy shorelines; above, rocky cliffs perch like balconies overlooking the Pacific.

The highest of these ridges, Mount Tamalpais, crests 2,600 feet above the ocean floor. It was named by the Ohlone tribe for a mythical princess; they saw in the gentle slopes a sleeping princess, her long hair cascading toward the bay. In the centuries before Spanish conquest, the coastal Miwok, a branch of the Ohlone, roamed here along with Columbian blacktail deer, harbor seals, and scores of bird species; the wildlife is still here though the Indians are long gone.

Narrow canyons dissect the hills. In spring, grasses compete with lupine and poppies for space on the slopes; in winter, rains restore the meadows to green and seasonal creeks run fast. Fog rises from the ocean each morning and night, draping the coastline in mystery, veiling the prominent peaks and ridges until they are only suggestions of a fantastic, untamed landscape. In summer, marine fog keeps the weather cool but not cold and the air moist—both requisites for the magnificent *Sequoia sempervirens,* the giant redwoods that form towering groves just inland from northern California's coast.

Until the 1940s, most of the houses in Marin were summer homes for San Franciscans. Before the Golden Gate Bridge was completed in 1938, the need to commute by ferry deterred most from establishing principal residences across the bay; but after the war, as people crowded into the region, southeastern Marin became much more attractive and accessible, and development proceeded apace.

Other than its water district lands, southern Marin County had only two publicly protected areas at this time: Mount Tamalpais State Park, with 870 acres, and Muir Woods National Monument, with 495 acres. On a map, the state park wrapped around the national monument like a crab's claw, ending abruptly at Panoramic Highway, with water district lands to the north. The paths I hiked on often took me over private land—still open space, but unprotected and ripe for development.

In more remote west Marin, the issues were different, but even more open land was at risk. Here, much of the native forest had been logged during and after the Gold Rush to meet San Francisco's booming demand for lumber. The meadows became grazing lands, and a century later most of the remaining private acreage was still in large parcels owned by ranchers. These ranches, however, were floundering economically. Thin topsoil, rugged terrain, and long, dry summers all worked against them, and generations of cattle had overgrazed the land, inviting erosion. With property taxes beginning to rise, many ranchers were struggling to make ends meet; land speculators were moving in.

But these problems were little known outside the local community, and when I began to voice concern about the fate of the ranch lands, people would sometimes retort, "Don't you like ranches? They're so picturesque." Those ranches had been in the same families for generations and would always remain that way, they said. Such responses expressed a romantic vision of the Old West, as well as the belief that private property was preferable to public parks because owners cared for the land better than the government did—a belief I once shared. These factors deflected my sense of urgency for some time.

Local consciousness of the need to preserve rural Marin was growing along with my own, however. Members of several conservation clubs around San Francisco Bay were working to help the state acquire particular plots of land, a few acres at a time. For example, I worked with the Sierra Club and other groups to acquire Dad O'Rourke's Bench, 300 acres on the western slope of Mount Tamalpais—one of my first acts of conservation.

As time passed, a piecemeal approach to protecting this irreplaceable open space became less and less acceptable to me and others. One Sunday afternoon in 1947, while hiking above Muir Woods, I sat down in the grass and thought about what an ideal version of Mount Tamalpais State Park might contain. A complete watershed—that is, the land and waters from ridge to ridge—should be protected. That would mean the entire south slope of Mount Tamalpais, for now still free from massive development. It wasn't enough simply to add a few acres here and there; nature doesn't divide herself into measured plots. A watershed encompasses the chain of life; if any part is developed, the integrity of the whole ecosystem is threatened. Understanding this fundamental natural order, following the land's natural topography, was critical to meaningful preservation of Marin's open space.

Sitting in that meadow, I sketched a rough mental map of the area that should be preserved: the entire south slope of the mountain down to Muir Woods and across Redwood Creek and up again to include the ridge on the opposite side. This set of boundaries—far more ambitious than anyone had yet proposed—would enlarge the state park from 870 to 6,300 acres.

A few weeks later I shared my vision with Jim Tryner, the official in charge of acquiring new acreage for the state parks system. Tryner agreed that it was a good idea to expand Mount Tam Park to include the entire watershed of Redwood Creek. However, his boss Newton Drury, the new chief of the California Division of Parks and Beaches, who had just spent eleven years as director of the National Park Service, did not. So the agency declined to pursue the plan.

During this period I found myself increasingly spending my free time working with the Sierra Club, which seemed like the perfect home for my burgeoning concerns about the San Francisco Bay Area landscape. In 1946, I joined the Club's Conservation Committee, which was formed before the war but now was becoming increasingly more active. And in 1949, I chaired the Club's first regional conservation committee—that of the San Francisco Bay Chapter, formed so that local concerns could be addressed without draining the Club's resources from other campaigns.

In 1948, AN imminent threat of losing precious land around Mount Tam kicked my preservation efforts into high gear: the 700-acre Dias Ranch was sold to speculators. Two-thirds of the Dias property lay in Frank's Valley, just south of Muir Woods, and was part of the area I hoped to include in an expanded state park. The parcel ran across Panoramic Highway to the edge of the town of Mill Valley. On behalf of the Sierra Club, I began to research the available options for acquiring the ranch as open space. Many pieces of the puzzle would have to be assembled: the landowners' cooperation, the will of public officials, and most important, the funding. The 1928 California State Park Bond Act had established a matching fund for the acquisition of public land, and there was still some money in this fund. Even if state officials could be convinced the land was worth preserving, however, more money would have to be found, probably through a new bond issue.

My next action was to enlist Bill Losh, a conservation-minded business-man who owned a downtown public relations firm. Losh discovered the identities of the Dias Ranch speculators: a San Francisco lawyer (later a federal judge) named Stanley Weigel, and Carl Priest, the manager of the western division of the Parker Pen Company. Weigel and Priest proved friendly and agreed to meet with Losh and me. We explained that our primary concern was for the 540 acres of the Dias Ranch that lay west of Panoramic Highway. If this land were developed, the magnificent views from the crest of the highway to the Pacific would be cluttered with rooftops and telephone poles. Moreover, that acreage was part of the watershed of Redwood Creek, which runs through Muir Woods and into the ocean at Muir Beach. Adding it to the park would protect the complete watershed and form an ecological boundary for lands already under protection.

Surprisingly, Weigel and Priest were receptive to our vision. They promised to develop only the acreage east of the highway—less than a third of the total they'd purchased. The 540 acres to the west would remain undeveloped until money for its acquisition by the state could be raised through a bond act. Such an act of generosity is difficult to imagine today.

However, the state still needed to be convinced that the acquisition of Dias Ranch was a priority. I arranged for state parks chief Newton Drury to tour the property in person, believing that the land, with its dramatic cliffs and sweeping views of the Pacific, would speak for itself. Arthur Johnson, chairman of the California Riding and Hiking Trail Committee of the State Park Commission, joined us on the visit to Mount Tamalpais. Unfortunately, nature didn't cooperate that day. The sky was overcast; fog blocked the view from the highway to the ocean, permitting only glimpses of the manzanita-covered slopes.

Neither Drury nor Johnson knew this landscape. Johnson lived in the southern half of the state, and Drury had yet to explore the Marin coastline. On such a day, they could not see or even imagine the drama of the steep cliffs and winding coastline, the miles of blue ocean stretching to the horizon like a flat blue sheet—all hidden below. "We've got lots of areas like this in southern California," Johnson said, clearly unimpressed. No ground was gained that day in the fight for an ecologically complete park—but we were just getting started.

NEWTON DRURY DID have a vision for enlarging Mount Tamalpais State Park, but it did not then include the Dias Ranch. Drury's plan focused on acquiring the Brazil Ranch, a 1,200-acre parcel bordering Muir Woods on the west and adjacent to the existing state park. For him, this location made Brazil Ranch the logical choice, and he wasn't convinced that development west of Panoramic Highway was an immediate issue. There would be time to secure that property down the line if necessary, he said.

I disagreed. It wasn't that I didn't want to include the Brazil Ranch; both parcels were important. This was the first of many times I would run up against an agency mentality that seemed to view land options in terms of mutually exclusive choices—either this land or that land—when really the park in question needed both. I came to think of it as the "either/or" philosophy. In this case, however, the Dias Ranch had to take priority; the land was already in the hands of real estate developers. Weigel and Priest were willing to hold off on developing—but only if the state demonstrated it was willing to purchase the property.

The debate over Dias Ranch was indicative of more than just a disagreement over priorities. It demonstrated a growing split between the methods of state park bureaucrats and those of emerging conservationists. Drury was anxious about adding too much too fast—more concerned with how his agency would finance and staff new park additions than in the need to secure large, important parcels. For me, the smooth running of a bureaucracy took a backseat to preserving special places. The vision was paramount; once it was clear, I believed, the answers would be found. But once a place was gone, it could never be retrieved.

During this period, from about 1948 to 1953, I testified several times before the California State Park Commission in San Francisco and Sacramento, acting on behalf of several conservation groups. This was a daunting task that involved arguing against parks chief Drury, and the process took several years, but in the end I prevailed. In 1955, the California Legislature passed a bond act for $700,000 to purchase the 540 acres of Dias Ranch for addition to Mount Tamalpais State Park. True to their word, Weigel and Priest had left the land untouched—for seven years.

BESIDES DEVELOPMENT OF the Dias Ranch, other such plans for southern Marin were lurking. In 1953, I learned that three men were in the process of buying thirty acres of the Brazil Ranch lands above the Dipsea Trail, adjacent to the headquarters of Mount Tamalpais State Park at Pan Toll. Each of the three planned to build a home.

I brought this information to the attention of the State Park Commission, a body appointed by the governor that oversaw the Division of Parks and Beaches. There were three commissioners, but usually just two attended meetings: Charles Kasch, publisher of Ukiah's daily paper, and Joseph Knowland, publisher of the *Oakland Tribune,* had both been on the commission for years. Knowland, the elderly chairman, slept through most of this 1953 meeting but woke up long enough to argue that the state had no right to interfere with the Brazil purchasers. They were buying the land fair and square; their rights had to be respected.

I believed that something more important was at stake: the future of what could become one of our greatest state parks. This purchase would set a dangerous precedent: the state might balk at acquiring neighboring lands on the grounds that the area was already developed. Fortunately, I managed to convince Commissioner Kasch, who told the buyers that the state would condemn the 30 acres because it planned to include the land in the state park. The buyers agreed not to pursue the transaction; the Brazil family returned their deposit, and the immediate threat was eased. It would be years, however, before the state would have the funds to purchase the entire Brazil acreage.

Even more potentially devastating was the California Department of Highways' plan to build a freeway through southern and western Marin County. The plan called for expanding the scenic, two-lane Highway One into a four-lane highway that would travel down to Muir Beach, then up the coastal ridge past Pantoll Meadow to intersect with Ridgecrest Boulevard at the crest, then over the entire Bolinas Ridge to meet Sir Francis Drake Boulevard north of the state park. The Department claimed the highway was needed to accommodate west Marin's anticipated population of more than a quarter million. To me, it sounded like a self-fulfilling prophecy: it's well known that freeways bring people. With the high-speed road in place, other infrastructure—power lines and water supply—would soon follow. Blocking the highway was of pivotal importance, I thought.

A public hearing on the highway plan was held in 1953. I was unable to make the hearing personally and requested that the Sierra Club send

Bruce Kilgore to make our case. Kilgore, then editor of the *Sierra Club Bulletin* and an eloquent voice for preservation, delivered compelling testimony, and the proposal was dropped.

THE COMPLICATED TASK of assembling lands to expand Mount Tam State Park would continue for decades. The 1955 bond act, which had earmarked $700,000 for park acquisitions, was deemed faulty after the fact, and another bond was passed in 1958 for $1.1 million—an increase indicative of increasing land values and of increased concern on the state's part. Several more years would pass before the state would actually purchase the Dias and Brazil properties.

While the bond provided money, the state still had to identify acquisition priorities. Around 1960, Beaches and Parks chief Newton Drury held a meeting to determine the order in which lands should be purchased. I was invited to represent local conservationists. Local landowners with properties for potential sale also attended. At that meeting William Kent Jr., a member of one of the area's most prominent families, made a critical offer to the state.

Kent's father, William Kent Sr., had donated the land for Muir Woods National Monument back in 1908, and his children inherited large portions of southern and western Marin, including Stinson Beach. In the succeeding decades, however, the Kent family fortune dissipated to the point that William Kent Jr. needed to sell some of its holdings. One of these was the Steep Ravine property, a 200-acre parcel on the southwest slope of Mount Tam, surrounding the trail Peggy and I hiked on our first date. He would sell Steep Ravine for public use, Kent told us, if the state committed to making this purchase first in line; otherwise, he would sell it to interested developers. This got the state's attention, and eventually the Steep Ravine acreage was acquired.

Kent took me aside at the meeting and told me a cautionary tale about another of their properties. Seadrift is a span of sand dunes bordering Bolinas Lagoon and stretching along the Pacific shore from Stinson Beach northward almost to the cliffs of Bolinas. In the 1930s, the Kent family offered Seadrift to the state for public use in lieu of paying back taxes but was turned down. In the early 1950s, the Kents again asked the state to acquire the property, this time for $50,000. Chief Drury rejected the offer, alleging that the state already owned enough of Stinson Beach. Today, Seadrift is the premier vacation development in Marin County. Its sands have been paved with roads, every inch of its ground subdivided into lots with million-dollar homes, and manned security gates keep out would-be trespassers. Seadrift is paradise for the few who can afford it—but it could have benefited so many more people as public property in its natural state.

Having had some success in expanding parkland close to San Francisco, we Bay Area conservationists were encouraged to explore other special lands in the region with a view toward protection. Early in my campaign to enlarge Mount Tam State Park, I had spoken with park supervisor George Holmboe, who essentially said, "We've got our hands full already; we don't need any large additions to the park. Why don't you go up north to Point Reyes?"

Point Reyes? I knew little about it, but in the late 1950s Peggy and I began spending our weekends exploring this peninsula, which reaches out into the Pacific, less than an hour north of San Francisco by car. We discovered a wild and varied landscape that some called an "island in time," largely unaltered since Sir Francis Drake sailed onto its shores in 1579. Steep, craggy cliffs frame miles of broad, sandy beaches. Tide pools carved into the rock hold starfish, sea urchins, and sea anemones, while near the peninsula's northern end, inlets known as *esteros* weave through marshes.

The Point Reyes peninsula is delineated by the San Andreas fault, which runs northwest through Bolinas Lagoon to Tomales Bay and out into the ocean, separating tectonic plates on the earth's crust. The peninsula lies on the Pacific Plate, while the mainland rests on the North American Plate. State Highway One traces the fault line; westward, the land rises from road level to 1,400 feet at the crest of Inverness Ridge. On our explorations, Peggy and I trekked through forests of bishop pine, Douglas fir, and bay trees, enjoying a feast of pungent fragrances, and crossed meadows of waving summer grasses and wildflowers. The land was abundant in wildlife: black-tailed deer, bobcats, foxes, hawks, pelicans, herons, egrets, and sea lions were all residents. In January, gray whales migrating south could be spotted from the shore near the Point Reyes lighthouse.

Except for the villages of Bolinas, Point Reyes Station, Olema, and Inverness, the area had not been developed. The weather could be chilly and the coast fog-laden, and the narrow, winding roads made for a long commute to the city. Indeed, most San Francisco residents had never seen Point Reyes. As in southern Marin County, most of the land was divided into ranches dating back to Spanish land grants. A 1955 National Park Service survey of the Pacific Coast included the peninsula on its list of sites worthy of national park status. But Point Reyes had not been designated as a national park, and few of its thousands of acres of beach, marsh, forest, and meadow had any protection.

Although few believed it was politically feasible to make Point Reyes a national park, I soon came to feel strongly that the attempt should be made, doubting that the land could be preserved if it remained as private property. Rising real estate prices, stricter state and county sanitary regulations, and thinning topsoil were conspiring to make ranching in this part of Marin economically difficult. And property taxes, based on the land's "highest and best use"—now deemed by the county to be subdivision into 40- to 60-acre ranchettes—were climbing fast. It was sad if understandable that most ranchers, faced with the choice of eking out a meager existence or selling their land to developers, would take the cash.

In the late 1950s, Clem Miller, congressional representative for the Point Reyes region, submitted a bill in the House of Representatives for the federal government to acquire most of the peninsula. Joel Gustafson, a professor of biology at San Francisco State University, chaired the newly formed Point Reyes Foundation to organize for the protection of these lands. Peggy was a founding member, and I became the Sierra Club's representative. Tragically, Miller died in a plane crash while campaigning for reelection in 1960. He was buried in the future park at Arch Rock, a serpentine cliff overlooking the Pacific. Fortunately, Don Clausen, a Crescent City resident elected to fill Miller's seat, continued to campaign for preservation of Point Reyes.

The Sierra Club became highly involved in the campaign, producing a short film about Point Reyes by Laurel Reynolds and Mindy Hoover as well as an Exhibit Format book, *Island in Time,* with stunning photographs and a text by *San Francisco Chronicle* staff writer Harold Gilliam.

It was by then a common Sierra Club campaign tactic to team with a local organization that would take the lead publicly. In this case, the Club worked behind the scenes as the main lobbying group, while the Point Reyes Foundation served as the up-front organization. Working with a grassroots group was a matter not only of combining resources but of political necessity. By the 1960s, after several national campaigns, the Sierra Club had grown large and powerful—too much so in the eyes of many—and our causes tended to win more public support if they were perceived as originating in a local concern.

The Point Reyes campaign also met with some local resistance. Unlike ranchers in the southern half of the county, the ranchers in northwest Marin hung on tightly to their homesteads even though economically beleaguered, loath to sell to the U.S. government.

Loggers also had come into the area seeking profitable timber, but they soon realized the trees weren't as good as those in northern California and Oregon. One of these speculating lumbermen, an Oregonian named William Sweet, had purchased thousands of acres. When he found he couldn't turn a profit from logging, he subdivided his land into 60-acre ranchettes, one of which he offered to sell to Peggy and me at a very reasonable price. (We turned him down.) I feared that subdivision could take place throughout Point Reyes if it were not protected.

The campaign won strong support, however, both in the Bay Area and in Washington, and in 1962, Congress approved Point Reyes National Seashore—as much in a memorial to Clem Miller as a result of our efforts. Congress agreed to purchase the ranches, which resulted in 58,000 acres being set aside. One of the local ranchers, Boyd Stewart, proved instrumental in persuading his fellow ranchers to sell their land to the government, letting them know that they could retain their homes as a lifetime estate, lease their former land for grazing, and avoid paying property taxes—benefits provided by the Miller bill.

The national seashore was a fine achievement as far as it went, but I wanted more. I had a vision of Point Reyes National Seashore connecting to the hills of southern Marin and Mount Tamalpais State Park, forming an unbroken stretch of public lands leading out of San Francisco and north through Marin. Such a super-park would be ample to accommodate the city's recreational demand and offer a rich panoply of landforms: mountain, forest, stream, marsh, estuary, beach, and coastline. It might also serve as an impetus for other parts of the country, since at that time no sizable national park existed adjacent to a major city. Coincidentally, in 1963 the President's Outdoor Recreation Resources Review Commission (ORRRC) issued a report urging more federal efforts to put parks in close proximity to where most people lived.

By the middle of 1969, the pieces of this puzzle were beginning to arrange themselves. Point Reyes was under national protection, and the state had acquired 6,300 acres of the south slope of Mount Tamalpais. Still, my vision of a continuous strip of protected lands from Point Reyes into San Francisco remained a dream, not a reality, while land values continued to rise and pressure to develop Marin intensified. I knew that if we didn't mount a major campaign for a large park soon, we would lose the only chance to save the wilderness in our backyard. And I was about to acquire the most committed and skillful ally I could have wished for.

I MET CONGRESSMAN Phillip Burton in 1964, shortly after his first election to the House of Representatives. I had been elected president of the Sierra Club for the first time in 1961 after having served for several years on the board of directors, and I was in Washington on several matters of business—one of which was to visit members of California's congressional delegation. I duly paid my respects to the Bay Area's newest representative, briefly introducing myself to Burton.

That evening, Bill Zimmerman, the Club's first lobbyist, took Peggy and me to dinner at the old Congressional Hotel, also the headquarters of the Democratic National Committee. At the next table, Phil Burton was dining with another new congressman, who left after an hour or so. Burton, a large man with piercing dark eyes, then drew up a chair to our table. We spoke briefly about conservation issues, including the Club's current campaign for a Redwood National Park. Burton listened intently. Unlike many politicians who gave lip service to conservation issues, Burton seemed genuinely interested.

After a time I said good-bye, and we started away. Suddenly I felt a huge ham of a hand on my left shoulder and turned around as Burton warned, "We'll be seeing a lot of each other." He was right. That chance meeting in a Washington restaurant sealed a new friendship.

Burton quickly became my closest ally on Capitol Hill and a close friend as well. He called me almost every time he was in San Francisco, often inviting me to dinner at his favorite restaurant, the House of Prime Rib on Van Ness Avenue. He would also ask me to appear at his political rallies, calling me his guru and soliciting my opinion on conservation issues—and on the trustworthiness of any conservationist who sought his support for a particular project.

Phil Burton could hardly be called a lover of the great outdoors. He didn't exercise; in Washington, a government driver chauffeured him the three blocks from his apartment to the Capitol. His conservation friends joked that the only time Burton ever took a walk was when he went outside for a cigarette at Ansel Adams's house. His diet consisted of prime rib, Stolichnaya vodka, and Chesterfield cigarettes. And on the surface, our personal styles couldn't have been more different. Burton was aggressive, at times bullying, his temper often flying off the handle. Other congressmen were physically intimidated by his rage, and Burton cultivated their fear. I, on the other hand, tended to avoid confrontation, preferring to rely on my southern diplomacy.

Our motives for preservation also differed. My clear goals stemmed from my ecological beliefs, but for Burton, a champion of the working class, parks held a different allure. He believed that parks could be a great social equalizer, offering respite to those unable to afford a private beach or a country home. What we shared, however, was a belief that people needed open spaces and the persistence to drive a campaign to its end. Although Burton is most often remembered for his welfare and social security reforms, he was, in fact, one of the greatest of environmental legislators—in my experience, the best.

By 1969, the political timing was right for a national urban recreation area. Walter Hickel, former governor of Alaska and President Nixon's newly appointed secretary of the interior, had just announced the administration's ambitious new plan, Parks to the People, which would establish new parks in urban areas. The National Park Service had already deemed fourteen sites worthy of consideration, including a Gateway East National Recreation Area outside New York City and a Gateway West National Recreation Area outside San Francisco.

Hickel was given further impetus to act when, in November 1969, a band of Native Americans took possession of Alcatraz, claiming the island on behalf of all Native Americans as compensation for lands taken by the whites. Nixon had little sympathy for the Indian occupation—they were creating a media sensation on federal land, and he wanted them off. Hickel suggested that the government incorporate Alcatraz into the Gateway West Recreation Area, and he directed the Bureau of Outdoor Recreation (a subdivision of the Interior Department) to work on a proposal.

I had little faith in Hickel's ability to generate a satisfactory park proposal. The Sierra Club had opposed his nomination as interior secretary. As governor of Alaska, he had supported the reckless development of the Trans-Alaska Pipeline System immediately after oil was discovered in Prudhoe Bay.

The Bureau of Outdoor Recreation worked on a Bay Area park proposal for three years but never formally released its plan. From my own connections in the Interior Department, I gathered that it amounted to some 3,000 to 4,000 acres, including Alcatraz and the U.S. military's obsolete forts in San Francisco and Marin counties. In 1969, Congressman William Mailliard of Marin introduced a skeletal bill to convert the surplus military land into park space—a minimal gesture compared to the great park I had in mind.

ONE KEY AREA for a gateway park outside San Francisco was the Marin headlands, the windswept hilltops just north of the Golden Gate Bridge. An earlier National Park Service survey had suggested the headlands as a possible park site. Several military forts had been located here, and during the 1960s, the Department of Defense ceded several parcels, 40 to 80 acres in size, as surplus. We urged the NPS to acquire these lands, but it declined—another case of bureaucracy before land, of details suffocating vision. Marin Headlands Inc., a private group founded by San Francisco artist Katherine Frankforter, continued to advocate that the federal government convert the surplus military land to park space. The group, of which I was a member, included about twenty prominent citizens, mostly businessmen and lawyers. Eventually we were fortunate enough to get the California State Department of Recreation and Parks, under Director Charles DeTurk, to accept these parcels—at least temporarily.

Attempts to develop the Marin headlands did not cease while citizen groups and politicians were drawing up their plans. In the 1960s, Gulf Oil purchased almost 1,200 acres adjacent to Forts Barry and Cronkite near Sausalito and hired a Boston developer, Thomas Fruge, to design a city of 25,000, including shops, apartment buildings, and a high-rise hotel, collectively to be known as Marincello. The Marin County Board of Supervisors granted Fruge a preliminary building permit, and Fruge cleared an access road through Tennessee Valley. However, Fruge died in 1970 with the project still in early stages, and in the next election most of the supervisors who supported Marincello were replaced, and the project stalled.

In San Francisco, more trouble was brewing. In 1970 the General Services Administration selected Fort Miley, in the residential Richmond district, as the site of a new archives building to house all federal documents concerning the western states. The proposed one-acre multistoried building and adjacent parking lot would take up as much as 12.5 acres— far out of proportion for the neighborhood. Across Clement Street from the site lived a young artist named Amy Meyer, who began organizing neighbors to block the plan. Amy brought her concerns to the Sierra Club's San Francisco Bay Chapter, hoping to enlist support, whereupon the Club made her chair of the San Francisco Bay Chapter Conservation Committee, charged with halting construction of the mammoth building. It was her first conservation campaign.

Around this time, the Bay Chapter began seeking me out to aid their own burgeoning efforts in local conservation. By now I had been working for twenty-five years to protect Marin's lands. Amy listened to my ideas about creating a sweeping, expansive park at San Francisco's doorstep and came to see her own fight to stop the Fort Miley development as part of such a broad plan. It was about that time that I coined the phrase "Wilderness begins in your own backyard." More and more people were beginning to see that we needed open spaces nearby, not only as a convenient refuge from the city, but also as a buffer for overcrowded national parks.

While the Sierra Club proved immensely sympathetic and helpful in the gateway park effort, it had many other issues on its plate. I realized that a small, single-purpose organization was needed to push our project ahead fast, so in 1971 Amy and I joined forces to create People for a Golden Gate National Recreation Area (PFGGNRA), to rally local support. A dedicated group of some twenty-five volunteers, including Bob Young and Diane Hunter, formed the core. I was the organization's chairman and architect, theorizing how large an area should be encompassed, designing and redesigning boundaries, while Amy organized letter-writing and telephone campaigns. She worked tirelessly, seeking the approval of every Marin and San Francisco supervisor, local service organization, and business.

We worked quietly for three months, through March of 1971. In April I flew to Washington to present proposals on behalf of PFGGNRA. In fact, I carried two proposals: the first ambitious, the second audacious. I presented the first to Marin County Congressman Bill Mailliard, who responded, "You're asking for an awful lot." This plan called for a park of 26,000 acres, 10,000 of which had to be acquired from private landowners—too large, Mailliard thought. It was 20,000 acres more than what Hickel had asked for. But Mailliard said he would go along. I then took the plan to California senators Alan Cranston and John Tunney. Like Mailliard, they weren't enthusiastic, but they would introduce and support a bill in the U.S. Senate.

Lastly, I visited Phil Burton. He studied my maps in silence for several minutes, then asked, "Is this what you want?"

I admitted it wasn't everything.

"Well, what *do* you want?" he demanded.

I explained my second "dream" plan, which included 8,000 more acres in the Olema Valley, the area between Point Reyes National Seashore and the Marin Municipal Water District. If we could get these acres, there would be a continuous corridor of undeveloped open public land from Tomales Point in Point Reyes National Seashore all the way to San Francisco itself. Another 17,000 acres belonging to the water district wouldn't appear in the bill, but since the land was already dedicated, it would in effect bring the total number of protected acres to well over 100,000.

"Why didn't you present that to me?" Burton wanted to know.

"I didn't think it was politically feasible," I said.

Burton erupted. "Get the hell out of here!" he thundered. "You tell me what you want, not what's politically feasible, and I'll get it through Congress!"

I was delighted, needless to say. Back in San Francisco, I spent the next two months working on a final draft of the proposal. When I returned to Washington in June with PFGGNRA's full plan, Burton again asked, "Is this what you want?" This time it was.

Burton introduced the bill in committee on June 16, 1971. The acreage now totaled 34,000. In addition to the 8,000 acres in the Olema Valley, the proposal included all of the area's obsolete military outposts: Forts Barry, Baker, and Cronkite in Marin; Forts Funston, Mason, Miley, and Point in San Francisco; more than 1,400 acres in the Presidio; as well as the Marin Headlands and Angel Island State Parks, Alcatraz Island, and Baker, Phelan, and Ocean beaches. Burton added a provision to stave off the multimillion-dollar housing development at Marincello with a stipulation that would forbid anyone from occupying a home built after July 1, 1971. Burton called the mayor of Sausalito and told him to relay the news to Gulf.

Burton also took away any future right by the military to develop the Presidio. Considered the army's jewel, the Presidio, with its rolling green forests and lawns and historic forts, extended to the edge of the bay at the base of the Golden Gate Bridge. Its Spanish tiled-roof architecture evoked the nineteenth century and California's ties to Mexico. Burton suspected that the base eventually would be closed, and he wanted to safeguard against the possibility that the land would be subdivided and sold as prime real estate.

Not surprisingly, our bill did not win the support of the military, who thought that even Mailliard's version was too generous. Military officials wanted to cut the bill by 10,000 acres and retain control of the Presidio, and San Francisco mayor Joe Alioto sided with them. Nor did the NPS endorse our bill, preferring the smaller version first proposed by Mailliard. Rogers Morton, who had replaced Hickel as secretary of the interior, likewise supported the smaller version.

However, the PFGGNRA bill had the support of many San Franciscans, including the board of supervisors and the Sierra Club as well as both California senators. It also was the pet project of Phil Burton. By 1971, Burton had gained considerable prestige in the House and was a member of the House Subcommittee on National Parks. He had discovered that public parks were one of the few issues that drew bipartisan support. Burton was one of the most brilliant and thorough politicians I have ever known, tracking and rechecking lists of every member of the House, personally speaking with each one, sometimes threatening reluctant colleagues, until he was sure he had enough votes to win. At times, he seemed to legislate through the sheer force of his will. Our bill passed the full Interior and Insular Affairs Committee virtually intact in August 1972, just over a year after its introduction. In contrast, the Sierra Club's proposals to establish a Redwood National Park had languished in committee for several years.

In the Senate, however, our proposal was being held hostage by the Subcommittee on Parks and Recreation, whose chair, Alan Bible of Nevada, persistently delayed hearings. Concerned, Amy Meyer called park activists in New York, where lobbying efforts had already succeeded in establishing the Gateway East National Recreation Area. Organizers there said they had faced similar procrastination until President Nixon had personally toured the area and endorsed their proposal.

With Interior Secretary Morton's help and that of his highly supportive assistant secretary, Nathaniel Reed, we immediately set about arranging a presidential tour of the proposed parklands around San Francisco. Nixon's reelection campaign staff seized upon the idea as a way to create positive television footage and boost the president's image in San Francisco, where he lagged in the polls.

The day before his arrival, Nixon's visit was heralded by Bill Thomas on the front page of the *San Francisco Chronicle* with the headline: "Nixon to Dedicate an Uncreated Park." Thomas, who had worked for Phil Burton and helped to expand Mailliard's original proposal, had since left

Burton's office to write for the paper, and his article read like a eulogy to the northern California landscape. In this atmosphere of expectation, Nixon arrived, touring the proposed area in a small military steamer, the *General Coxe*.

At the U.S. Coast Guard dock, Amy and I stood in the receiving line to greet the president. As I shook his hand, he said to me, "You get the Congress to pass this bill. I'll sign it." Two days later, Senator Bible finally scheduled hearings, where, in a dramatic change of allegiance, Secretary Morton altered his final testimony before the National Parks Subcommittee. He took out his speech and ripped it in half.

"I'd prepared a speech for today," he said, "the speech the NPS wants me to give, but my friend Dr. Wayburn has convinced me otherwise." His last helicopter flight over the area, he explained, had changed his mind. The landscape had moved him. "I support the large park," Morton testified.

With such clear signs of approval from the president and the secretary of the interior, we were able to add the Olema Valley acreage to the Senate version of the bill. Burton thought that even if the president considered the additional lands excessive, he wouldn't dare risk his popularity by vetoing the bill. Ranchers were offered generous sums for their property and lifetime estates. The PFGGNRA bill passed the House October 11, 1972, one month after President Nixon toured the proposed park. The Senate approved it the next day. Two weeks later, just days before his reelection, Nixon signed the bill into law.

Phil Burton's political power had proved critical. While other public parks took years, sometimes decades, to be established, Burton pushed the Golden Gate National Recreation Area through Congress in just sixteen months.

In 1972, WHILE in the process of helping to outline the final boundaries of the GGNRA, I received a letter from a woman who had inherited the remainder of the old Dias Ranch—the 240 acres east of Panoramic Highway that Bill Losh and I had agreed years before would remain in the hands of Priest and Weigel. Miraculously, this land had remained undeveloped, and now its heiress wanted to see the property included in the new park. Through her desire, the entire Dias Ranch became public land.

Conservation cannot be left exclusively in the hands of government agencies. I trust the National Park Service no more than I do the U.S. Forest Service or the State Department of Parks and Recreation. It's not that these agencies are staffed by bad people. As public officials, however, they are influenced by a variety of people around them, including those who would sacrifice the earth for personal gain: timber and mining interests, oil companies, and real estate developers.

The conservationist's role is to be one of those influences and to be as clear and constant a voice as possible. Phil Burton was just such a voice.

Burton died in April 1983 of a ruptured abdominal aneurism. He was just fifty-six. For years, family and friends, including myself, had implored Burton to see his doctor, cut down on the alcohol and cigarettes, take time to relax. But he knew how to function at full throttle only, and his drive was never satiated. I once told Burton staffer Clive Pinnix that Burton was like a train; the job for the rest of us was simply to lay track. In any event, he ignored all pleas to take care of his health, often growing irritable at the mention. His death was not only untimely, but needless and preventable. It was also a great loss for conservationists everywhere. Phil Burton did more to protect the American landscape than any other legislator of his time.

In June 1991, eight years after his death, I attended the dedication ceremony for the Phil Burton Memorial on the lawn of San Francisco's Fort Mason overlooking the Golden Gate. A bronze statue of Burton stands ten feet, larger than life, as the living man often seemed. His trousers are rumpled, his tie hangs askew, one arm stretches forward as if arguing a point, the other raised as if indicating the whole of the bay, the Golden Gate, and the Marin headlands rising from the opposite shore. Thanks to his efforts, those hills contain only grasses, trees, and a few crumbling bunkers.

It is fitting that Burton, who considered himself an advocate for working people, should be memorialized here at Fort Mason, headquarters of the GGNRA. This facility offers recreational and cultural opportunities not usually associated with national parks. The former embarkation buildings now house art studios, intimate theaters, restaurants, and office space for arts organizations and nonprofits, all of whom are able to lease space at a fraction of San Francisco's sky-high rents.

From north to south, the Golden Gate National Recreation Area spans some twenty-five miles and 75,000 acres in all. At its widest, it's a mere six miles across, yet it includes seventy-five miles of serpentine coastline ripe for exploration. Its external boundaries encompass Mount Tamalpais State Park—only 870 acres in 1948, it now comprises 6,300. Point Reyes National Seashore, which was unprotected as late as the 1950s, now has 74,000 acres in public hands. The total acreage of public land in Marin and San Francisco counties is about 200,000, an astonishing figure for a metropolitan area of 6 million people. With a car, any Bay Area resident can reach one of its remote refuges in less than an hour and a half, or can visit its shoreline by public transportation.

Administratively the area remains a mishmash: two national park units; several state parks including Tomales Bay, Hearts Desire, and Samuel P. Taylor; as well as county and municipal recreation areas. It is not, however, as the NPS feared, too large. Its lands are always in use and, in some places, teeming with crowds. On weekends beginning in the spring, Panoramic Highway backs up for miles with visitors eager to get to Stinson Beach. In the 1950s children used to run among the redwoods of Muir Woods, playing hide and seek behind the massive trunks. Now visitors traverse a boardwalk so as not to overtamp the soil, giant redwoods loom from behind protective fencing, and cars overflow from the parking lot, spilling out to line the sides of the road.

Yet if we didn't have this wilderness in our backyard, the damage would be much worse—not just to Muir Woods, but to the character of the entire area. Unlike some other parts of the Bay Area, Marin developed a strong conservation ethic. The consequences of failing to develop one can be seen in San Mateo and Santa Clara counties, south of San Francisco, where the landscape is dominated by congested concrete avenues and business parks. Very little open land remains, most of it trampled by suburban sprawl and outgrowth from Silicon Valley.

I have continued to follow the fates of the Golden Gate National Recreation Area, Point Reyes National Seashore, and Mount Tamalpais State Park as a member of the Citizens' Advisory Commission for GGNRA and PRNS. Of all the issues that have emerged, the most notable has been the recent conversion of the Presidio of San Francisco from a military base to a national park inside the GGNRA. A congressional mandate transferred the administration of 80 percent of the Presidio from the National Park Service to a separate public/private organization, the Presidio Trust, which is directed to make the park self-supporting by the year 2013. This has created an enormous challenge for that institution. Although there has been progress in finding new support to replace what used to be a $25 million annual expense to the federal government, the fate of the Presidio as a national park remains uncertain.

Otherwise, both the Golden Gate National Recreation Area and Point Reyes National Seashore are fulfilling the promise we envisioned when they were established. They stand as islands of hope and solace for a large, nearby metropolitan constituency.

Each weekend for more than twenty-five years, Peggy and I drove across the Golden Gate Bridge to our house in Bolinas. There, wilderness does begin literally in our backyard, from where we could gaze onto the Pacific Ocean, Bolinas Lagoon, Stinson Beach, and beyond, along the craggy coastline. On a clear night, San Francisco sparkles in the distance. To the east, across the (still) two-lane Highway One, rises Mount Tamalpais; its forested bulk unmarred. Peggy and I and our four children spent countless weekends climbing Mount Tam. We explored its trails so often that the children came to call it "our mountain."

I hope others have called it theirs.

I am now ninety-six and no longer able to hike eighteen miles as I used to. While I still walk whenever possible, my enjoyment of the hills is more likely to be the view from a chair than from the trail. Yet Tamalpais, the headland hills, and the Point Reyes coastline continue to inspire me. Wilderness is enjoyed not only by the young and hardy. Sometimes it is simply enough to know it exists—to remember and to dream.

CHAPTER THREE

EXPLORING, DEFINING, AND PROMOTING WILDERNESS WITH THE SIERRA CLUB

❧

*It is only in very recent years—less than a century, in fact—
that an attentive attitude toward undisturbed and unutilized
nature has begun to emerge.*

—A. Starker Leopold, *"Wilderness and Culture,"* 1957

WHEN I SIGNED UP for a Sierra Club burro trip in 1939, I had no idea how closely my life was to become entwined with the organization over the next six decades. As noted, I was already an enthusiast about the Sierra Nevada back then but in no sense an active conservationist. Nor did I see any point simply in joining an exclusive organization; I was not really a joiner. However, my continuing education in wilderness exploration—much of it on Club trips—and my exposure to the ideas and traditions of conservation through contact with fellow members and Club leaders were shaping me irrevocably.

In retrospect, I think the Sierra Club and I were made for each other, and our meeting was timely for both. As the postwar years began, the Club was compelled to evolve rather quickly from a tight cadre of outdoor enthusiasts into a large, well-organized, national force in the realm of U.S. public land policy—partly under the urging of younger members like myself who witnessed with alarm the pressures exerted by postwar growth on our beloved landscapes and wanted to work effectively with others to preserve our natural heritage. The Club and I grew up together, in a sense, the organization's expanding scope and outlook mirroring my own growth as a conservationist.

But this is only a broad outline. What made me fall in love with the Club—in the same way I in fell in love with the Sierra Nevada, as well as with Peggy—lay in the details of my experience. So I'll share a few details from those early, formative times and describe where they led me.

SHORTLY AFTER RETURNING from military service in 1946, I was set to depart for a backpacking trip, but my partner had to cancel at the last minute. Lacking other options, I showed up on the Sierra Club's doorstep at 220 Bush Street in San Francisco hoping to find a replacement. No one was available.

"Why not try a High Trip instead?" a staff member asked. The famed "High Trip" had been the Club's chief calling card since early in the century: these highly organized expeditions took large groups of Club members into the Sierra Nevada two or three times each summer, with massive amounts of gear packed in on mules. That summer, three two-week trips were in the works, each in need of a trip doctor. Participants on each trip numbered about 150, as well as a young support crew and a dozen packers, each responsible for five mules that carried stoves, food, dunnage bags, and even an outhouse!

Six weeks out in the Sierra; didn't that sound like a dream come true? Actually, no. I balked at the idea of spending even two weeks in the Sierra with a group that constituted a roving town—hardly the antidote for someone seeking to get away from it all. My idea was to escape civilization, not to bring it with me into the mountains. But no backpacking partner was forthcoming, and the staff was persistent. I was needed, they said. I explained that I couldn't possibly spare the six weeks: my medical practice needed rebuilding. What about two weeks? they countered.

I reluctantly agreed to accompany one High Trip, feeling somewhat suckered. I joined the group at our starting point on the east side of the Sierra, near the town of Lone Pine. (Participants drove their own vehicles to the mountains, offering rides to the carless.) Our route would take us up an abandoned road that was originally intended to cross the crest of the range, then by trail over Army Pass. The east side is desertlike, more sand than dirt, a landscape of sage scrub and pine trees, at least at the lower elevations. I had explored the eastern Sierra on earlier trips and wasn't sure this one would hold many new discoveries for me.

Our group was led by Richard Leonard, a San Francisco lawyer and chair of the Outings Committee, then the Club's largest and most prominent branch. Leonard also was known locally as an expert climber. Fifteen years earlier, when a law student, he had founded the Cragmont Climbing Club, a small group that practiced on the rocky outcrops of the Berkeley hills.

Typically on a High Trip, the whole group moved to a new camp every one or two days. Once settled at each destination, trip members dispersed in pairs or small groups to take day hikes or scramble up peaks near camp. Miraculously, considering this scattering of such a large group, no one was lost. At night, we gathered for dinner and then around the campfire, telling stories or singing to strumming guitars. There was a sense of cama-raderie within the group, as well as a genuine devotion to the mountains' preservation. Members were respectful of the campsites, scoping the ground for litter each morning.

Far from becoming restive with the size of the group, I found myself growing more and more enamored of the High Trip and its participants. These were people I respected, who in addition to their regular professions were also amateur experts on the Sierra's history, geography, geology, and botany. Even more important, they were men and women of strong char-acter, who encountered the land with love and respect. Who wouldn't want to be included among their ranks?

Two days out, we watched a lone figure descend a mountain pass to meet our party. It was Francis Farquhar, a certified public accountant, climber, and former Club president, who in the 1930s had traveled to Washington, D.C., as the Club's representative in its big campaign of that decade, the establishment of Kings Canyon National Park. I enjoyed getting to know him, and later in the trip would climb the steep slopes of Mount Williamson with Francis and his wife, Marge, as well as Cliff and Verda Heimbucher, using ropes. The whole High Trip group climbed Mount Whitney, the tallest mountain in the lower forty-eight but much easier to climb than Williamson.

One day Dick Leonard led us across a miserable stretch of sand called Guyot Flat, a plateau about 5,000 feet high, south of Mount Whitney. The day was hot and dry, and our boots ground against the cracked earth, sending up sprays of dust. The plain stretched five or six miles across without the shade of a tree in sight. After an hour of trekking I caught up with Leonard to question the choice of terrain; the Sierra had so many vistas and valleys to offer, I wondered why the group had to tramp through this barren desert.

"Couldn't we have gone another way?" I demanded.

Socratically, he answered with another question: "Have you ever read John Muir?"

I admitted my unfamiliarity with the Club's revered founder. "But I will," I promised.

"Well, you should," Leonard said. "Muir described the beautiful wildflowers of Guyot Meadow before they were destroyed by herds of sheep."

I was astounded by this remark. Sheep had not grazed this land for two generations, and yet it remained devoid of vegetation. Grazing was so common; it was difficult to believe it could have such lasting repercussions. To me the Sierra Nevada, with its jagged peaks, ice-capped cornices, and rushing waterfalls, had seemed majestic, invincible. Yet the survival of its living parts, I suddenly realized, was tenuous. For eons the range had weathered nature's cataclysms, but it had not developed immunity to acts of human domestication. I resolved to read Muir's writings, and though I didn't find time for some years, they made a powerful impression on me when I finally did so.

At the end of the two-week outing, we circled back to the lowlands. No one's life had needed saving; in fact, the trip ended without medical incident. Not called upon to be a doctor on this trip, I was free simply to enjoy the experience of being a Sierra Club member among other members. Back at the trailhead we met the next group starting out. They were led by another Berkeley climber, a former army trainer who had been stationed in the Italian Alps during the war. Tall and blonde, he cut an impressive figure. I stopped just long enough to shake hands with the man with whom I was to work in tandem for many eventful years: David Brower.

That September, I attended the Club's annual banquet dinner at the Fairmont Hotel on San Francisco's Nob Hill. President Bestor Robinson, an Oakland attorney, looked dashing in his tuxedo as he presided over the ceremonies. I never imagined that someday I would be in his position.

As IT TURNED OUT, I rose quickly through the Club's ranks. I became a member of the national Conservation Committee, which set nationwide conservation priorities for the organization, in 1946. In 1947 I successfully ran for the executive committee of the San Francisco Bay Chapter and was elected its chair the following year. In 1949, I formed the first chapter-level conservation committee devoted to regional conservation problems, such as Mount Tamalpais State Park.

The first task I took on for this committee—really my initial venture in conservation work—was attempting to persuade the city of San Francisco to reject a new proposed road at Lands End that would run below the Palace of the Legion of Honor, a majestic art museum perched high on the cliffs overlooking the Golden Gate. The rock there was serpentine, and prolonged heavy rains could turn this rock to mud. The previous roadway adjacent to the building had collapsed for that reason. The city engineer listened politely to me, then patted me on the back and said, "Young man, this time we'll do it right." They put the road in, and in the next huge storm, about three years later, the road fell thirty feet and had to be abandoned.

Although I maintained a flourishing medical practice, with every year I allowed myself to become more and more involved with the Sierra Club. Each decision to enter a Club election was in effect a choice between medicine and conservation; each position would require more time away from my practice and leave fewer hours for teaching and research.

I had never considered myself an organization man, but the Club offered me opportunities and resources I could never have had on my own. As a college student I had dreamed of saving the world through medical research, like Sinclair Lewis's protagonist Martin Arrowsmith. I had done some research and published a fair number of scientific articles in the 1930s and 1940s. However, the sum of my contributions to scientific medicine was relatively small; most of my time had been spent caring for individual patients. I could have pressed further in research, but conservation promised the chance to make an impact on a totally different scale. Instead of working with single human beings, I would come to study watersheds and ecosystems, exploring how such natural systems could remain healthy when confronted with human development. Although the interrelation of medicine and ecology is clear in retrospect, I did not appreciate the connection at the time. Nor was my growing involvement a deliberate decision. The truth is, I was getting hooked on conservation. I enjoyed the people, the ferment of ideas and strategy, the challenge. I had the vague feeling that I was on the verge of something big.

My wife, Peggy, for her part, would soon come to embrace the Sierra Club and its ideals with a fervor nearly equal to mine. As her wedding gift to me in September 1947, she gave up her two-pack-a-day cigarette habit. In 1948 she agreed to participate in the Club's High Trip. She didn't actually imagine she would enjoy trekking around the mountains, but she was determined to support her new husband's interest. Three months pregnant with our first child, suffering from morning sickness, and with no high expectations of the trip, Peggy hit the trail—and quickly found herself seduced by the same camaraderie I had discovered. A lively addition to the nightly campfire entertainment was young Paul Kaufman, who overturned the storage canisters and beat them like drums. And there was photographer Cedric Wright, who would meet weary hikers at the base of a mountain pass with a hot tub of water and wash their feet. Also a violinist, Wright brought along his violin and nicknamed the portable outhouse—a pyramidal, curtained affair—the "straddlevarius."

It helped that a Sierra Club High Trip was not a trial of survival but, rather, a kind introduction to a gentle wilderness. Our meals were cooked for us, and a team of packers carried thirty pounds of gear and food per participant. It seldom rained, so we slept under the stars. One night in particular, camping in Paradise Valley above Kings Canyon, turned into an indelible memory for Peggy. Around 11 P.M. she lay in her sleeping bag, staring at the constellations as the campfire embers slowly died. The steep cliffs surrounding us were little more than vague silhouettes against a dark sky. In the distance she heard a rumble that soon grew to a roar. It was a big rock slide, we later realized. She listened, breathless, enthralled by the noise that seemed to rise out of the earth itself. Then all was quiet. At that moment she realized she loved the wilderness.

Over the next fourteen years and throughout three more pregnancies, Peggy would continue to take part in the High Trips, as well as accompany me on most of my independent explorations. We would coauthor many articles for the *Sierra Club Bulletin,* and eventually she came to write natural history and outdoor travel books for the Club. She would become a noted conservationist in her own right.

UNTIL THE EARLY 1950S, the Sierra Club expanded its scope of interest only gradually, remaining focused on recreation and a narrow concept of conservation in parts of California. An overall environmental ethic had yet to be integrated into the Club's mission. Soon, however, an environmental philosophy—many related philosophies, really—would evolve out of necessity. The postwar years brought a tremendous boom in population and land development, particularly in the San Francisco Bay Area. Suddenly there was more of everything: more houses, more people, more cars, more freeways. The flip side of this surge was, of course, less open space, less forest, less wilderness.

In response to a growing urge on the part of conservationists to articulate the concept of wilderness, the first Sierra Club Wilderness Conference was held in Berkeley in 1949. The idea came from Club director Ike Livermore (later to serve as resources secretary to Governor Ronald Reagan). Livermore owned two packing outfits in the Sierra and had witnessed the degradation of the high country firsthand. Naturally enough, the first conference focused on the High Sierra and ideas for improving its management. In addition to members of the Sierra Club, attendees included members of other environmental organizations such as The Wilderness Society and the Audubon Society, as well as employees of federal land management agencies such as the National Park Service, the U.S. Forest Service, and the U.S. Fish and Wildlife Service. Also invited were industry users of wilderness: lumbermen, stockmen, guides, and packers. As at future conferences, papers were presented, followed by discussions among the participants.

But before the group could formulate plans for protective management of the Sierra, it had to resolve some basic questions. What exactly *was* wilderness, and how important was it? While most of the conferees agreed that wilderness was necessary, there was no consensus on why. Most attendees praised wilderness in terms of its scenic, scientific, and recreational benefits to humankind—its anthropocentric value. A few, however, insisted that wilderness was essential apart from its usefulness to humans. Richard Leonard and David Brower were among those advocating a biocentric view of wilderness: the belief that unmanaged lands hold intrinsic value and do not need people to justify their existence.

The Wilderness Conferences continued on a biennial basis. Peggy and I took a keen interest and were involved in administering the conferences from 1961 to 1965. Early meetings focused on developing a concise, marketable view of wilderness. In 1951, Howard Zahniser, executive director of The Wilderness Society, had first put forth the idea of promoting a wilderness act as a piece of national legislation. By 1956 he had come up with an eloquent definition. In the preamble to the first federal wilderness bill, introduced in Congress that year by Senator Hubert H. Humphrey, he wrote:

> A wilderness, in contrast with those areas where man and his
> own works dominate the landscape, is hereby recognized as an
> area where the earth and its community of life are untrammeled
> by man, where man himself is a visitor who does not remain.

Zahniser's proposed legislation outlined an eight-point plan for wilderness preservation that he wanted to see adopted by the U.S. Congress. From 1956 on, a wilderness bill was introduced in every session of Congress. Eight years later, Zahniser's seed finally bore fruit with the passage in 1964 of the Wilderness Act.

Up to this time, "wilderness" was a tenuous designation from the standpoint of official protection. In the 1920s the U.S. Forest Service passed its so-called L regulations, which offered a series of protective classifications called Primitive Areas. Areas so labeled were not, however, immune to roads or logging. Under the later, more stringent U regulations, the chief forester could bestow a "wilderness" designation on a particular area—such as New Mexico's Gila Forest Wilderness, established in 1924 and the country's oldest declared wilderness. But this wilderness designation was not permanent. It was administrative, not legislative, and subject to being revoked at any time. The need for a more formally recognized concept of wilderness, and federal legislation regulating it, was becoming urgent to leaders of the growing conservation community.

Although the conferees differed in their arguments for wilderness, all agreed it must be safeguarded. But did the majority of Americans share this sentiment? Given that they probably did not, how could the concept of wilderness be sold to the American people in the midst of such a materialistic, development-minded era? The Club even hired a public relations consultant, Bill Losh, to help package its ideas.

Having worked with Losh during my earlier efforts to expand Mount Tamalpais State Park, I recognized the importance of "selling" conservation. Outside the Club I was often challenged by the question, "Why are you people always against something?" The question implied two problems with the general perception of conservation. First, those who wanted to help preserve wild spaces were considered different—outsiders, "you people," a minority out of tune with the rest of the country. Second, conservation was seen as a negative stance: you were against what others were working *for*. The Club was "against" miners, against loggers, against developers—against progress, it was said. (It's interesting that, half a century later, conservationists still face the same typecasting.)

I was resolved to reverse these perceptions and to present the Club's work and mine in a positive light. Wilderness would have to be packaged, I believed, not only as an integral part of our American heritage but as a democratic resource available to all. (Congressman Phil Burton, my cohort on the GGNRA campaign in the 1970s, was the great exponent of open space "for the people.") Any park proposal I espoused, any campaign to establish or expand wilderness, would have to be expressed in such terms: not "locking up" resources but saving them, not setting aside open space for the enjoyment of a wealthy few but the stewardship of special places for all Americans, including those yet unborn.

Wilderness proponents also would have to counter charges of elitism. Most members of environmental organizations were highly educated: doctors, lawyers, academics, and businessmen. Not only did the Sierra

Club require that new members be sponsored, but until the end of World War II, its defining activity, the High Trip, required substantial free time at a time when paid vacations were not the norm.

The Wilderness Conferences, which continued through 1975, were fertile ground for the rising environmental consciousness. Ideas budded, cross-pollinated with others, and generated new lines of argument. What role should humans play in shaping the planet? And what role did wilderness play in shaping humans? Many participants agreed with Aldo Leopold that wilderness possesses its own value and that wild places also contain a moral strength, the power to elevate man's base instincts—in essence, that humanity's salvation lies in wilderness. By the late fifties, in any case, a well-defined wilderness ethic began to emerge. Some would adopt this ethic as a personal philosophy; others would take up the call to environmental activism with religious zeal.

While the debate over biocentric and anthropocentric views of wilderness continued, I believed that it unnecessarily polarized wilderness advocates and diminished our effectiveness in marketing wilderness to the unconverted. Wilderness is important both in and of itself and because it helps humankind. True, unmanaged lands do not need human use to justify their existence—but humans do exist, and our spirit yearns for contact with wild places. That both views were valid made wilderness preservation even more important.

IN 1950, THE CLUB'S Conservation Committee decided to reach out to the Federation of Western Outdoor Clubs (FWOC), an umbrella organization of thirty-one mostly local groups such as the Seattle-based Mountaineers and the Portland Mazamas, with the Sierra Club as the largest group. The federation had yet to become a strong voice for conservation, so the committee agreed that we ought to take a more active role in shaping the organization as an ally for the Sierra Club's aims.

The outreach task fell to me. In 1950 I briefly visited an FWOC meeting, and in 1951 I attended the federation's convention as the Club's delegate. A furious debate was under way: delegates were arguing about the reclassification of a U.S. Forest Service area I'd never heard of—the Three Sisters Primitive Area in central Oregon. (The Three Sisters is a group of stunning peaks in the Cascades Range of central Oregon.) The Forest Service had announced it intended to change the status of the land from primitive area to wilderness, but with boundaries that would reduce its size. The new proposed western boundary followed a stream called Separation Creek. Whatever land lay outside the boundaries would, of course, be subject to logging.

The FWOC convention was willing to accept the Forest Service proposal, the sole dissenting voice being that of a biologist named Ruth Hobson. Hobson, near tears, pleaded for a boundary at Horse Creek, which would include a larger area. She was quite distraught, and the federation's leaders were at a loss for how to respond.

They turned to me, the delegate of the largest member organization. "What's your opinion?" asked forester L. A. Nelson, who, along with insurance executive Ding Cannon, led those in favor of the smaller Forest Service area.

I admitted I didn't have one. I'd never been to the Three Sisters.

"Well, come back next year and give us your opinion," Cannon said. They decided to table their decision until they had more information. "The federation will adopt your stand."

I can't say exactly why they were so willing to trust the opinion of a newcomer. Perhaps they just wanted a fresh perspective. At any rate, I agreed to do some fact-finding, and the next summer Peggy and I joined district ranger Brit Ashe on a "show me" trip of the area. In keeping with the Forest Service's policy of evenhandedness, Gus Arneson, a lumberman from Springfield, Oregon, was also invited. We rode by day and argued by night.

The Three Sisters region was a revelation to me: an entirely new expression of wilderness. The shapes and patterns of the Oregon Cascades differed sharply from the above-timberline experience of Yosemite and Kings Canyon and even more dramatically from the coastal canyons of the Bay Area. The Three Sisters area boasted vast columns of Douglas fir, ridge-to-ridge forests, and snowcapped volcanic ridges. After spending five days exploring, I concluded that Hobson had been right to include Horse Creek—but even her proposed boundary didn't stretch far enough. Creeks are not natural dividing lines. In order to safeguard the watershed, the land needed ridge-to-ridge protection. I concluded that the boundary should be even farther west, encompassing the Ollallie ridge west of Horse Creek—an additional 53,000 acres.

When I returned to the FWOC convention in 1952, Nelson and Cannon quickly sought me out and asked me for my opinion.

"You're not going to like it," I told them.

But they stuck to their word, and the federation adopted my suggestion as its official position. In 1953 I was elected president of the FWOC, a position I would retain for the next two years. The Sierra Club's hopes for transforming the FWOC into a force for conservation succeeded more quickly than anyone had anticipated. It would take ten years, however, for the Forest Service to resolve its reclassification of the Three Sisters, and ultimately it chose Horse Creek as the boundary—not as far west as I had hoped. Nevertheless, this effort exemplified the value of not compromising early on. The wilderness area was smaller than we wanted but larger than it would have been had the Forest Service not met with opposition. Local conservationists continued to battle for the deleted acreage, and some of it was eventually restored, though some was lost to logging.

As THE SIERRA CLUB began to enlarge its field of operations, so did I. I became chairman of the Conservation Committee and in 1957 was elected for the first time to the Club's national board of directors. And throughout the 1950s and 1960s, taking whatever time I could away from my medical practice, Peggy and I embarked on a series of journeys exploring the mountain ranges of the west. We would load the car with our four children and camping supplies, drive hundreds of miles, and then venture forth by foot. These whirlwind tours were designed to cover as much territory as possible. They were flavored with a sense of urgency, of the west's diminishing open spaces, and—as we entered the 1960s—our hopes for passage of a wilderness bill, which promised to save some of what remained. In essence, we were creating our own map of the western wilderness.

With each trip we ventured farther afield, looking for places still "untrammeled" enough (as Zahniser put it) to be considered worthy of wilderness protection. Each trip revealed more and more places that deserved such protection. I had not expected to find landscapes rivaling the beauty and scale of the Sierra Nevada, but we discovered that wilderness came in a multitude of climates and colors, shapes and formations. The Sierra Club rightly wanted to protect California's wilds, but these were not the only areas worthy of our attention. The entire west was a monument to the possibilities of wilderness.

Our exploration of Oregon's Three Sisters area in 1952 was the first of these journeys. In 1955 we reconnoitered Mount Rainier, and in 1956, 1958, and 1959 we visited the Washington Cascades. Steeper than the Sierra, the Cascades are tall, rough-edged volcanic peaks, often snow covered most of the year. In 1960 and 1961, I served as the doctor on a Sierra Club Special Trip to the Sawtooth Mountains of Idaho. (Special Trips were so called because they took place outside California.) As a result of this, the Club lobbied for a Sawtooth Mountain National Park, but we were blocked by resistance from an Idaho congressman. The compromise was a national recreation area, which gave the mountains much less protection. While in Idaho, we briefly visited the region that became the Frank Church Wilderness of the River of No Return, traveling down that famed river, the Salmon, the lifeblood of this land.

In 1962 we explored Wyoming and Montana, visiting the Grand Tetons and Yellowstone and Glacier National Parks, as well as the more remote Wind River Mountains, part of which would become the Bridger Wilderness. We returned to the Wind Rivers again in 1964, 1965, and 1966, contributing many suggestions to the Forest Service on their prospective wilderness areas there. Our introductory visits to the ranges of the west included spending a little time in the Ruby Mountains of Nevada, which also became wilderness—though not until 1989.

We came to know one part of the Colorado Rockies very well courtesy of our eldest daughter, Cynthia, who chose to board at the Rocky Mountain High School in Carbondale. For three winters, we traveled on the Western Pacific Railroad to Glenwood Springs, rented a car, and drove up to visit Cynthia, then on to Aspen for a week's skiing. Aspen offered the best skiing I've ever known, and we grew enamoured of the surrounding mountains.

In 1966, I led a Sierra Club High-Light Trip (as the name suggests, these were high-elevation expeditions with a minimum of gear) through the Maroon Bells–Snowmass Primitive Area, scheduled to be reclassified as wilderness. As a result of that trip, I recommended that the Forest Service increase its wilderness proposal from 90,000 to around 115,000 protected acres, but for nine years I received no response. Then in 1975, while traveling in Alaska, I received a letter from the Forest Service that read, "Dr. Wayburn: you will be pleased to know that the suggestions you made for the Maroon Bells–Snowmass Wilderness have been accepted!" Given the intensive resort and vacation-home development in the immediate Aspen area since then, it's clear how important and timely it was to preserve the magnificent slopes and meadows of the Maroon Bells.

To me, 1952 remains the pivotal year in the Sierra Club's history—a time I have often described as "the turning of the hinge." That year saw three critical events: the Club's decision to grow large, to expand nationally, and to hire a professional staff. Soon the organization would shed its regional identity and its primary focus on outings in the Sierra Nevada to become the foremost advocate for the nation's environment.

The Club's shift in this direction was accelerated in 1951 by an unusual and pressing issue. The U.S. Bureau of Reclamation (the agency of the Interior Department responsible for public works on federal land) was moving forward with plans for the Upper Colorado River Project in northeastern Utah and northwestern Colorado. Based on the perceived need for more power and water to support the west's growing population, ten dams were proposed.

What most troubled the Sierra Club about the project was that two of the dams, Split Mountain and Echo Park, would be built within Dinosaur National Monument—a park that sprawls across both states, in theory protected within the national park system. However, President Truman's secretary of the Interior, Oscar Chapman, had already given his approval to the plans; construction was expected to begin soon. Newton Drury, then director of the National Park Service, was opposed to the dams, but Chapman forbade Drury from criticizing the project openly. Under pressure from Chapman, Drury would soon resign—his next post was heading up California's Division of Beaches and Parks when we were fighting for more protected land around Mount Tamalpais (see chapter 2).

The Club's decision to wage a national campaign against proposed federal dams in Dinosaur National Monument originated within the Conservation Committee—a group of Club leaders and policymakers that formed the strategic heart of the organization. Its recommendations were passed on to the board of directors, which usually adopted them. At this time, the committee was an eclectic group of mostly Bay Area members who met at the home of chairman Harold Bradley on Durant Avenue, adjacent to the University of California's Berkeley campus. Bradley, a retired professor of chemistry at the University of Wisconsin, would later serve on the board of directors and as the Club's president; his father, Cornelius, had been a founding member.

Once a month, twenty to forty members met to discuss and debate conservation issues. At that time the Club's focus was still strongly regional, centered on California's parks and forests, and typically the issue involved an existing or proposed state park such as Mount Tamalpais or the Big Basin redwoods or Butano forest in the Santa Cruz Mountains.

Dinosaur, then, represented a long step afield for the Conservation Committee, few of whose members had even heard of the place. Even fewer knew exactly where it was: some thought the park might lie entirely in Colorado or in Utah. Only a handful of members, including Bradley and Dick Leonard, had ever explored the expansive Colorado Plateau, especially the region around the confluence of the Green and Yampa rivers—tributaries of the Colorado—where Dinosaur was located. The plateau is a vast network of high-elevation canyons encompassing the Grand Canyon, Zion, and Bryce National Parks and such renowned Native American cliff dwellings as Mesa Verde and Cañon de Chelly. Although the Bureau was contending that Dinosaur was merely a hot, dusty desert containing dinosaur bones, Bradley and Leonard thought otherwise. Within Dinosaur's canyons also lay intriguing gorges and mesas carved from golden sandstone, including Steamboat Rock, rising 800 feet from the floor of Echo Park.

The proposed dams in Dinosaur—Split Mountain on the Green River in Utah and Echo Park on the Yampa, just upstream from where it joins the Green, in Colorado—were troublesome not just because they threatened to flood pretty places. At stake was the integrity of the national park system.

National parks were supposed to be untouchable, sacrosanct. The national monument status of Dinosaur should have afforded it the same level of protection. The damming of rivers within Dinosaur could set a dangerous precedent: how many other dams would find their way into national parks?

For me and most of the others gathered in Bradley's living room, Dinosaur marked a significant development in conservation philosophy. I opposed damming Dinosaur on principle rather than from experience, whereas my earlier conservation efforts had sprung from direct contact with the land. When I worked to save parts of the Sierra and Mount Tamalpais from development, it was because I had walked their trails and topped their ridges. I knew these places intimately, and my desire to help save them was rooted in that experience. I had never been to Dinosaur, however. Deciding to protect it represented a leap of faith for both me and the Club. If we could not stop development in such places now, what would happen in the future, as the population, with its energy and water demands, continued to increase?

Most of the committee felt similarly, though some argued that the Sierra Club had no right to enter this debate—that a national monument in Utah was beyond its scope. They believed that our effectiveness depended on maintaining a narrow geographic focus. Others did not want to provoke antagonism in the federal agency and felt that outright opposition was not in keeping with the Club's character; they wanted the Club to stick to its traditional role of advising. Former Club president Bestor Robinson asserted that the Club could not successfully oppose both dams; one of the sites would have to be sacrificed.

Although we debated late into the night, the committee could not reach a consensus. At midnight we agreed to hold a lunch meeting the following day: whoever could make that meeting would decide the course of action. I was among the eight members who gathered at a downtown San Francisco restaurant; also present were Bradley, Leonard, Dave Brower, Charlotte Mauk, Art Blake, and Lewis Clark. We were unanimous in opposing the dams. At its next meeting, after brief deliberation, the board of directors adopted our position.

The campaign to save Dinosaur National Monument spurred thousands of new members to join the Sierra Club, more than doubling its membership by 1960. This expansion of the Club's ranks, with many of the new members residing in urban areas, pushed the organization more and more toward involvement with national issues, while increasing its diversity of views. Issues championed by new members would range from concerns about clean air and water, to energy sources and use, to preserving the integrity of national parks and the health of national forests, and ultimately to protecting vast wildernesses in places they might never see—such as Alaska.

As its membership expanded, the Club was compelled to address concerns about elitism. A precipitating incident occurred in Los Angeles, in which an African American man had been denied membership in the Angeles Chapter. Ansel Adams, in particular, was outraged by the chapter's bigotry, and the ensuing debate focused on the outdated sponsorship requirement. Finally, in the mid-1960s, the Club dropped this requirement and opened its doors to all. Entry into its ranks would no longer be a matter of knowing the right people; a small check for dues would suffice. There was also a growing sense that if the Club was going to conduct national campaigns, it would need a wider base of support. Its influence would be based on its collective membership rather than on the prominence of its individual members.

Of course, such a momentous decision was not without compromise. With greater numbers and diversity would come greater contention. And, ironically, the influx of new members made it less likely that a campaign such as Dinosaur could emerge so quickly and from the actions of so few people—for example, the consensus of eight committee members over lunch.

AMONG THE WATERSHED events of 1952 was the Sierra Club's hiring of David Brower as its first professional manager. Growing membership, by then more than seven thousand, warranted such a position; gone were the days of Will Colby's administration, when the Club's records were kept in a cigar box. The president and board—all volunteers—had become overwhelmed with duties, meetings, and memos.

Brower's qualifications were exemplary. In addition to leading Club outings and serving on the board, he worked as an editor at the University of

California Press under its publisher, August Frugé, and served as managing editor of the *Sierra Club Bulletin*. When first hired in 1952, Brower worked on a 5/7-time basis; later he became full time and more.

His accomplishments over the next two decades would be extraordinary and prolific. He represented the Sierra Club at countless legislative hearings. He led the Upper Colorado River campaign, disproving "with ninth-grade arithmetic" (as he himself claimed) Bureau of Reclamation figures showing the benefits of dam construction in Dinosaur National Monument. Later, he led the campaign to save the Grand Canyon from dams. During this period, membership rose by 15 percent a year, on average.

It was Brower who envisioned what would become a Sierra Club trademark: the Exhibit Format series of books. In 1959 he produced the first such book, *This Is the American Earth*, adapted from an exhibit of Ansel Adams's photographs at the Club's LeConte Memorial Lodge in Yosemite Valley. Adams's black-and-white photos were accompanied by the exhibit's poetic text, written by Nancy Newhall.

This Is the American Earth received universal praise as well as several publishing awards. The oversized format and Adams's powerful images created a stunning visual testimony to America's wilds and the threats they faced. Adams intended the book to connect viewers to the landscape emotionally, communicating the necessity of wilderness on a basic, instinctual level. *This Is the American Earth* sold well, and Brower would increasingly devote his time to such publications, arguing that the books, more than anything else, brought in new members. The claim is hard to prove or disprove; in any case, by 1961 the Club would more than double its 1952 membership to reach 16,500, and by the Club's seventy-fifth anniversary in 1967, membership had shot up to 55,000.

The Sierra Club's maturing in size and professionalism coincided with intensifying pressures on America's wildlands. In the 1950s, both the National Park Service and the U.S. Forest Service—the agencies that wield the most power over the nation's public lands—launched plans to reclassify and change the management of their holdings. At the Forest Service, Chief Forester Richard McArdle began a Timber Resources Review—an inventory designed to reclassify the national forests according to their "highest use."

Growing up in Georgia, I had developed great respect for the U.S. Forest Service. It had undertaken since the 1930s, among other projects, a major replanting of pine trees, which controlled dust and whose branches provided shade from the wet heat of a southern summer. Before World War II, the Sierra Club had a good working relationship with the agency and its foresters, often taking the role of a conciliatory advisor. In the postwar years, however, the Forest Service's vision of the nation's forest resources narrowed to a tight focus on logging, and more and more the agency and the Club became adversaries.

The Forest Service has always been a utilitarian agency; its motto is "The greatest good for the greatest number in the long run." In the 1950s, the greatest good was interpreted to mean harvesting timber to meet the demands of a growing population and an expanding economy. Chief Forester McArdle wanted the Forest Service to mirror the country's boom, so what had been, until then, in considerable part a custodial agency was reinvented as an enterprise specializing in timber. Before this time, an aggressive, large-scale timber program would not have been economically feasible due to poor access to some of the best stands, more readily accessible private timber sources, and a weak economy. All that was changing: private timber was growing scarcer, the economy was thriving, and if the agency had its way, roads would soon penetrate the remotest forests in its empire.

The Timber Resources Review called for inventorying and reclassifying all the Forest Service's holdings. The Sierra Club did not in principle oppose such a review as long as, in cataloging their lands, the agency included areas that should not be developed. Unfortunately, wilderness held a precarious place in the Forest Service's value system. Its "wilderness" designation, remember, was subject to administrative review. Future chief foresters, perceiving a need to develop such lands, could revoke the designation and open the area to logging.

However designated, no forestlands were inviolable. In addition to being vulnerable to logging, most of the western forests contained private mining claims. Upon proving that an area could produce even a minimal amount of minerals, any individual or company could demand the right to build access roads and, after a certain waiting period, acquire the claim for a small fee. Vast stretches of public land were thus lost to private enterprise. Thousands of such claims were filed in the west as a result of the 1872 Mining Law.

It soon became clear that in its reclassification, the Forest Service was chiefly beholden to a criterion known as "multiple use." Multiple use required foresters to consider equally an area's economic and non-economic values before classifying it. By the 1950s the term had became so pervasive in every conversation and correspondence between the Forest Service and the Club that it came to sound like a mantra. We joked that foresters were required three times a day to bow to the east and chant, "Multiple use, multiple use, multiple use."

In the 1950s, the Forest Service outlined and submitted to Congress a multiple-use bill, which the agency hoped would serve as an overall management plan. According to the bill, the five recognized uses of the national forests were: 1) watershed protection, 2) wildlife protection, 3) the safeguarding of clean water sources, 4) wilderness, and 5) logging. Although wilderness itself was just one of the listed uses, we at the Sierra Club noted that wilderness actually was consistent with all the uses except logging. The Club supported passage of the Multiple-Use Sustained-Yield Act of 1960; it would be the first time that the importance of wilderness would be officially recognized as a primary use of the national forests.

In theory, the multiple-use doctrine showed promise. In practice, however, multiple use too often meant logging plus another use, generally termed "recreation." In 1953, in my capacity as president of the Federation of Western Outdoor Clubs, I had lunch with Regional Forester Clair Hendee, who stressed the importance of building roads throughout the national forest system without delay. He told me that completing a good road system now would save having to go back into the forest with new roads when it came time to relog the stands or when it was decided to open an area for recreation.

For Chief Forester McArdle, the definition of wilderness was limited to a certain type of terrain—usually high, rugged country with few trees and in which "the commercial values are slight," as he wrote in a letter to the Sierra Club. McArdle also belittled the value of wilderness, calling the designation "highly restrictive" and asserting that such lands were "used by a minority." Since the Forest Service was bound to pursue "the greatest good for the greatest number," McArdle's critique of wilderness did not portend well for protected lands. Add up these factors, and the result was that in the mid-1950s, only 10 percent of national forest lands were designated as wilderness. And the majority of these wilderness lands were not forested, since trees were deemed to have a higher or more appropriate use: as timber.

As evidence of the Forest Service's drive to harvest timber began to mount, the Sierra Club began to question the agency's management strategies. One area where concern focused early was a few thousand acres in the Mammoth Lakes region along Highway 395 near the California-Nevada border, a place known as Deadman Summit. Here, among the sagebrush and pumice flats, stood a forest of lodgepole pine, red fir, and virgin Jeffrey pine—the finest stand of this species in the west, some said. Blue crater lakes dotted the lower elevations. In the 1860s, the headless corpse of a miner had been discovered in one of the streams, forever earning it the name of Deadman Creek.

Though assigned to a timber or "working" circle, the area remained unlogged until the early 1950s. Then a local resident, John Haddaway, observed that Forest Service personnel were cutting down trees on the side of the highway, contrary to the usual agency policy of maintaining scenic roadside "corridors." Upon inquiring, Haddaway was told by the district ranger that Deadman Summit was to be designated as a recreation area and that the cuts were for "sanitation" reasons, to keep the remaining trees free of pests and disease. Other foresters, however, gave Haddaway other reasons why the trees were being cut. One said the trees were not diseased at all; another said they were being cut for sale as timber, despite the fact that Jeffrey pines had little commercial value. Haddaway suspected the Forest Service lacked a clear plan for the area. Meanwhile, logging also began in the trees at the edge of the summit, near Glass Creek.

After the Sierra Club formally expressed its concern, the Forest Service invited Harold Bradley, Dick Leonard, and me to view the cuts at Deadman Summit. At Glass Creek, I saw trunk after trunk marked with a telltale slash of paint—denoting trees slated to be cut. Locals and tourists enjoyed driving through the roadside stands, but it was during this trip that I realized the potential trickery of such tree-lined corridors. They provided verdant facades for automobile tourists, but what lay beyond? As I walked deeper into the forest, the number of trees marked for cutting did not diminish. These were not around planned campsites or picnic benches; how could they be considered hazard trees in need of "sanitation cuts"? Since that trip, I have never advocated the establishment of scenic corridors. While affording a pretty roadside view, such facades too often are shielding the public's view of destructive cuts going on behind them.

In the spring of 1955, I met with the assistant regional forester for California, Millard Barnum, who gave me a written outline of the Forest Service's plans for logging at Deadman. The document stressed that conservationists would be consulted before any further cuts were made. I saw the plan as a small victory: at least the Forest Service was formally acknowledging that conservationists should have a say in the future of our natural resources. A published plan also seemed like a step in the right direction. But the cuts did not stop, nor was the Sierra Club always consulted before further logging began.

That October, Peggy and I published an article in the *Sierra Club Bulletin* titled "The Fate of Deadman Creek." Although it did not condemn outright the Forest Service policy there, it suggested that the agency had not considered the ramifications of so much logging:

> How far should development go in areas zoned primarily for recreation? Can the Forest Service open up undeveloped lands for recreation without cutting? Can it not maintain areas of natural forest outside its wilderness areas as buffer zones? If a "high-risk" cut is necessary, should it take 25–30 percent of the merchantable timber as it does at Deadman Creek?

And in terms of Sierra Club policy, had Deadman established a precedent we wanted to follow? Would we accept Forest Service logging to create recreation areas, for example, knowing that considerable commercial logging would precede the "recreational" use? Peggy and I weren't convinced. We wrote: "Is it our obligation to plan the management of our comparatively few remaining primitive areas now?"

In another article, "Our Vanishing Wilderness," in the January 1957 *Bulletin,* Peggy and I again urged Club members to take note of our disappearing forests. Most members, not to mention the general population, did not realize that change was afoot, assuming the Forest Service was continuing to manage its lands for posterity. The article attracted considerable attention and served as a wake-up call. It goes without saying today that Club members should concern themselves with forest management, but this was not so in 1957. Most members had yet to be rallied to active conservation, much less to challenging the management policies of the Forest Service.

THE BROAD POSTWAR trends of increased income and leisure time were also having an impact on the country's national parks. In 1956, National Park Service director Conrad Wirth unveiled "Mission 66," a ten-year plan designed to upgrade the national parks' infrastructure in time for the NPS's golden anniversary in 1966. This overhaul of the system's resources was necessary, Wirth explained, since the parks were hosting twice as many visitors as they had been designed to accommodate. The solution, as expressed in Mission 66, was to plan new or improved roads and major new construction of buildings in many parks. Inherent in this approach was a vision of a new kind of American tourist—one anchored to an automobile, who demanded quick access to the nation's geographical wonders.

The NPS presented an eight-point plan, most of which focused on expanding existing facilities such as hotels, campsites, employee housing, and roads. The agency's decision to refurbish existing facilities seemed sound, but I questioned the plan's priorities. Wirth indicated, for instance, that maintaining trails took a backseat to improving roads. Expansion of campgrounds was listed after establishment of adequate parking areas. And maintaining wilderness areas came last of all. If the parks were flooded by visitors, it would seem logical that the NPS would have wanted to expand their boundaries. But acquisition of new parklands was not a part of Mission 66.

Details about this plan were not quickly forthcoming. Wirth told the Sierra Club board of directors that they would be consulted immediately about Mission 66, yet years would pass before the Club learned more than just a general outline. And although the NPS seemed amenable to questioning, its answers failed to provide the level of detail the Club needed to offer constructive criticism. In truth, Wirth was not really looking for an active dialogue between the NPS and the Sierra Club or any other environmental organization.

The NPS assured us that they were giving prime consideration to the great park principle of wilderness preservation, along with the emphasis on construction and development. But as Peggy and I concluded in another *Sierra Club Bulletin* article, "Lacking details, we have to wonder how these two basically incompatible concepts are being reconciled." The clearly divergent views of the NPS and the Club on how to handle increased pressure on the parks stemmed from each group's perception of the role of national parks and the profile of their visitors. With NPS's emphasis on road expansion and realignment, it seemed clear that the organization was tailoring the parks to automobile tourists rather than to those seeking a wilderness experience.

One detail of Mission 66 that, in retrospect, stands as a significant failure for the Sierra Club was the NPS's plan to improve or "realign" the old Tioga Road, which crossed through northern Yosemite National Park from the east side of the Sierra to the west—first built to access the Tioga mines, long since closed. Even the realignment of a road in a national park raises questions not easily answered. What is the purpose of roads in national parks? Is it the same as for a highway: to expedite travel by moving cars as efficiently as possible from one spot to another? Is it to expose a park's scenery, to permit travelers visually to access a park's wonders from inside a car? Or should both these purposes take a backseat to some larger value? Some argued at the time, and still argue, that roads in parks should be, at most, tolerated intrusions designed to get travelers to a wilderness entry point and no farther. Forty-five years later, these same questions are being explored with regard to current plans for Yosemite Valley, where road traffic has taken a significant toll on the valley's peerless natural beauty.

The National Park Service first seriously pursued the idea of constructing a trans-Sierra highway in the 1930s. There were good roads running north–south on both sides of the range, but park officials projected that more and more visitors would need to traverse the Sierra west to east and vice versa. Then, as in the 1950s, the old Tioga Road was the proposed route, and to placate the Sierra Club, the NPS argued that an improved Tioga Road would draw Yosemite tourists away from the crowded valley floor and into the higher elevations. In the 1930s, Club leaders Will Colby and Walter Huber agreed to the idea, envisioning the proposed road as two narrow lanes winding up from the valley floor, cresting at Tioga Pass, and exiting the park at the small town of Lee Vining, near the Nevada border.

For various reasons, however, the earlier Tioga Road project was delayed and the idea did not surface again until the era of Mission 66—by which time road design and construction had changed significantly. In general, roads were designed to be wider than in prewar years, and new machinery made it possible to drill into hillsides and rock formations that previously would have been skirted. Roads no longer had to bend to the landscape—they could simply cut right through it. So when the NPS resuscitated its proposal for a "realigned" Tioga Road, it called for a significantly wider road with a different route—one that would cut through a rare formation of glacier-polished granite just west of Lake Tenaya, an area of superlative natural beauty.

Ansel Adams, whose passion for Yosemite rivaled that of John Muir himself, was furious. He considered Tenaya the single most beautiful spot in the park and demanded that the Club renounce its support of the road; if not, he intended to resign from the board. Club policy forbade board members from criticizing the integrity of the management agencies, and he wanted to be free to criticize park officials openly. Other Club leaders—Dave Brower, Dick Leonard, and I among them—also opposed the road and believed that, given its new size and route, the Club was not beholden to promises made twenty years earlier.

Yet many board members, because that promise had been made, felt uneasy about committing our resources to fighting the road. They feared the Club would be accused of going back on its word, of lacking moral principle. In the end, Adams was the only board member willing to wage an all-out fight, while Leonard argued that the Club should rely on its longstanding strategy of persuasion.

Persuasion ultimately failed, and the road was built. Adams was persuaded not to resign but was heartbroken. In the early 1960s, by then president of the Sierra Club, I attended the road's opening ceremony. The night before, Peggy and I camped in the high country at the Sierra Club's Soda Springs property in Tuolumne Meadows (later sold to the NPS). The next morning a crowd of officials wearing shiny leather shoes and city suits gathered at a site where the polished rocks had been lacerated to make way for asphalt. Clad in khaki slacks, flannel shirt, and boots, I added visual contrast and a somber note to the proceedings as I expressed regret for this symbol of "progress."

The Tioga Pass Road has fulfilled its promise all too well. Despite the magnificent views it offers, the road is used primarily as a thruway for travelers from the northern California coast or the San Joaquin Valley headed for the eastern side of the Sierra and Nevada. The road also lures traffic into Yosemite's backcountry, which should be the realm of those seeking a wilderness experience. Yet Yosemite Valley remains more packed than ever, with crowding in the summer months reaching crisis levels.

Later in the 1960s, the Forest Service proposed yet another new trans-Sierra highway. This one would originate near Clover Meadow on the west, pass south of Yosemite through what is now the Ansel Adams Wilderness, and end at the town of Mammoth Lakes. The scenario echoed Tioga in that Sierra Club leaders in the 1930s had agreed to such a proposal in principle. But the Club had learned its lesson from the Tioga Pass debacle and was adamant in opposing the Mammoth road. Fortunately, our stand was supported by Ike Livermore, California secretary of resources under Governor Reagan, and that road was never built.

THE CAMPAIGN TO PRESERVE one special place in the Northwest touched on all the prominent features of conservation in the 1950s and 1960s—the coordinating role of the Sierra Club, key point work by local organizations, adamant resistance by federal management agencies, and the necessity of impassioned, persistent individual effort.

In 1955, the Sierra Club put on one of its earliest non-California trips—a special High-Light Trip—to the Sunrise area on the northern flank of Mount Rainier. The trip's charismatic leader was Oliver Kehrlein, then in his seventies, who always was surrounded by a bevy of women of all ages; his assistant was Alfred Schmitz. Sunrise was a beautiful place, 7,000 feet in elevation, just below the perpetual snow line. During our first days there we were visited by the grand old man of the Seattle Mountaineers, a mattress-maker named Leo Gallagher. Standing with Leo in an absolutely gorgeous field of wildflowers, I admired the lovely landscape aloud.

"If you think these flowers are wonderful, you should see the meadows of Glacier Peak," Leo answered.

At that time, almost no one in the Club knew about Glacier Peak—a so-called Limited Area of the Forest Service in the North Cascades of Washington, due for reclassification in the next few years. Intrigued, I persuaded Kehrlein and Schmitz to stop by the area on their way east to scout the next year's planned Special Trip, to Lake O'Hara in the Canadian Rockies. They traveled up Lake Chelan via steamer to Holden, hiked up the canyons into the Glacier Peak region, and were so entranced that they never got to Lake O'Hara. The next year they led the Club's first trip to Glacier Peak; I went along as doctor.

We camped and hiked up the canyon for twelve days, going from Holden on Lake Chelan to Cloudy Pass, then crossing Suiattle Pass and going as far as Image Lake—one of the more exquisite places in the mountain world, reflecting Glacier Peak in its still waters. In addition Grant McConnell, then a professor of political science at the University of Chicago, who owned a cabin on the Stehekin River, wrote to executive director David Brower about the extraordinary value of the Stehekin–Glacier Peak region, urging that the Club take action to protect it. Later that summer, Brower came along on a second trip to Glacier Peak, and he too fell in love with the area. To support a planned campaign, Brower and I hired Phillip Hyde to take photographs documenting the region. And in 1958 Ansel Adams accompanied Peggy and me when we explored the north fork of the Stehekin and the Cascade Pass region, bringing back memorable images.

During the next few years, a great deal of activity took place around protecting the Glacier Peak wilderness. I recall sitting by the campfire at the FWOC's annual convention with Ed Cliff, who later became the

Forest Service's chief forester, and Ed Crafts, the future first director of the federal Bureau of Outdoor Recreation. (At the time, both were associate chief foresters.) In vain I argued that a large Glacier Peak wilderness would best serve the place and the public.

Smoking his ever-present pipe, Cliff asked, "Which would you rather have: a larger Three Sisters or a larger Glacier Peak Wilderness? You can't have both." The project of reclassifying the Three Sisters area had been under way since 1952 (see page 75), and it was maddening to be faced again with an either/or choice.

Peggy and I spent our summer vacations of 1956, 1958, and 1959 in the North Cascades working for the permanent protection of this magnificent region, where we wanted to see a sizable designated wilderness centering on Glacier Peak. A local, single-purpose organization, the North Cascades Conservation Council, was founded by Club member Patrick Goldsworthy to be the spear carrier for conservation endeavors.

But Glacier Peak found its most passionate champion in a nineteen-year-old student named David Simons, who first began exploring the area as a volunteer for the Club. Dave Brower later hired him for a pittance—all the Club could afford—to survey the area, and Simons came to regard Brower as a father figure. I remember seeing him around Glacier Peak on several occasions: a tall, blond, skinny kid with a huge camera hanging from his backpack.

Simons quickly became convinced that Glacier Peak should become a national park rather than remain in the hands of the Forest Service. At first I resisted the idea because it would provoke more antagonism from the Forest Service. Moreover, I was not enamored with the National Park Service just then because it seemed bent on developing roads and facilities. The Forest Service pitched itself as the more responsible agency, claiming it would keep such development out of Glacier Peak. Simons grew frustrated with me, calling me as stubborn as a "ton of concrete." Glacier Peak soon became such an obsession for Simons that his grades dropped, and he became eligible for the military draft. Tragically, he fell ill and died just weeks after arriving at boot camp.

I and other Glacier Peak advocates were determined that David's devotion to this land would not have been in vain. After giving the Forest

Service plenty of time to establish a wilderness designation, I came around to supporting national park status when the Forest Service did not. Washington senator Henry M. (Scoop) Jackson, then chairman of the Senate Interior Committee, championed the park proposal, and in 1968 Congress established a North Cascades National Park and Recreation Area totaling more than 700,000 acres. Later, an adjacent Glacier Peak Wilderness was established as well. Probably the transfer of jurisdiction over such a large chunk of wildlands to the National Park Service rankled the Forest Service enough that it finally took action to protect some of the area on its own.

CHAPTER FOUR

NAVIGATING ROUGH WATERS AT THE CLUB

❧

Surely the task of statesmanship is more difficult today than ever before.

—Walter Lippmann, *A Preface to Politics,* 1913

I FIRST RAN FOR THE SIERRA CLUB board of directors in 1956 but lost to Clifford Youngquist, an outings leader. Dave Brower was furious. Where were the Club's priorities, he fumed, if an outings leader won more votes than the chairman of the Conservation Committee? It's true that my profile was different from that of most previous Club leaders. I was not a talented rock climber or a native Californian or an outings leader; rather, I had risen through the ranks of the conservation program. The following year Brower campaigned actively for me, and in 1957 I was elected to the board—a position that, minus the required "term-limit" rotations off, I would retain for the next thirty-six years.

Dave and I worked well together, especially in the first decade of his tenure, and we agreed on most of our objectives. We both wanted the Club to grow in membership and to pursue an active conservation program. We both thought of conservation in large terms and opposed compromise for the sake of expediency. Many of the Club's greatest legislative accomplishments, to my mind, took place in the fifties—the first half of the period in which Brower served as executive director. For my part, I was elected vice president in 1959 and continued to chair the Conservation Committee until 1961.

In 1961, John F. Kennedy entered the White House, and I was elected president of the Sierra Club for the first time. These were exciting times for conservation. The Kennedy administration promised to be a breath of fresh air. Young and energetic, the Democrat from Massachusetts recognized the need to preserve the planet's dwindling open space. We also had high hopes for new Secretary of the Interior Stewart Udall, who had demonstrated an unusual knowledge of conservation problems. We at the Club hoped that such a progressive administration would be more receptive to conservation than the development-minded Eisenhower administration of the 1950s.

Through most of the 1950s, Brower had been the Club's point man legislatively, often going to Washington to meet with lawmakers. As we entered the 1960s, that mantle was passed to me as Dave became increasingly occupied with the publications program. Beginning in 1961 I was frequently in D.C. for congressional hearings or meetings with members of Congress and the lobbyists the Club had begun to use around that time. I generally took a red-eye flight so as to miss as little time as possible from my medical work. During this time I came to personify the Sierra Club for many on Capitol Hill.

The Club's stepped-up involvement in legislative activity and lobbying came with a price, however. By the late 1950s, Club directors had begun to worry about the issue of tax deductibility for donors to the Club, even though legislative matters still represented only a small proportion of the Club's work and budget. Anticipating increased fiscal scrutiny, the Club in 1957 formed an affiliated organization called Trustees for Conservation, whose members were mostly Sierra Club directors. It was chartered as a civic league, or 501(c)(4) organization under the Internal Revenue Code, for the express purpose of lobbying the U.S. Congress—the assumption being that the Sierra Club itself would no longer do this. Ansel Adams was the first president of Trustees, and I was the second. Bill Zimmerman, the Sierra Club's first Washington, D.C., lobbyist, became the lobbyist for Trustees as well. Through him, Trustees lobbied for passage of the wilderness bill and for the North Cascades National Park.

But this organization failed to attract contributions as the Sierra Club did, because it was not, like the Club, a known quantity. After a few years Trustees was abandoned, and the Sierra Club resumed its direct lobbying role. To guarantee that contributions would continue to flow without conflicting with lobbying efforts, Club leaders in 1960 launched another organization, the Sierra Club Foundation, "for the purposes of furthering the principles of the Sierra Club," as its charter resolution stated. Two hundred of us gave $100 each in seed money to get this new entity off the ground.

The foundation was designed to guard against future actions by the Internal Revenue Service against the Club, and for its first eight years it was essentially a sleeper organization. In 1968, however, when the IRS ruled that the Sierra Club could no longer assure tax deductibility to its contributors, the foundation—a 501(c)(3) organization under the Internal Revenue Code—assumed a much more aggressive role in soliciting and distributing contributions for education and related charitable activities. As president of the foundation for seven years, from 1971 to 1978, I presided over a tremendous increase in the magnitude of funds it handled. Today the foundation annually raises more than $60 million and disburses more than $26 million in program grants.

EXECUTIVE DIRECTOR Dave Brower and I—as chair of the Conservation Committee and later as president—quickly forged an agreement on our division of labor. As the number of potential campaigns escalated, the Club's directors identified five priority projects. Of these, Brower would spearhead the campaign to save the Grand Canyon from the Bureau of Reclamation's dams, while I would devote myself to the creation of a Redwoods National Park in northern California. We both would work toward the remaining three goals: passing the wilderness bill then moving through Congress, expanding the national park system, and establishing a large Glacier Peak Wilderness Area (later the North Cascades National Park; see chapter 3).

Dave and I worked closely together, our weekly lunch meeting often taking place in my medical office at 490 Post Street in San Francisco. We also met at Peggy's and my home on Sea View Terrace, Dave sometimes bringing his ad copy or book proposals for the Exhibit Format series. Although we meshed on our philosophies of wilderness, we often differed on how to sell our ideas to the general public—on tactics and strategy. I had already concluded that any campaign needed to be presented in terms of positive action rather than negative reaction. The Sierra Club was *pro,* not con. I also believed that, insofar as was possible, the Club should remain on cordial terms with land management agencies, even when strongly opposing an agency's plans. Under no circumstances did I consider ridicule or derision appropriate. My approach relied on patience and the recognition that campaigns often took a decade to achieve resolution. I was known as a diplomat.

Dave, on the other hand, was never concerned about appearing contrary. In fact, I believe he relished it. He coined the phrase "Not blind opposition to progress but opposition to blind progress." He was impatient: the earth was in a state of crisis; the time for action was always now. Nor was he above using guilt as a primary motivator for preservation. "If enough people care" was one of his pet phrases in ads and books. Brower displayed no reservations about saying he was against anything or anyone, routinely referring to the Forest Service as "the enemy." His tactics prompted Russell Train of the World Wildlife Fund to say, "Thank God for David Brower—he makes the rest of us look so reasonable."

Passionate in speech and bold in gesture, Brower was confident and charismatic, physically impressive, an expert climber, a gifted writer. He easily won attention—sometimes notoriety—and followers, especially young people. Dave served as a father figure to two young men who would play significant roles in the Club: David Simons, advocate for a North Cascades National Park (see chapter 3), and attorney Phil Berry, a future Sierra Club president. For better or for worse, David Brower would increasingly be seen as the person responsible for the Club's growth and public image. To many, including himself, he became the embodiment of the Sierra Club.

Psychologically, Brower felt it was critical for him and the Club to distance themselves from the land management agencies. He was particularly distrustful of the agencies' citizen advisory boards, which, he felt, were designed to turn environmentalists against each other. Agencies would feed such boards "confidential" information, he argued, in an effort to win their allegiance, and then send them back to their parent organizations as agents of compromise. He certainly felt this way about Dick Leonard and Bestor Robinson, who knew many of the federal managers personally. Brower viewed diplomacy as ineffectual and negotiations behind closed doors as conspiracy.

Many older members felt uneasy about the Club's new direction and Brower's aggressive tactics, pining for the earlier days of gentlemanly counsel. One such member, Joel Hildebrand—a well-known professor of chemistry at the University of California, former Club president, and honorary vice president—resigned in 1965 after Brower published a blanket criticism of pesticides in the *Sierra Club Bulletin*. In a written response to Brower, Hildebrand stated that he could no longer ally himself with an organization that unleashed such loose attacks, but his article was rejected by the *Bulletin's* editor, Hugh Nash, a devoted follower of Brower.

Other older directors continued to serve but found that their ideas were out of sync with the new Club. Bestor Robinson, for example, served on the board of directors until 1966 but with shrinking influence. Robinson had argued that the Club would have to compromise on Dinosaur National Monument; later he supported the siting of a PG&E nuclear plant at Diablo Canyon (see page 112) and a proposed ski development by the Walt Disney Corporation in the Mineral King area of the southern Sierra Nevada.

Robinson enraged Brower with such stands, but I had a different take on the veteran Club leader. An experienced attorney, Robinson was eloquent and well trained in argument. He also thought like a lawyer, wanting to settle issues out of court. Sizing up a situation, Robinson would calculate the point of eventual compromise and urge that the Club make a stand there. But I knew that if we took a compromise position from the start, we would end up with much less. Still, to me Bestor was one of the board's most valuable members. When he presented a case, I knew his arguments would be echoed on the outside by the management agencies and politicians. Debating with him gave me the chance to prepare counterarguments.

Difficulties between Brower and the board had begun to surface in the late 1950s, and by the spring of 1961, several directors were expressing concern that Brower disregarded their requests. Others questioned his agenda for his publications program, now larger than anyone had anticipated. The Club's balance sheet, which up to this point had always been in the black, was now registering a deficit. Such questions would be raised over and over in the years to come. Brower always maintained that the nature of publishing required a certain financial leeway and that book sales were not the sole measure of the program's success. At first the board took him at his word, satisfied that the books were fostering membership and making important contributions to the Club's campaigns. But the deficits continued to increase, and the Club was depleting its capital at an alarming rate.

August Frugé, the volunteer chair of the Club's Publications Committee and Brower's former supervisor at the University of California Press, was the first to make a serious challenge against the publications program. For Frugé, the question went beyond the issue of finances: he felt that publications had become the tail that wagged the dog. Ansel Adams, also on the committee, strongly disagreed. He thought the publications were the Club's most important activity and wanted to see the program expand even further.

I was concerned that work on the publications was siphoning Dave's energy away from our legislative program and from implementing the decisions of the board. More and more, he was occupied with books rather than administrative needs or legislative analysis. He was also becoming increasingly difficult to deal with personally, often appearing to resent the board's requests, at times overtly rude. This attitude seemed out of line—not only because Dave was employed by the board but also because its volunteer members gave so generously of their own time. There was also a mounting sense of self-imposed drama; his absence at a luncheon meeting would be chalked up to a "last-minute crisis."

Yet Dave's dedication to conservation was beyond question. He persisted relentlessly in the fight to save the Colorado River from proposed dams. In January 1963, after a lawsuit by the National Parks and Conservation Association against the secretary of the interior to stop construction of a dam at Glen Canyon, Utah, was thrown out of court, Dave flew to Washington to appeal personally to Interior Secretary Stewart Udall. Rising waters from Lake Powell, behind the Glen Canyon Dam, threatened to flood Rainbow Bridge National Monument, a magnificent sandstone arch held sacred by the Navajo, and countless beautiful side canyons.

His pleas were to no avail. Glen Canyon was lost to the lake waters but served as a lesson: while opposing the Dinosaur dams, the Sierra Club had not also opposed other dams already proposed on non–federally protected land. Few had seen Glen Canyon before Congress's decision to authorize the dam. Those who did see it between then and its destruction recognized that its scenic value surpassed that of Dinosaur.

After Glen Canyon was already drowned, Brower produced *The Place No One Knew,* a collection of color photographs of the region by Eliot Porter, taken before the dam construction. Some on the Publications Committee questioned the value of a book about a place already lost. But for Brower, *The Place No One Knew* served both as a requiem for a place he had treasured and as an act of retribution—a visual reminder to all who had conspired in this crime against the earth. Dave would neither forget nor forgive the damming of Glen Canyon. In an interview with the *East Bay Express* in 1999, a year before his death, he admitted he still felt a personal sense of guilt at not being able to stop the dam. Brower was eighty-eight; Glen Canyon was thirty-six years behind him. Few have burned so fiercely for so long.

In the early 1960s the biennial Sierra Club Wilderness Conferences were acquiring considerable stature. Peggy and I organized three of the conferences of that decade: in 1961, 1963, and 1965, Peggy serving as either general secretary or chair and I as chair or vice chair. As participation increased, the guest list began to include many top-level officials. The 1961 banquet was a momentous occasion: the governor of California, Edmund G. Brown, introduced an associate justice of the Supreme Court, William O. Douglas, and he in turn introduced the evening's speaker, the new secretary of the interior, Stewart Udall. That year the conference made the front page of the *San Francisco Chronicle.* This was also the meeting at which Peggy first suggested to Secretary Udall that he establish a Redwood National Park.

Beyond advocating for wilderness preservation, the conferences began to examine broader environmental questions and burgeoning ecological concepts. Conferees sought to define not only what should be officially designated as "wild," but also how humans needed to protect areas *outside* of wilderness. They expressed a growing awareness of the interconnectedness of earth's species, and recognized that certain behaviors of the human species were in dire need of modification. They articulated the idea that wilderness alone would not suffice: if people did not curb themselves, we would ultimately destroy the wild places we strove to preserve.

The first federal wilderness bill was drafted—largely by the Wilderness Society's Howard Zahniser—during 1955 and early 1956, and introduced in the Senate by Hubert H. Humphrey (D-Minn.) in June 1956. Representative John P. Saylor (R-Pa.) sponsored it in the House. Lobbying for this legislation became one of the Sierra Club's chief endeavors, from the introduction of the first bill until final passage of the Wilderness Act in 1964. An intensive eight-year campaign finally overcame formidable opposition by western industrial and extractive interests, conservative western legislators, leaders of the federal land management agencies, and the Eisenhower administration. The Kennedy administration's firm support made the difference, and President Lyndon Johnson signed the landmark legislation on September 3, 1964.

Throughout the battle for the Wilderness Act, I said repeatedly that I didn't care how long it took to pass a wilderness bill—the fact that it was in Congress would make the Forest Service hesitate to log in the Primitive Areas under consideration. This proved true—the limelight shone on Forest Service areas by legislative action meant that the agency did not dare reduce their levels of protection.

Relations between the Sierra Club and the Forest Service were strained in this period, because the Club strongly supported the wilderness bill while the agency opposed it, fearing that a legislated mandate would take away its management flexibility and severely constrain its freedom to act. Officials argued that there was no need for legislation: they could protect wild areas adequately by administrative means. They also balked at the proposed transfer of Forest Service lands to the National Park Service. The Forest Service sent Associate Chief Ed Crafts to a meeting of the Sierra Club board in 1960, at which he and I were the principal duelists in a contest that left our relations unchanged. I regretted the antagonism, but in this case it was unavoidable.

For Peggy and me, a highlight of our work with the Wilderness Conferences was meeting and getting to know Supreme Court Justice William O. Douglas, one of the principal speakers at the 1961 conference. An outdoors enthusiast and world explorer, Douglas did not limit his appreciation to remote wilds. In 1954 he mounted a crusade in his own backyard of Washington, D.C., to save the historic Chesapeake and Ohio Canal. When the *Washington Post* endorsed a plan to turn the canal into a motor parkway, Douglas challenged its editorial staff to walk the canal's 180 miles. They accepted the offer and afterward withdrew their endorsement.

In his book *My Wilderness: East of Katahdin,* Douglas described a winter's day on the C&O:

All was silent, except the crunching of the snow underfoot. When I stopped I could almost hear my heart beat. Yet, I was less than a dozen miles from the heart of Washington D.C. My wilderness, though small and confined, was real. It was in miniature the immense northland stretching to the Arctic Circle and beyond.

Douglas would later journey through the Arctic, and his account of running Alaska's Sheenjek River would strike chords that resonated with my own experiences.

I actually met Douglas for the first time in 1959. Although he had explored mountains in Europe, the Middle East, and Asia, Douglas admitted he'd never set foot in the Sierra Nevada. Dave Brower, Bob Golden, Peggy, and I planned a special five-day trip for him. Climbing the east side of the Sierra from June Lake, we made our way up to Donohue Pass, from which we would traverse the John Muir Trail southward. Late the first afternoon, each of us made our way into camp at the ridge crest—except Douglas. We waited, but he did not appear. Alarmed, I started down the trail with a horse, finding Douglas at least two miles from camp. He was blue in the face and moving very slowly.

"Bill, I've got a horse here for you," I offered.

Douglas looked up, his jaw clenched. "Don't bother me," he waved me away. "Go on! I'll get there."

And he did. Having reached the top and rested, he resumed his usual amiable demeanor and told us bawdy stories. Later I learned that ten years earlier, in 1949, he had been seriously injured when a large mule had stumbled and fallen on him. The accident left him with twenty-three broken ribs and only one functioning lung.

Douglas was a perceptive writer about the outdoors and a visionary wilderness advocate. The concept of wilderness as an American heritage had been recognized by others, but Douglas would take this argument to a new level. In *A Wilderness Bill of Rights,* he rooted wilderness firmly in American law. In Douglas's legal opinion, wilderness was not only desirable; it was a right as fundamental as any found in the Constitution. Lovers of wilderness, he asserted,

> are important in our pluralistic society. Though these actual
> participants constitute a minority, they have rights the majority
> should respect. The Bill of Rights, which makes up the first ten
> amendments to the Constitution, contains in the main guarantees
> to minorities. When it comes to Wilderness we need a similar
> Bill of Rights to protect those whose spiritual values extend to
> rivers and lakes, the valleys and the ridges, and who find life in
> a mechanized society worth living only because those splendid
> resources are not despoiled.

Douglas was also an ecologist when most others still had an anthropocentric view of wilderness. The role of humans was to be stewards, he thought: "We who come this way are merely short-term tenants. . . . Our power in wilderness terms is only the power to destroy, not to create." Many of the ideas contained in *A Wilderness Bill of Rights* would be incorporated into the Wilderness Act.

In 1960 some of us persuaded Douglas to run for the Sierra Club board of directors, and he won a seat easily. During his tenure, he tried to persuade me to get the Sierra Club headquarters moved from San Francisco to Washington, claiming, "That's where the action is." But the Club has always been a grassroots organization with its roots firmly in California. We have been happy and fortunate to remain outside the Beltway.

Although elected to a three-year term, Douglas resigned after two years. He correctly anticipated that environmental cases would come before the Supreme Court and did not want to have to recuse himself for conflict of interest. His presence on the bench would later prove critical in the Sierra Club's attempt to stop the Disney Corporation from developing Mineral King Valley (see page 127). I suspected, however, that Douglas's decision to resign from the board also stemmed from the Club's growing internal arguments.

Douglas and I remained friends. He dedicated one of his books to our eldest daughter, Cynthia, and flirted incorrigibly with my lovely wife. Although he is gone, his books continue to inspire. I return to them again and again; at times his words convey my experiences better than my own.

THE WILDERNESS CONFERENCES, though mainly a setting for animated discussion, were sometimes swept into the fiery disagreements over conservation in the 1960s. In 1963, Rachel Carson's editor, Paul Brooks, was invited to speak at the conference on her controversial new book, *Silent Spring*. With its claim that pesticides were destroying wildlife and were unsafe for human consumption, *Silent Spring* had created an uproar among those in the chemical sciences.

Tom Jukes, a cofounder of the Sierra Club's Atlantic Chapter and a noted chemist who worked for the American Cyanamide Company, was furious that the Club had extended this invitation to Brooks. Like many scientists, Jukes heaped scorn on Carson's "unscientific" book; Carson herself was dismissed by many as "hysterical." Jukes wrote Brooks a scathing letter expressing his outrage at Carson and at Brooks for publishing the work. Brooks read the letter just minutes after arriving at the Palace Hotel, the conference site. Visibly shaken, he offered to cancel his talk, saying "I'll go quietly." But Peggy and I took him aside and convinced him that we were eager to hear him. Paul and I remained close until his death thirty-five years later.

Another hot topic at the conferences was population control. Some participants—notably Paul Ehrlich, who would soon write *The Population Bomb*—argued that unless environmentalists worked toward zero percent growth, the world, let alone wilderness, would not be able to sustain itself.

In 1965, Harvard professor Lincoln Day talked about his work on population control, advocating a limit of two children for responsible parents. At the press conference, George Duchek of the now-defunct *San Francisco News* asked Day how many kids he had; Day replied that he had had a vasectomy after the birth of his second child.

Duchek then turned to me: "Dr. Wayburn, how many kids do you have?" There was no escaping the fact that Peggy and I had four children. I reminded him, however, that we were from a different generation, when four had been perceived as the magic number. Nevertheless I strongly believed the conference was right to broadcast a wake-up call.

By January 1963, it was clear that the Sierra Club was operating at a deficit. In fact, part of almost every board of directors meeting during my presidency would be devoted to the club's financial straits. At the 1963 meeting, director Nate Clark argued that the publications program was eating up the budget. Brower countered by saying that outside gifts would replenish funds. Bestor Robinson acknowledged that the program had grown but felt that our concurrent membership growth and conservation success warranted the expense. He and treasurer Cliff Heimbucher asked for a fixed publications budget, which proved an elusive goal. A bookkeeper was hired to sort through the mishmash of 1962 accounts; most of his time was spent tracking publishing receipts.

Dave missed more meetings. The December 1962 edition of the *Bulletin* was delayed until February 1963 because he insisted on rewriting the photo captions. I grew frustrated as the executive director always seemed to find something more important to do than what the board or I had requested. In April 1963, Dave disappeared for several days. When I asked where he was, his staff told me he had gone to Glen Canyon, but he had not cleared his plans with the board or me. Dave was brilliant but demanded absolute self-rule. One of his most-used expressions was "Follow me."

I felt that some decision by the board was inevitable. Either the directors would have to elect a figurehead president (as some organizations did) and turn over the Club to the executive director or they must deliver an ultimatum. "How much should the organization reflect the ego . . . of a single individual," I wrote in my journal, "as he progresses from one series of endeavors to the next, leaving the previous ones behind?"

Also in 1963, August Frugé intensified his criticism of the publications program. As Publications Committee chair, Frugé felt he was not being adequately consulted about upcoming projects. He had not been given the full text for *The Place No One Knew,* for example, until the book was already in production. Of the year's list of seven books, Frugé had seen the complete text for only two. And Brower was advertising books that had never been authorized by the committee. His latest proposed book, on the Galapagos Islands, did not win the approval of Frugé, who felt not only that the Club was spreading itself too thin in financing the books, but also that Dave's chosen material lacked focus and, at times, quality. Could the Sierra Club really hope to be effective in protecting wilderness, Frugé argued, if it took up the battle cry for every inch of the earth?

Frugé considered resigning as committee chair but stayed on at the board's request. At a heated meeting at the Palace Hotel, both he and Francis Farquhar asked for firm budgets. A livid Brower stormed out of the room but soon returned. Ansel Adams and Martin Litton, the travel editor for *Sunset* magazine, came to Brower's defense. Adams felt that Frugé was denying the emotional appeal of photographic images and the potential of art to transform people's views of wilderness and reminded him of the books' success in bringing in new members.

As Brower's contention with the board increased, he would confide in me, saying he was going to resign if the board crossed him again. So far, his threats had proved to be no more than dramatic displays; he would threaten to leave and the board would ask him to stay. But beginning in 1962, I warned him to abandon such tactics. "Don't do it, Dave," I told him. "The board will accept your resignation." The threats stopped.

As the Sierra Club continued to grow, its leaders were forced to deal with the consequences. At its December 1963 meeting, the board considered the question: How would all of the Club's new members shape its identity and purpose? Ten years earlier most members had joined because of the outings program, but the membership was no longer a homogenous group. With the Club's increasingly public campaigns, many members joined to support and take part in conservation programs. How could the new Club welcome a spectrum of interests and yet remain a cohesive, effective organization?

Active participation at the chapter level, coordinated nationally, would be key. When the Club admitted its first chapters outside California, in the 1950s, they were regional in scope: the Atlantic coast, the Pacific Northwest, and so on. As membership swelled, these subdivided into state-based chapters. (California, the Club's home state, remains the exception, encompassing thirteen chapters.) Larger chapters formed smaller units known as "groups" to focus on particular places or issues. As chapters proliferated in the 1960s, the board envisioned that each would carry on its own grassroots and lobbying efforts, led by conservation representatives who would also link their chapters with the national hierarchy.

The board of directors—fifteen leaders elected by membership-wide vote to staggered terms of three years each—governs the Club nationally and elects the president and vice president from its ranks, as well as other officers. These plus one other director comprise the executive committee, which can make urgent administrative decisions in the absence of the full board. The board is advised by the Sierra Club Council of Club leaders, consisting of a delegate from each chapter.

My first presidency lasted until 1964, when Will Siri—a biophysicist at the University of California—took over, and I became vice president. By then I had already served for three years rather than the customary two, and I was about to become president of the San Francisco Medical Society.

In 1966, the Club elected George Marshall, an economist, as president; I continued as vice president. Marshall, who lived in Los Angeles, soon found the job too exhausting. He had not really wanted to be president, doubting his ability to govern such a large and contentious organization, but had acquiesced at the board's request. His physical distance from the Club's main office in San Francisco made it difficult for him to follow day-to-day developments or stave off conflicts before they escalated. Marshall would refuse to run for a second term in 1967.

Because I lived in San Francisco, I was frequently called in to help with administrative and political issues. It was during Marshall's tenure that Ansel Adams, who had been such a staunch advocate of the publications program, turned emphatically against Dave Brower. The last straw for Adams was an Exhibit Format book Dave was determined to go forward with, even though it had been turned down by the Publications Committee. Ansel claimed that the text and photographs were not up to the Club's standard. Concerned chiefly about Dave's defiance of the committee, I confronted him and production came to a halt.

Dave's unilateral campaign promotions were about to land the Club in fiscal hot water, and with almost no warning. One of his favorite tactics was placing provocative full-page ads in major newspapers—ads whose copy was usually approved by the board or president. In June 1966, as part of his ongoing efforts to stop construction of dams on the Colorado River, Dave ran an ad in the *New York Times* and the *Washington Post*. A Club member in New Jersey had suggested the headline for what became the Club's best-known ad: "Should we also flood the Sistine Chapel so tourists can get nearer the ceiling?"

The ad claimed the proposed dams would threaten the Grand Canyon and held Secretary Stewart Udall and his brother, Arizona congressman Morris Udall, directly accountable for the projects. Udall was taken aback, as were many in the Club. Richard Leonard, who seemed to grow more conservative with each passing year, saw the criticism of Udall as slanderous and unprofessional. Still, the ads undoubtedly were effective and brought immediate response. Coupons attached to the ads resulted in thousands of new memberships as well as many letters to officials, arousing new involvement in conservation.

On June 10, 1966, shortly after the full-page ad ran in the *New York Times,* a faceless man in a dark blue suit walked into the Sierra Club offices and hand-delivered a letter from the Internal Revenue Service. It stated that the Club's status as a charitable organization under Section 501(c)(3) of the Internal Revenue Code was under question and that gifts to the Club could no longer be guaranteed as tax deductible. The IRS saw the ads as substantial lobbying activity, beyond what a charitable organization was allowed to engage in.

The loss of charitable status was serious. While the ads had stimulated membership growth and increased income from annual dues, the Club at that time was also receiving charitable gifts amounting to a considerable (for that time) sum—just over $100,000 a year. These gifts made possible the Club's publications program as well as research then under way to identify areas eligible for protection under the recently signed Wilderness Act.

The board determined to resist the IRS action. At that time the Club was still essentially an educational and scientific organization with less than 5 percent of its budget devoted to lobbying efforts. (Currently more than half of the Club's budget goes toward influencing legislation.) On the recommendation of members Don Harris and Fred Fisher, who had represented the Club in environmental legal actions on a volunteer basis, we hired Gary Torre—the partner in their firm responsible for tax matters— to take the Sierra Club's case to the IRS.

Gary, who had once clerked for Justice William O. Douglas, undertook an intensive review of the Club's expenditures and activities, which made it quite clear that the expenditure for ads and other lobbying activities was a tiny part of total annual expenditures. It was equally clear that staff and volunteer time dedicated to lobbying was minuscule compared to the time spent exploring, maintaining, and protecting the environment. Gary submitted a substantial brief to the IRS, but the case was rejected— leaving judicial action as the only means by which the issue could be contested. But such proceedings would be costly, and at a time when the club could afford little. Instead, Gary advised, the Club should accept the status of a 501(c)(4) organization, which could engage in unlimited lobbying activities and expenditures. He pointed out that the Sierra Club Foundation, already formed, could be the channel for tax-deductible contributions for educational, nonlobbying activities.

Thus began the Sierra Club Foundation's long and successful career in seeking funds and supporting related organizations engaged in work that complemented the Club's programs. As a qualified 501(c)(4) organization with expanded scope for lobbying activities, the Club put itself in position to become the country's leading organization lobbying for environmental protection—which it is today.

THE BROWER CONTROVERSY aside, other issues arose in the contentious sixties that deeply split the Sierra Club's leadership, reflecting the gap between older members inclined to work with development interests and more radical younger members.

In the late fifties, I'd received a letter from a resident of Bodega Bay, a coastal community fifty miles north of San Francisco. Rose Gaffney's letter informed me of the Pacific Gas and Electric Company's plan to build a power plant next to her home. Although Bodega was only an hour and a half drive, I had never been there, and as chair of the Club's Conservation Committee, I thought I should see the proposed site firsthand. Peggy and I and the children drove up one weekend and discovered a quiet seaside town at the mouth of Tomales Bay, just north of another area I would come to know intimately: Point Reyes. A few dozen houses nestled in the gentle coastal hills, and a rocky peninsula called Bodega Head jutted into the Pacific; it was here that PG&E wanted to build. At the town limits, flat, golden sand beaches stretched northward for miles.

It was obvious that Bodega deserved protection. Before returning to San Francisco, we headed inland to Santa Rosa, where the Club's new Redwood Chapter was holding its first meeting. Bodega fell into their territory, so I briefed the group on what I had just seen, asking them to research the project and give me a full report. The brand-new chapter lacked the resources for such an investigation, however, and no report was ever forthcoming.

The Club's board of directors did vote to oppose the plant but did not authorize a real campaign. Then-president Harold Bradley did not consider a struggle against a power plant appropriate to the Club's mission. The sustained fight to save Bodega Bay came from two young Club members, attorney Phil Berry and forestry school graduate Dave Pesonen. Berry and Pesonen felt the board was dragging its feet, and they kept the debate over the plant alive for the next several years—during which they discovered that the new plant was to be a nuclear facility.

Various lines of argument emerged. Some board members—Leonard and Siri among them—felt that Berry and Pesonen lacked adequate scientific training to rule out nuclear plants. Others argued that it was unrealistic for the Club to oppose California's growth. Berry and Pesonen's staunch opposition never wavered, but in 1963, with plant construction about to begin, the argument became moot. As foundation holes were being drilled into the rockbed, seismologists discovered an earthquake fault line running beneath Bodega Head, and construction ceased.

The Bodega controversy was soon overshadowed by a much bigger and more protracted debate over another PG&E nuclear plant. In 1962, Kathleen Goddard Jackson (later Jones), a coastal activist and the first chair of the Sierra Club Council, appealed to the Club for help to stop the building of a plant at the Nipomo Dunes, north of Santa Barbara. PG&E had already optioned the land, so we had to move quickly.

I appointed Kathy Jackson chair of a special task committee to organize the Club's efforts, and I personally toured the area. In my estimation, there is no part of the California coastline undeserving of protection, and the Nipomo Dunes were no exception. Previous National Park Service surveys had mentioned the dunes as a possible national park site. I thought the dunes were worthy of being a state park at the very least; they needed some kind of protection. When we confronted PG&E about Nipomo, the company predictably balked at changing its plans but after two years of negotiating agreed to search for an alternative site farther up the coast.

The place they fixed on was Diablo Canyon on the central coast, west of the town of San Luis Obispo, which PG&E claimed lacked Nipomo's scenic values. None of the Sierra Club directors, however, learned about the selection of Diablo Canyon until 1964, after the end of my first stint as president. My successor, Will Siri, and Kathy Jackson entered into negotiations with PG&E and agreed to Diablo as a suitable site; Siri introduced this proposal at a board meeting in the spring of 1966. He and Jackson agreed that the site's scenic value did not compare to the Nipomo Dunes; the land was mostly grazed and crossed by service roads. As Jackson would later describe it, Diablo Canyon was a suitable place for a "county picnic park."

Also involved in the negotiations for an alternative site was a three-person team called Conservation Associates. Consisting of Dorothy Varian, wife of the cofounder of the energy company Varian Associates; Richard Leonard's wife, Doris; and George Collins, a retired NPS planner, Conservation Associates attempted to be a bridge between conservation and industry. They too gave their approval to the Diablo site.

▲ Ed and Peggy Wayburn skiing near Echo Summit, south of Lake Tahoe, after Christmas of 1947. PHOTOGRAPH COURTESY THE WAYBURN FAMILY.

▲ Edgar Wayburn in 1957. Photograph courtesy the Sierra Club.

▲▲ On the Sierra Club's 1949 High Trip, Ed Wayburn led a side trip to Mt. Whitney. Photograph by Cedric Wright courtesy the Sierra Club. ▲ Ed helps Peggy wash her hair on a Sierra Nevada backpacking trip. Sierra Club Outings photograph courtesy the Sierra Club.

▲ ▲ The Sierra Club board of directors, 1963. Back row, left to right: George Marshall, Cliff Heimbucher, Ansel Adams, Nate Clark, Will Siri, Alex Hildebrand, Lewis Clark, Fred Eissler. Front row, left to right: Randal Dickey, Polly Dyer, Ed Wayburn, Charlotte Mauk, Dick Leonard, Bestor Robinson, Jules Eichorn. PHOTOGRAPH COURTESY THE SIERRA CLUB.

▲ A Sierra Club board of directors meeting, ca. 1964, with most of the same personnel, including Adams (left) and Wayburn (across the table); Dave Brower in the right background. PHOTOGRAPH COURTESY THE SIERRA CLUB.

◄ Ed and Peggy Wayburn at the 1963 Sierra Club banquet with U.S. Forest Service regional forester for California, Jack Deinema, and Mrs. Deinema.
PHOTOGRAPH COURTESY THE SIERRA CLUB.

May 1966 bring peace, prosperity —
and a great Redwood National Park!

The Wayburns

▲ ▲ In the view room at the Wayburn family home on Seaview Terrace, San Francisco, where conservation plans were hatched. Left to right: Laurie, Cynthia, Ed, Diana, William, and Peggy. PHOTOGRAPH BY BILL OWEN COURTESY THE WAYBURN FAMILY. ▲ The Wayburn family, Christmas 1965. Left to right: Laurie, Diana, Bill, Cynthia, Peggy, and Ed. Gwendy, the first of many vizslas, is also present. PHOTOGRAPH BY BILL OWEN COURTESY THE WAYBURN FAMILY.

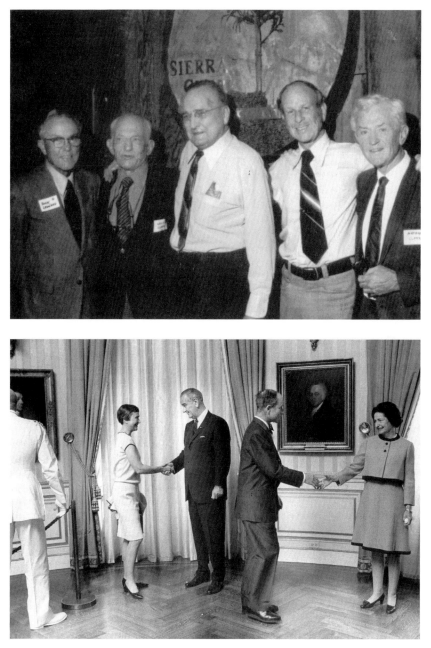

▲ ▲ Sierra Club president Ed Wayburn with past presidents in the mid-1960s. Left to right: Dick Leonard, Lewis Clark, Bestor Robinson, Ed Wayburn, and Nathan Clark. PHOTOGRAPH COURTESY THE SIERRA CLUB. ▲ Ed and Peggy Wayburn with President Lyndon Johnson and Lady Bird Johnson in the White House, 1968, after the signing of the bill establishing Redwood National Park. PHOTOGRAPH COURTESY THE WHITE HOUSE.

▲▲ A field trip with the Bureau of Land Management at Tebay Lakes in Alaska's Chugach Mountains in 1968. PHOTOGRAPH COURTESY THE BUREAU OF LAND MANAGEMENT. ▲ "That great day on the Toklat" in Denali National Park, Alaska, summer 1968. Left to right: Peggy Wayburn, Gordon Haber, Ed Wayburn, Sigurd Olson. PHOTOGRAPH BY BILL EVERHART COURTESY THE NATIONAL PARK SERVICE.

◄ Ed and Peggy Wayburn on West Chichagof Island in Southeast Alaska in the summer of 1968. PHOTOGRAPH BY JACK CALVIN COURTESY THE WAYBURN FAMILY.

▲ ▲ On a 1972 field trip with Secretary of the Interior Rogers Morton in Chitistone Canyon in Alaska's Wrangell–St. Elias National Park. PHOTOGRAPH COURTESY THE NATIONAL PARK SERVICE.

▲ The Wayburns and Jack Hession on the Mulchatna River on a 1974 field trip to inspect the future Lake Clark National Park. PHOTOGRAPH BY JIM ROUSH COURTESY THE WAYBURN FAMILY.

▲▲ Dave Brower, Ansel Adams, and Ed Wayburn at a reunion in the early 1970s at the home of Ansel Adams in Carmel Highlands. PHOTOGRAPH BY MARK PALMER COURTESY THE SIERRA CLUB. ▲ Ed with Congressman Phil Burton, who received the first Edgar Wayburn Award at the Sierra Club banquet in 1979. PHOTOGRAPH COURTESY THE SIERRA CLUB.

Siri seemed to expect the directors to simply go along with his stand, but his and Jackson's private negotiations were troubling to some. Although I thought he should have consulted the board before committing the Club to a position, I stood by Siri's actions. I felt personally obliged to do so—not only had he supported me in opposing the Nipomo Dunes site, but he had inherited the problem of finding an alternative. Siri and Jackson also maintained that approving Diablo Canyon was rooted in the Club's tradition of helping to identify alternatives and that going along with PG&E would keep open the lines of communication between the two organizations.

In the following vote, only Fred Eissler opposed the Diablo site. Polly Dyer and Paul Brooks abstained, but the rest of the board voted to uphold the Diablo agreement. Dick Leonard wrote a cordial letter to PG&E president Shermer Sibley, thanking him for his cooperation.

During this time, director Martin Litton had been traveling abroad and returned home to learn about the board's vote. Litton, who had a volatile temper, was outraged. He'd seen Diablo Canyon, and the board had been duped, he claimed. He scoffed at the idea that the power plant was necessary to California's burgeoning population, believing that more power would only encourage more people to settle. Litton, too, wrote a letter to Sibley, but it took a very different tone, asserting that the board's assent had been fraudulently obtained and that the company had been deliberately misleading about the area's scenic qualities.

In the hope of allaying growing concern within the Club's ranks, PG&E sponsored a "show-me" trip to Diablo Canyon. I was among several directors who boarded a Lear jet. When the pilot turned around to greet us, he looked strangely familiar—not surprising, since he was revealed to be Danny Kaye, who besides being the premier comedian of his day also rented out his self-piloted plane for special tours.

The tour itself did little to assuage my concern that the board had acted in haste. Diablo Canyon was not a barren, mediocre strip of land but a finely sculpted coastal range area shaded by old oak groves. It was not as striking as, and certainly was different in topography from, the Nipomo Dunes but was worthy of preservation all the same. Furthermore, the proposed route of the power line connecting Diablo to the main PG&E grid, which PG&E had claimed would remain invisible from the coast, would, in fact, travel over a ridge top and dominate the local landscape.

I now felt our decision to accept the Diablo Canyon site had been a mistake. Eissler and Litton had been right; PG&E was not to be trusted. Siri and Jackson, in their fervor to save one beautiful place, had condemned another, and, as with Glen Canyon dam, the board had voted for an alternative that few had seen firsthand. With the advantage of hindsight, I would have chosen a different path from the start, but still I felt morally obliged to stand by Siri. The Club had reached a consensus; integrity demanded we stick to it. But the debate would drag on for several years—a strange aberration, a nonpriority issue that sparked a battle of personalities and aggravated tensions on the board.

The Diablo Canyon baton would be passed from president to Club president. By the time it landed in the hands of George Marshall in September 1966, the directors were bitterly divided. Now Eissler and Litton were joined by Polly Dyer. Jules Eichorn also changed camps, claiming he was not beholden to a decision based on PG&E's misrepresentations. Adams, Leonard, Siri, and I advocated maintaining the Club's position. Eissler wanted Diablo Canyon put to a vote of the entire membership, and a referendum, the first in the Sierra Club's history, would appear on the 1967 ballot. (Dave Brower, though without a vote on the board of directors, had not originally opposed the Diablo site but came around to that view after lobbying by Eissler and Litton.)

Personally, I was growing frustrated by the amount of time devoted to this single issue. I felt Diablo was worth saving but the question had been blown out of proportion; our campaigns in other places such as the Redwoods, the Grand Canyon, and the North Cascades were on a larger scale, involving vast areas of public wilderness. For the board, however, this decision had assumed symbolic importance, reflecting the changing composition and modus operandi of the Club's leadership. What would take precedence—the land or the integrity of the board?

In the spring of 1967, the Sierra Club membership voted two to one to uphold the board's original decision to accept Diablo Canyon as an alternative site for PG&E's nuclear plant. The problem seemed put to rest, but the respite would be temporary.

Throughout the mid-1960s, the board–Brower relationship continued to deteriorate. At a 1967 meeting, Dick Leonard presented the board with a letter signed by many Club leaders, including seven former presidents. It outlined what they saw as the executive director's failings: his emotionalism, his aggressive tactics, his maligning of public officials, his disregard for the Club's finances, and his general tendency to do first and tell later. The letter called Brower "irresponsible and uncompromising" and demanded that the board of directors regain control of the Club's policy and publications.

Adams reiterated his concern about the publishing program, saying he regretted not heeding August Frugé's earlier warnings. Forty percent of the club's budget was now being expended on publications. Adams especially disliked another of Dave's projects, *On the Loose*—a collection of philosophy and photographs that its young authors, Terry and Renny Russell, hoped would serve as an ecological manifesto for their generation. The book looked like a potential best-seller, but Adams thought the material was subpar.

Ansel's criticism of Brower was fierce; his intense hostility was troubling to many, including myself. Certainly his resentment could be traced in part to his belief that Dave had compromised artistic standards that Adams demanded in his own work. But perhaps Adams also discovered, at least in the Diablo case, that he was not necessarily the wilderness radical he considered himself to be. Always an unknown quantity on matters of policy, he now blamed Brower for all the Club's troubles.

Reacting to Adams's criticism and to the letter presented by Leonard, President Will Siri proposed to reorganize the Publications Committee into a discrete entity with a hard budget. The motion passed, but in practice little would change. The board edged closer toward a bitter disintegration, a tense period I would come to call "the Brawl."

The night before the Club's annual meeting of May 1967, the board met in a stormy closed session at the St. Francis Hotel. The current board was split internally, with four newly elected Brower supporters forming their own camp: photographer Eliot Porter, nuclear engineer Laurence Moss, hydrologist Luna Leopold, and attorney Phil Berry. Discussion centered on whether to retain Brower as executive director, and whom the board should elect as its incoming president. I was asked if I would take the job again: I was considered a statesman, a moderate, respectful of both sides. And I seemed to be the only director with whom Dave was able to work, the only one he seemed to trust, and therefore, perhaps, the only one who could control him at all.

The decision to take up the presidency again was not an easy one. Anticipating the call, I had already discussed it at length with Peggy and our children. Our time together would inevitably suffer, as the post now amounted to a more than full-time job and entailed considerable time away from home. The Sierra Club now had fifty thousand members; within six months, that number would climb to more than fifty-seven thousand. And the president would have the support of, at best, half the board.

The day after the emergency session, the new board met publicly for the first time. It decided to retain Brower and formally elected me president. I had made it understood we would need to clear the air. In this spirit, Ansel Adams—who recently had been so fiercely critical of Brower—proposed a vote of confidence in the executive director. It passed. After the meeting, Dave expressed happiness at my return. "Now you'll be able to carry out your mission in the Redwoods more easily," he said. "We can work together."

I WANTED HIS WORDS to be true, and for a few months it seemed to be so. But the board's divisions had merely been swept under the rug. The Diablo Canyon issue, in particular, just wouldn't go away. A group of directors pressed for continued discussion; some were concerned about the effects of nuclear pollution on the local marine life. I tried to postpone Diablo Canyon until September, saying that our focus had to remain elsewhere until then.

Before the September meeting, however, eight of the fifteen directors authorized their names to be used on a letter to PG&E president Shermer Sibley, informing him that the Sierra Club board of directors was again reviewing its policy on Diablo. Brower, who had helped draft the letter, agreed at my request not to send it, but Martin Litton, believing he had the support of a majority of the board, sent it on his own. Sibley called me in confusion. Was the letter real? he asked. Was the Sierra Club going back on its word? The letter had put me in an incredibly awkward situation of trying to explain the Club's position—a position I did not support. Local newspapers got wind of the letter; several criticized our wavering stance.

The September board meeting exploded over Diablo. It ended with the board passing a resolution acknowledging that it had erred in its initial acceptance of the Diablo Canyon as an alternative to Nipomo Dunes. The resolution cited Diablo's "unique scenic values"; it did not mention opposition to nuclear energy per se. The directors also reaffirmed the Club's policy of opposing any power plants along the California coast.

Litton argued that the board could not pass such a resolution and then fail to act on it. Fearing that this issue would paralyze our efforts in our other campaigns, I sent a telegram to each of the directors:

KEEP FOREMOST IN YOUR MIND ALL THE GREAT GOALS
AND PURPOSES FOR WHICH WE HAVE WORKED SO LONG.
OUR ACHIEVEMENTS HAVE NEVER BEEN GREATER. OUR
DISSOLUTION OVER DIABLO CANYON OR ANY OTHER
SINGLE ISSUE OR DECISION CAN MAKE A DIFFERENCE...
100 YEARS FROM NOW.

As 1967 drew to a close, the argument over what action to take on Diablo Canyon, if any, was eclipsed by a larger ongoing problem: Dave Brower's continued fiscal irresponsibility and deepening divisions in the board over how far to support him. His strong and vocal opposition to the Diablo arrangement merely fed the fires.

In February 1968, the board directed Brower to obtain the approval of the president before making any significant withdrawals from the executive director's fund. Until that point, these monies had been labeled a "contingency fund" but now were classified as "discretionary." Although this was little more than a verbal slap on the wrist—a reminder to Dave to exhibit discretion in spending the Club's money—the move exacerbated Brower's longstanding resentment of the older, more conservative directors. He repeatedly told me, "The board is out to get me."

Earlier, his fears had seemed paranoid, but now he had genuine cause for concern: a growing contingent of the board was set on removing him from office. It's also possible that Dave himself was inciting the showdown in hopes of emerging from the next election with a board solidly behind him. It was an ironic situation: externally, the Sierra Club had never exerted so much influence, on the edge of victory in its campaigns for the Redwood National Park and the North Cascades National Park. Internally, the Club's leadership was disintegrating. It was a very difficult time to be president, and despite my constant efforts to hold things together, I feared we were headed for a blowout.

In the face of mounting criticism, Dave continued to act without consulting the board or even me. In the spring of 1968, he published an issue of the *Sierra Club Explorer*—a sporadic supplementary periodical—in which he advertised a new two-volume book on the Galapagos Islands edited by his son, Kenneth. Dave saw *The Flow of Wildness* as the flagship title in an "Earth National Park" series he envisioned. He claimed the *Explorer* issue was funded legitimately by membership dues and that he had been forced to publish it because I'd forbidden his advertising the book in the *Bulletin*. Indeed, I had forbidden any ads, because the book's publication had been unauthorized. The *Explorer* mailing came at considerable cost—every member received a copy.

At the September 1968 board meeting, Ansel Adams, Dick Leonard, and Richard Sill asked for the executive director's resignation, but no definitive action was taken then. In October, the trio followed up with a list of particulars: Sill claimed Brower had added book royalties to his discretionary fund to endow his personal campaigns privately. Adams protested that Dave ignored directions from the board and the Publications Committee, citing the unapproved Galapagos book as an example. Leonard focused on Brower's fiscal irresponsibility, compiling a history of the Club's finances that showed the publications program registering a deficit for the last five years—and that because of this, the Club repeatedly had been forced to dip into restricted funds to keep afloat.

Although all these arguments were valid to a considerable degree, I came to Dave's defense. Some of the accusations were merely assertions until proved in writing. And 1968 had been a very good year for conservation—the Club and its allies had won passage of a 700,000-acre North Cascades National Park and Recreation Area, and we had successfully

118

waged a tough battle for a Redwood National Park. Certainly the executive director deserved some credit for these successes.

Adams shot back by criticizing the Club's redwoods campaign (which I directed). He claimed that we had been unethical in failing to endorse the proposal of another conservation organization, the Save-the-Redwoods League, and that this lack of unity had compromised the ultimate size of the park.

The trio of Adams, Sill, and Leonard began to formulate a platform for the April 1969 board election, when Adams and Frugé would be up for reelection. Calling themselves the CMCs—Concerned Members for Conservation—they were joined as candidates by Superior Court Judge Raymond Sherwin, real estate executive Maynard Munger, and Nicholas Clinch, a popular mountaineer and outings leader who had led expeditions to the Andes and the Himalayas. I was not asked to join their slate.

On January 14, 1969, I was in bed with the flu when I received a telephone call from George Duchek at the *San Francisco News*. "What's this 'Earth National Park' ad you've got in the *New York Times*?" he asked.

"What ad?" I replied. Brower had not informed me of any new advertisements, despite his new requirement to get the president's authorization. However, for some weeks, I'd been getting hints from the staff that something might be going on.

Duchek sent me a copy of the ad, which showed a satellite photograph of the earth. The headline urged: "New Sierra Club publications advance this urgent idea: An international program before it is too late, to preserve Earth as a 'conservation district' within the Universe; a sort of 'EARTH NATIONAL PARK.'"

The ad played on the fervor surrounding the recent moon landing, telling readers that unless their idea of home included taking an "evening walk in an oxygen helmet and a space suit," they had better start taking care of their home planet. What followed was a hodgepodge account of international environmental threats: the depletion of oxygen-producing plants, the dangers of pesticides, proposed dams in Asia and Africa. Brower envisioned the planet as "a wildlife preserve of a sort, except that we are the wildlife." The language was flighty and unfocused—fodder for the kind of criticism routinely flung at conservationists.

Included in the ad were three cut-out-and-mail coupons. One asked President Nixon to launch an international conservation program; one solicited prospective members and purchasers of Club publications, including *Galapagos: The Flow of Wildness.* The third was addressed to me, as treasurer of the Sierra Club Foundation and the manager of tax-deductible gifts, urging me to help fund an ambitious new line of "some one hundred books."

The ad totaled one and a half pages, and its cost to the Club, I later learned, was $10,500. Another $5,500 had been spent on its preparation, including work contracted out to a San Francisco advertising firm. The board had never authorized announcing such an international program; the idea had been broached at the December 1968 board meeting but had not been approved. Even if we had wanted to undertake such a program—which would require a change in the Club's bylaws, as our mission was then limited to the United States—we didn't have the money to finance it. The Club was virtually bankrupt.

Brower had pushed too far, and I sent him a telegram immediately suspending his ability to make further financial commitments for the Sierra Club. Brower protested my action first to the executive committee and then to the board, claiming I had no authority to do so. By the end of January the executive committee confirmed my action; the full board's endorsement was harder to gain. Dave had succeeded in packing the board with people who were true conservationists but inexperienced about Club management. The executive committee consisted of longstanding members, including attorney Phil Berry, who had been a devoted follower of Brower but had gradually withdrawn his allegiance.

Berry warned Dave that he would be legally responsible if he entered into further contracts. In early February the board did decide (by a close seven to six vote) that Brower would take a leave of absence until after the April elections. He agreed, stating that he would run for the board of directors and if elected, would resign as executive director. In the interim, Michael McCloskey, who had done outstanding work for the Club both as the Northwest conservation representative and as conservation director, would serve as interim director of the staff.

In 1892, JOHN MUIR founded a club to explore, enjoy, and preserve the Sierra Nevada. The leaders of my generation expanded that club, carrying Muir's vision beyond the mountains of California to embrace an overall wilderness ethic and the fight to preserve all of America's wilds. Perhaps more than any other individual, Dave Brower was responsible for that growth in size and vision. But the Sierra Club was larger than any one person's agenda, any one vision of its future. The ongoing struggle over Brower's role undercut our responsibility to our membership, most of whom were put off by the strife and recognized that it impaired the Club's conservation activities. Most important was our continued commitment to the earth itself. If the Sierra Club folded due either to financial disaster or personal dissension, who would be left to carry on Muir's work? If the loudest voice for wilderness was quieted, who would hear the call?

Had our only criterion for a successful executive director been sound financial judgment, Dave would have been fired much earlier. The Club was in serious financial difficulty; had we been a business, we would have had to declare bankruptcy. But I would not allow that. The first step was to restrain Brower's spending. Dave didn't care about money per se—he used it as a vehicle for his books and media appeals to the public. And without the authority to use Club funds to promote his ideas, Dave would resign his position, I was sure.

I did not actually fire him, though, or propose firing him. Despite all of Dave's indiscretions and abuses of authority, his bad judgment, his failure to comply with requests or carry through with projects, and despite the fact that every recent president except myself had wished him gone, he had accomplished too much, had drawn too many people into the Club, and was too dedicated to conservation to be cast out summarily. At his best, he had been an inspiration.

For years, Brower had warned that outside forces—corporations, advisory boards, management agencies—would try to divide the Club's ranks. Now, ironically, he had become the instrument of the Club's division. Dave had wanted to provoke the board, to create tension and, ultimately, confrontation. I believe he thought he had enough support on the board to win the imminent face-off.

As the April election approached, candidates for the board of directors formed election slates for the first time in the Club's history. On February 7, 1969, Donald Aitken, a physicist at Stanford University, held a press conference to announce the formation of the Committee for an Active, Bold, Constructive Sierra Club—also known as the ABC. Aitken, the committee chair, sought to "cut through the hysterical charges . . . made against Dave Brower." Brower headed the ABC ticket, which also included George Alderson, Polly Dyer, Fred Eissler, and David Sive. At the press conference, Brower declared that the real issue facing the Club was not himself but the Club's inability to move beyond "polite protests" and get in sync with the changing needs of the conservation movement.

Adams, Frugé, Sherwin, Munger, and Clinch continued their campaign as the CMC. Two more candidates—Virginia Prentice, a research geographer at the University of Michigan, and Sanford Tepfer, a botanist and a biology professor at the University of Oregon—positioned themselves as outside the controversy, but neither was expected to garner significant votes. From the onset, both sides expected the voting to center on one or the other of the competing platforms, though many CMC supporters feared Brower would win a seat on name recognition alone.

Committees were formed, and brochures outlining the respective parties' aims were drafted and mailed to every member of the Club. The CMC's primary goals were not surprising: a return to fiscal responsibility, a closely defined publications program, increased involvement of volunteers and chapter committees in making Club policy, and David Brower's resignation. A CMC brochure outlined at length Brower's indiscretions and concluded in Adams's words, "Our greatest conservation goal today is the conservation of the Sierra Club itself."

Whereas the CMC platform focused on restoring order to the Club's internal organization, the ABC's rhetoric sounded like an urgent call to war: "In the struggle to save the Earth's wild places and environment, it is now the eleventh hour. Anything short of total commitment in this battle . . . is reprehensible." The Club had a choice: to "revert to its days as a society of companions on the trail" or to "be an eloquent, successful voice for causes that might otherwise have no voice." The ABC characterized the CMC as outdated and ineffective. "These opposition directors are not bad men. But they just wish that things could somehow be simpler, more polite, less cosmic, and less risky—they are uncomfortable with what today's struggle requires."

The media seized on the Club's internal strife in reporting on the upcoming elections, often presenting Brower as a visionary martyr persecuted by a provincial old-boys network. Stirred by such inaccuracies, the distinguished author and one-time Club director Wallace Stegner was moved to speak up. In an article in the *Palo Alto Times* of February 11, 1969, Stegner asserted that Brower had been "bitten by the worm of power" and described how those who opposed Dave had once been his ardent supporters:

> Those whom his recklessness and insubordination have driven
> into opposition are not senile fuddy-duddies—he almost calls
> them birdwatchers—but some of the most distinguished,
> experienced, and dedicated conservationists on the planet.
> They oppose him, as I do, because they fear that in his grab
> for absolute power he will wreck the Sierra Club.

The article would be widely reproduced by the CMC slate in the months before the election.

Until late February I ran for the board as an independent. A sizable group, Volunteers for Wayburn, which included Stegner, George Marshall, Phil Berry, and Will Siri, had formed to help campaign for my reelection. I was not on unfriendly terms with the CMC but for a time was not considered in their camp because I had refused to fire Brower in the fall of 1968. I was considered a middle-ground candidate—once again the diplomat. It was a fair assessment. For six months, I had been trying to hold the board together and to avoid conflict at a time when others invited it, remaining as far from the mudslinging as I could.

With Brower's suspension, however, the CMC and I both decided we had more in common than not. I was asked to join the CMC slate, with Nicholas Clinch voluntarily withdrawing so I could stand as the fifth candidate. By the end of February my name appeared officially on CMC publications. Among my supporters, Marshall and Siri added their names to the list endorsing the CMC slate but did not officially join the party; Phil Berry would steadfastly refuse to endorse either slate.

To my dismay, the acrimony only worsened as April drew near. Partisans on each side derided the other and created weekly newsletters that read like gossip sheets. Some claimed ABC stood for "Aggressive Berserk Conservation"; the other side spelled out CMC as "Conservatives for Minimal Conservation." For myself, I did not relish muddying Brower's name publicly, but I did not attempt to control the CMC publications calling attention to Dave's indiscretions and the state of the Club.

Club members suffered the most. Although the local chapters generally supported the CMC slate, it was impossible for the average member to sort out the veracity of either side's claims on the basis of their literature. As president and a known moderate, I received dozens of letter from members appalled by the infighting. One high-school-age member summed up her frustration in a letter to the *Yodeler,* the San Francisco Bay Chapter's newsletter: "I have just spent four hours . . . attempting to decipher the various statements, accusations, etc. with which the two 'sides' of the Sierra Club have been flooding the mails. It is my opinion that if anything destroys this wonderful organization, it will be the feud . . . now going on."

On March 7, the situation worsened, if possible, when I suspended Hugh Nash from his duties as editor of the *Sierra Club Bulletin.* Nash, who was totally beholden to Brower, had refused to print more than a scant two paragraphs about Brower's suspension. I felt that an event of this magnitude warranted deeper coverage, that membership was entitled to more than a cursory summary of the board's actions. Nash held out, accusing me of trying to use the *Bulletin* as a propaganda tool for my own reelection. The ABC would use Nash's suspension as proof of my desire to ride roughshod over the staff. Meanwhile, the March *Bulletin,* already three weeks behind schedule, waited incomplete in the Sierra Club offices; it would not be mailed until five days after election ballots had been sent out. Some members, on receiving their ballots, did not realize that the ABC's principal candidate was under suspension.

The results of the April 1969 election were conclusive. All five members of the CMC slate were elected. David Brower, the ABC candidate winning the most votes, came in sixth; even so, he received 25 percent fewer votes than the lowest-scoring CMC candidate, Maynard Munger. Because all the victorious candidates were from the CMC, the new executive committee contained no members of the ABC party. On the lingering issue of Diablo Canyon, members voted three to one in favor of the board's original resolution. The Diablo controversy would finally be put to rest. The CMC owed its success to the many volunteers who had donated both time and money and to the local chapters that had endorsed its positions.

I had hoped to be reelected president to ensure that I could carry out my conservation programs, long delayed by the internal battle. But although I had led its slate, the CMC considered me too close to the center of the controversy. Ironically, the CMC directors voted for Phil Berry, while the Brower supporters remaining on the board voted for me. I lost by one vote and accepted the position of vice president, on the condition that I would take charge of the conservation program. In fact, losing to Berry proved a blessing in disguise; I was able to concentrate on conservation work while Phil traveled around the country visiting chapters and healing the wounds of the past year.

In May, at the first meeting of the board of directors after the election, David Brower submitted his resignation. The board accepted it, acknowledged Dave's contributions to the Club, and wished him well in his future endeavors. Dave spoke briefly and calmly of parting ways and then left the meeting. Within months he would found a new environmental organization, Friends of the Earth. Some of his former staff at the Sierra Club would follow him.

THE NEXT FEW months amounted to a housecleaning. In addition to Brower, Hugh Nash was let go. Brower's departure left a void in the position of executive director that many, with good reason, were hesitant to fill quickly. Rumors circulated that former Interior Secretary Stewart Udall would accept the position if asked, but most board members were reluctant to take on another high-profile personality. What we needed was someone who knew the organization and could work quietly and effectively to set our house in order.

We found that person within our own staff ranks—a candidate with solid conservation experience on both the regional and national level. J. Michael McCloskey came to the Sierra Club in 1961 as our first staff representative based in the Northwest. By that time, both the Club and the Federation of Western Outdoor Clubs felt they needed a representative stationed in the region, but neither organization had enough money to hire someone. So we pooled resources, with Leo Gallagher, a dedicated FWOC member, funding the federation's portion.

Karl Onthank, who had succeeded me as FWOC president, was associate dean at the University of Oregon. He knew a law student more interested in environmental work than in the practice of law—and thus it happened that Mike McCloskey went to work for the Sierra Club while still in law school. From the start, McCloskey proved extremely able in handling conservation issues in the Northwest. He understood that if the Club wished to be a viable force legislatively, it would need to beef up its proposals. It was Mike who would later take up the issue of the North Cascades National Park, transforming David Simons's survey of the Glacier Peak Wilderness Area (see chapter 3) into comprehensive analysis and proposed legislation.

Mike already had been serving as interim staff director during Brower's suspension; at the May 1969 board meeting he was officially named to that position. He continued to prove extremely able and within a year was appointed executive director.

Unlike Dave Brower, who used the force of his personality to challenge officials and enlist followers, Mike would bring a new level of professionalism to the Club's campaigns. He recognized the need for detailed legislative analysis and used his law training to the Club's advantage. His reports gave the Club's positions a historical perspective, provided detailed analysis to support them, and preempted arguments against them. He did not use his position to try to influence the board of directors; rather, he took his cues from their agenda. Never did he use his position to seize the limelight.

When Raymond Sherwin was elected Club president in 1971, he felt he needed an assistant who would report directly to him. He proposed Phil Berry for the job, and the board seemed ready to accept him. McCloskey was uncomfortable with the idea of someone being interposed between the chief of staff and the president and board—but he was still young and not yet confident about speaking up for himself. I took him aside and gave him a pep talk; it was up to him to put the directors straight. Later in the meeting, Mike did speak up. I remember him buttoning his suit vest, straightening his shoulders, and declaring, "From now on, you're going to see a different Mike McCloskey." Berry did not get the job after all.

Mike remained the Sierra Club's top staff member for seventeen years—the same amount of time Dave Brower served as executive director. But when Mike presented his resignation, everyone was disappointed to see him go.

As THE 1960s moved into the '70s, the Club continued to seek new ways of defending the environment, developing new programs, and even spinning off new, affiliated entities—as it had in forming the Sierra Club Foundation. The Club had explored using litigation to protect the environment in the '60s, taking part in several legal actions, and this was an area to which Mike McCloskey brought his professional expertise and enthusiasm. Earlier, Dick Leonard had hired Bob Jasperson and Greg Archbald to run an organization called the Conservation Law Society of America, but because the Internal Revenue Service would not grant the society (c)3 status, Mike—together with Don Harris and Fred Fisher from the Club's Legal Committee—started thinking about an independent nonprofit.

Around 1968, McCloskey outlined the prospects and shape for such an organization. In 1970 I had the privilege of offering at the board of directors meeting a motion to authorize the establishment of an independent, nonprofit organization to be called the "Sierra Club Legal Defense Fund." The first case it brought aimed to prevent the Disney Corporation from building a ski resort in the southern Sierra Nevada, in a valley known as Mineral King. The case was filed in June 1969 and would drag on in one form or another until 1977, with many advances and setbacks. The opinions expressed by the U.S. Supreme Court when it considered the Club's appeal of a lower court ruling resulted in "a new and much broadened definition of *standing* in environmental law."

Those opinions included a celebrated dissent contributed by my old friend Justice William O. Douglas, which broke the ground in which the seed of environmental law could germinate: "Conservation organizations should have standing to defend natural wonders before the courts . . . those people who 'know' its values and wonders will be able to speak for the entire ecological community."

Mineral King ultimately was preserved, and this case—along with the formation of the Legal Defense Fund as an environmental law firm—signaled the advent of litigation as a principal tool for environmental protection.

WITH THE APOLLO moon landing, America moved from the industrial age into the space age. For many, the event symbolized a new frontier of space exploration. For conservationists, the dramatic views of Earth from space served as a reminder of our planet's smallness and fragility. Some viewed space exploration as a misplaced priority: what the earth needed was restoration, not expensive escape rockets. Still, NASA's program provided a rich metaphor for conservationists. The phrase "spaceship earth" would be invoked throughout the Wilderness Conference of 1969 and widely repeated afterward in Club dialogues and publications.

In 1969, President Phil Berry urged the board of directors to expand its horizons by promoting the emerging ideas of survival environmentalism. It wasn't enough to preserve wild places, Berry claimed; without campaigns for the "gut" issues of human existence—clean water, air, population control, and strict regulations governing pesticide uses—wilderness was irrelevant. The Club had to embrace a comprehensive environmental platform, he argued, to attract and engage an increasingly urban membership. Berry, and the board in general, sought an ethic that translated beyond ideas into practical ways of sustaining life, an environmental code for everyday living.

Most of these ideas had been discussed for a decade in the context of the Wilderness Conferences, but integrating them into the Club's practical agenda was a different matter. Personally, I was cautious. For decades I had worked to preserve wilderness—it was the basis for my relationships and work in the Club. In 1969, I was still deeply entrenched in several campaigns: the Golden Gate National Recreation Area, Alaska's wilderness areas, and heightened protection for California's redwoods, since the first Redwood National Park Act had proved inadequate. I was concerned that the Club would spread itself too thin. Did we have the resources to fight for all the survival issues and still maintain effective campaigns to which we had already pledged ourselves? Even more to the point, were issues of environmental survival a logical extension of the Club's mission?

A pattern was repeating itself. Twenty years earlier I had been among the young turks pressing the older, more established members for a more aggressive Club. Now Berry's vanguard was pushing our boundaries to include a meaningful expression of the next generation's concerns. In 1970 the board passed resolutions confirming the importance as a national issue of sustaining livable conditions and urging that the United States work actively toward zero population growth here and abroad.

I soon overcame my resistance to this brand of environmentalism and developed my own take on it. In March 1970, I published an editorial in the *Bulletin* stating that for the Club's purposes, "Survival is not enough." So-called conservationists and so-called environmentalists would need to recognize that they were two sides of the same coin. A case in point was the Club's recent role in defeating the proposed National Timber Supply Act, which would have opened many wilderness areas to logging. The two groups had recognized a mutual interest in stopping the bill. Traditional conservationists rallied against the loss of wild and scenic areas, while "environmentalists" recognized that fewer trees would mean less oxygen, more carbon dioxide, more erosion, and more polluted waterways. As I wrote then,

> these "new" issues are not so removed from the "old." And we
> speak for the vital importance of the "old" values in their own
> right; they must not be lost in the present spotlight on survival.
> We cannot afford to let up on the battles for the old-fashioned
> Wilderness Areas, for more National Parks, for preservation of
> forests and streams and meadows and the earth's beautiful wild
> places . . . they will become ever more precious in a world which
> must be increasingly structured and restricted to insure man's
> survival. . . .
>
> As highly skilled technologists we are capable of cleaning up
> our environment. We can win the fight for good air and orderly

cities . . . in short, we can survive. We can also end up living in a concrete world and subsisting on algae, if survival is our only aim. The earth was meant to be a livable, beautiful and varied place; none of us must settle for less.

A month later, in April 1970, the nation celebrated its first Earth Day. Mike McCloskey edited a special volume for the event, a small paperback collection of essays written for the most part by young Club leaders. *Ecotactics: The Sierra Club Handbook for Environmental Activists* became a best-seller. For many, the Earth Day celebration symbolized an ideological victory: conservation had attracted enough attention that its principles were being recognized by the public at large. For the Sierra Club, Earth Day represented a shining moment in its long journey—but not one to linger over.

CHAPTER FIVE

RESTORING NATURE'S CATHEDRAL

The Battle for Redwood National Park

❧

Tall and straight the last redwoods stand . . .
they are our captives; their death has been decreed.
There is still time to stop the execution—
but time is running short.

—François Leydet, *The Last Redwoods*

IN THE WINTER OF 1955, a series of heavy storms pelted the coast of northern California in what was deemed a hundred-year flood. Rain soaked the region's redwood belt—the only substantial forest of *Sequoia sempervirens* remaining in the world, patches of it protected since the 1920s in a series of state parks strung along the coast. Hardest hit of the protected areas was the Rockefeller Forest, a magnificent bottomland grove growing along Bull Creek in the heart of Humboldt Redwoods State Park—the southernmost of the large parks. Eroded hillsides above the grove slid away. Avalanches of mud and silt deluged Bull Creek, causing the stream to overflow with a wash of debris that slammed into the trees along the banks. Trunks logjammed in the water, creating tangled pileups. Waterlogged soil loosened the roots of other redwoods.

As the storms raged on, one after another of the 250- to 300-foot giants toppled. When the trunks were counted, more than five hundred great redwoods had been felled by the storms. Another hundred were badly damaged and would have to be cut.

While periodic floods had swept through the region for thousands of years, the 1955 destruction was not an inevitable part of nature's cycle

131

of death and rejuvenation. The catastrophic loss of trees could be traced directly to manmade causes—to a watershed whose headwaters had been stripped bare by logging.

The Bull Creek watershed comprises some forty-one square miles; vertically, it spans several thousand feet. Before the 1950s, its upper ridges were swathed in thick stands of Douglas fir, gradually mixing with increasing numbers of redwoods as the hills settled into the bottomlands. Below the redwoods, willow and alder lined the clear creek waters where trout and salmon came to spawn. John D. Rockefeller Jr., a benefactor of the Save-the-Redwoods League, purchased the land and donated it to the state in 1931, when Bull Creek became a part of Humboldt Redwoods State Park.

But while the Rockefeller Forest itself was on protected land, the slopes of its upper watershed remained private property. The postwar building boom had generated intensive logging of these ridges, and by 1954 half of the upper Bull Creek watershed had been logged bare. Reckless logging, chute trails, and tractor ruts had reduced the park's lush green perimeters to a wasteland. And without their protective cover and root network, the hills literally washed away in winter storms. Once-clear creek waters grew clogged with mud and slash, destroying the salmon breeding grounds. What had taken nature millions of years to achieve, humans had destroyed in the span of a single generation.

In the years following 1955, the damage was compounded as weakened roots gave way to further erosion and deepening ruts. Even in normal seasonal rains, the redwoods continued to fall. As it did in 1955, the industry would blame the area's unstable soil while acknowledging no responsibility for having exacerbated that condition.

LOOKING AT NEWSPAPER photographs of the flood damage, I felt an almost personal sense of guilt. I had been so busy with other conservation campaigns that I had overlooked the peril of our country's grandest trees. Like others, I assumed that because many redwoods were on protected land and under the eye of such a notable conservation group as the Save-the-Redwoods League, the trees were well guarded.

At that time, no national park existed to protect the redwoods, which are not just the tallest but also among the oldest tree species on earth, with roots in the Jurassic Period of 130 million years ago. Ancient redwoods had thrived across much of the Northern Hemisphere in the subtropical climate of that era, but the ice age glaciers had inexorably contracted their range until this stretch of California coast became their last bastion. Still, the only federally protected redwoods were in Muir Woods, a national monument just north of San Francisco, established in 1908. Heavily visited to this day, it consists of a single grove in a small canyon on less than 500 acres donated by William Kent, a conservation-minded citizen.

California began setting aside redwood lands as early as 1902, when it created Big Basin Redwoods State Park, south of San Francisco. Prodded by the Save-the-Redwoods League, which was formed in 1918 by a group of influential conservationists, the state continued to set aside north-coast lands throughout the 1920s and '30s, in discrete parks scattered along Highway 101 for some ninety miles. Altogether these state parks— Humboldt, Prairie Creek, Del Norte Coast, and Jedediah Smith Redwoods state parks—totaled only a little more than 70,000 acres, about half of which represented true virgin growth. While picturesque, these parks fell short of providing a true wilderness experience. More important, they proved too small to adequately protect their own stands.

In the late 1950s Peggy and I began making trips up the coast to Humboldt and the other redwood state parks. We would make a long week-end of it; our favorite campsite was in Prairie Creek, a three-hundred-mile drive from San Francisco. There we pitched our tent alongside the giant roots of a toppled tree and hiked through green, wet rain forests as wisps of morning fog wove around the groves. Unlike a pretty vista viewed from a distance, the redwoods surrounded us, immersed us in their existence. Ferns plumed from the bases of trees, re-creating an ancient, primeval landscape. Tall rhododendrons with blossoming red canopies billowed over the edges of the trails, moss draping from their narrow branches.

Most magnificent of all were the redwoods themselves, the tallest living things on earth. We peered through a lattice of branches that filtered the sun so that its light reached the forest floor only in pale speckles. The trees rose in thick columns, supporting the leafy dome of one of nature's finest cathedrals. To see their full height, we had to crane our necks until our hair grazed our backs. Standing next to a trunk, we appeared tiny and insignificant. There was a divine grace about the forests, and Peggy and I became ardent converts.

Redwoods have an exceptionally long life span and extraordinary natural defenses. Their trunks resist fire and disease; verdant sprouts grow from the base of defunct stumps. Under natural conditions, redwoods indeed seem capable of living forever. However, as John Muir wrote in an essay called "Save the Redwoods," "Any fool can destroy trees. They cannot defend themselves or run away."

Indeed, we had only to walk to the edge of some parks to see the clear-cuts with their shaved hillsides. Driving from town to town along Highway 101, we noted huge lumberyards with stacks of redwood logs destined to become decks, wall paneling, and grape stakes. Above the lumber plants, smokestacks billowed in brown streams, filling the air with the smell of burning wood and sawdust. From 1945 to 1948 alone, the number of sawmills in the area had more than tripled, though many endured no longer than a single round of cutting. Once the land was clear-cut, the loggers moved on. Of the 2 million acres of redwood forest that had covered the northern California coast in the 1830s, this "cut-and-get-out" mentality had destroyed nearly all.

Since the nineteenth century, Humboldt and Del Norte counties had relied on the redwoods to fuel a single-industry economy. Except for the state parks, all the significant forests were owned by major lumber companies: Georgia-Pacific, Arcata Redwood, Simpson Lumber Company, and Miller-Rellim Redwood Company. Their employees and other residents lived in small towns like Garberville, Arcata—a quaint university town of clapboard cottages and Victorians—and farther north, at the mouth of Prairie Creek, tiny Orick, a handful of storefronts. Eureka served as the area's industrial and commercial anchor, seconded by Crescent City just below the Oregon border. Except for a few restaurants, hotels, and Humboldt State College in Arcata, the logging industry was virtually the area's only employer. Yet the entire region was economically depressed, with unemployment hovering around 15 percent—twice the national average.

As a boy, I had witnessed the shortcomings of a single-crop economy. Season after season of cotton planting had destroyed the once tree-laden hills and grasslands of my native Georgia, exposing the red clay soil. In summer, the dust blew until we coughed; in winter, rains turned the soil into red sludge. But as with cotton in the South, logging in Del Norte and Humboldt counties represented more than just a job. It was a way of life, each year delineated by the rhythms of logging. Men without other prospects for success felt empowered by felling giants hundreds of times their size—the mind-set that had made Paul Bunyan a folk hero.

By the early 1960s, only about 10 percent of the original 2-million-acre virgin redwood forests remained, including the stands within the state parks. Logging was quickly destroying all the remaining forests. Feeling it had done its duty, the state had no interest in acquiring more lands. The more time Peggy and I spent in redwood country, the stronger grew our conviction that federal protection was the only hope for the redwoods' long-term survival. If a national park were not established soon, the only redwoods left would be the state park groves—and even those were not safe, as the fate of Bull Creek demonstrated. But establishing a national park would require not only money; it would require change. That, we suspected, was something the logging interests would fiercely resist. What we couldn't have suspected was that the fight for a national park that could truly sustain the redwoods would take most of the next two decades.

Peggy's article "The Tragedy of Bull Creek" appeared in the January 1956 issue of the *Sierra Club Bulletin*. It acknowledged that the Save-the-Redwoods League and the state operated with the best intentions in acquiring lands for state parks, but it also detailed how, in failing to acquire the upper watersheds, they had abetted the eventual demise of so much of the Rockefeller Forest. The problem was that acquisitions had not been made according to natural boundaries. Peggy's text concluded, "Protection of the whole ecological unit of land is essential if there is to be a valid protection of any part at all." Large-scale land buying, and specifically watershed protection, was needed.

Later in 1956 I convinced the Sierra Club's board of directors to make the establishment of a redwood national park one of its five priority campaigns, and it was agreed that I should head up the Club's efforts. I was so busy with other projects, however, that it would be several more years before we began to work concertedly on the redwoods issue.

Nineteen sixty-one was a pivotal year—my first as Sierra Club president and Peggy's first as general secretary of the Club's Wilderness Conference, a biennial event since 1949. The conference banquet that year was the scene of some of our first national lobbying on behalf of redwoods. At the conference banquet, Supreme Court Justice William O. Douglas introduced the evening's speaker, newly named Secretary of the Interior Stewart Udall. As president-elect of the Club, I wanted to get to know Udall and win his support for our objectives, so I had arranged to meet him at his hotel earlier that evening.

When I arrived at his suite at San Francisco's Palace Hotel, Udall was shaving in front of the bathroom mirror, stripped to the waist. Catching my eye in the mirror, he said, "Oh, I know what you're after. Take a look at what's on the wall." Taped to the wall was a long roll of paper. On it a crude bar graph drawn with marker spelled out the conservation accomplishments of each president since Theodore Roosevelt. A tally of national park acreage was penciled by each name, beginning with a very long line for Teddy Roosevelt. The lines grew shorter for each succeeding president—Taft, Wilson, Harding, Coolidge—until another long line marked the terms of Franklin D. Roosevelt. Short ones followed for Harry Truman and Dwight Eisenhower, and the longest line of all stretched from John F. Kennedy's name. I couldn't have been more pleased, and told Udall so.

Peggy had arranged the banquet seating so that she was next to Udall, and over dinner she fed him stories about our journeys north and our ideas for a redwoods national park. The secretary admitted he had never seen a redwood and knew nothing about them. But Peggy's enthusiasm piqued his interest, and he promised to come out for a firsthand look at the redwoods.

Udall himself never made good on that promise, but in 1962 he did send his assistant secretary for fish, wildlife, and parks, John Carver. We took Carver to Humboldt State Redwoods Park and the Blue Creek redwoods of the Klamath River region. In the 1920s, Madison Grant, one of the founders of the Save-the-Redwoods League, had recommended this region as a potential site for a national park—but the Klamath River redwoods had since been reduced to patches, the slopes too scarred to be worthy of national park status. Disappointed, Peggy and I decided to focus our efforts elsewhere. Already, chainsaws were dictating the boundaries of the future park.

In THESE EARLY days of the campaign and the years leading up to it, we were gathering information and impressions that would shape our vision of the kind of park required to sustain the redwoods indefinitely: that is, an ecological whole rather than a scattering of impressive groves and road-side corridors.

For years, the timber companies had tried to persuade the public that they practiced responsible, sustainable logging of redwoods. They had posted signs along their roadside holdings, directing tourists to "tree exhibits," which purported to demonstrate how the industry was maintaining its forests by planting new trees to replace the redwoods they cut. What they failed to disclose was that the new trees were not redwoods but Sitka spruce and Douglas fir. The companies also emphasized that redwoods are the fastest-growing trees on earth, failing to mention that they are also among the slowest to mature. Unlike other species that can be successfully logged in fifty-year cycles, redwoods remain comparatively spindly for nearly their first century of existence.

Lacking such information, many visitors left the exhibits satisfied that the companies were logging responsibly, cutting down "overmature timber" or "commercial redwoods" on slopes rather than the "scenic redwoods" of the bottomlands. Such arbitrary classifications and jargon were used to justify clear-cutting. People got back in their cars believing the redwoods were in good hands. They did not realize that the roadside stands—intended to prove the industry's benevolence—were nothing more than green facades camouflaging the brutal clear-cuts beyond.

In 1963, two years after the Wilderness Conference, Secretary Udall publicly announced the Department of the Interior's support for a Redwood National Park. This was welcome news at that stage of the campaign; however, extensive ground surveys would be necessary before Interior could endorse specific boundaries, and the National Park Service claimed it lacked the funds necessary to conduct them. Fortunately, the National Geographic Society agreed to cover the costs. The joint NPS–Geographic team, including NPS landscape architects Chet Brown and Paul Fritz, arrived in northern California in May 1963. We hoped that in addition to collecting data, the team's work would focus public attention on the park issue.

It did indeed. Martin Litton, a Sierra Club director, private pilot, and travel editor of *Sunset* magazine, had become familiar with redwoods country while doing story research. He arranged to meet the government team on the banks of Redwood Creek, a privately owned stretch of land eight miles upstream from the town of Orick. This pristine area had struck Litton as potentially important. Turning to Chet Brown, the flippant Litton slapped the trunk of the nearest redwood.

"For all you know, Chet, this could be the world's tallest tree."

Gazing up the seemingly endless trunk, Brown thought Litton could be right and had his team measure the tree by triangulation. They estimated that it was over 367 feet tall—indeed the world's tallest tree ever measured. Photographs of this redwood, dubbed the "living Mount Everest," later appeared in the pages of *National Geographic*. Litton was amused but as a writer recognized the potential impact of such coverage. He was right: superlatives like "the tallest" captured the American imagination and helped greatly in attracting public support for a park. For Litton, however, as for most of us at the Sierra Club, the tree's record size was of little importance. The important thing was that it be saved.

After the discovery of these giant groves, Peggy and I explored the Redwood Creek watershed more thoroughly; Litton flew us over the area several times in 1963 and '64. We saw that the land unfolding below us contained most of what we were seeking for a park: the northeast slope was uncut green forest growing from the ridge to the creek. Redwood Creek was really a river in everything but name. From Orick, where it flowed quietly into the Pacific in a flat, wide band, it stretched upstream for about eighteen miles, intersected by several tributaries, including Prairie, Bridge, Devil's and Coyote Creeks. Although a mill existed near the mouth of Redwood Creek, by some miracle the watershed remained largely unlogged. (The lack of such uncut slopes at Bull Creek explained why it had flooded.) The land had traded hands several times in previous decades and had suffered some cutting on the southwest slope, but for reasons unknown most of the groves were left intact.

We didn't question our good fortune. Here were the ecological boundaries we had been seeking. We nicknamed the northeast slope "the lawn," and Redwood Creek became the nucleus of our park proposal. Still, the fact that most of trees had not yet been cut was in no way a guarantee of their continued survival. We knew from the Klamath experience how clear-cutting could destroy a watershed in the span of a few years.

Ground surveys of the redwood lands being considered for park inclusion proved difficult. Arcata Redwood Company owned 22,000 acres of the watershed, including the northeast slope above Redwood Creek—the jewel in its crown—and often refused conservationists' requests for permission to visit their holdings. Trespassing was potentially dangerous; we had been told that the loggers rode two to a truck with the second man riding shotgun. After Arcata repeatedly denied our requests for access to the northeast slope, we decided to explore it anyway. As we walked along the logging road, we listened for the sound of engines; when we heard one, we would leave the road and hide in the forest. One day, however, when accompanied by local activists Lucille Vinyard and Dave Van de Mark, we failed to hear the motor of a logging truck until it was nearly upon us. As the truck rounded the bend, we dove into the ditch beside the road. We survived.

Peggy and I returned to the redwoods many times, either camping out or staying in Orick at the Hagood Motel, run by the redoubtable Jean Hagood, one of the few locals who favored a Redwood National Park. The motel quickly became our base of operations; other concerned Club members and a handful of sympathetic locals would join us there to talk and plan. When Martin Litton wasn't available to fly us on scouting trips, Arcata resident Kay Chaffey, a former Women's Army Air Force pilot in World War II, took us up in a rented plane. And sometimes we met in the Eureka home of Ru Flo Harper Lee, another local campaign worker—for her safety parking our car two blocks away. We took inspiration from the support and local wisdom of these women and their families. They were not only dedicated volunteers who stayed with the campaign to its end, but also incredibly brave individuals to stand against the powerful logging interests and mounting local hostility surrounding the park campaign. Peggy and I worked hard, but at the end of the weekend we could return to the safety of our San Francisco home. Jean, Kay, Lucille, and Ru Flo could not. For publicly supporting the park, they were ostracized by their communities. All received anonymous threats.

In 1963, a new threat to the park effort became urgent when the California Department of Highways (now Caltrans) announced its plan to build an extension of the Highway 101 freeway north to the Oregon border. This was part of a network of freeways conceived to streamline links between states and, in the misguided vision of the Eisenhower administration, to offer a windshield view of America's natural wonders. As planned, the new freeway would cut through Prairie Creek and Jedediah Smith State Parks.

The Save-the-Redwoods League, in a perfect example of "either/or" philosophy, opposed routing the freeway through Jedediah Smith but was willing to compromise on Prairie Creek. Its secretary at the time was Newton Drury, earlier head of the NPS and of California Parks and Beaches (he and I had clashed over Mount Tamalpais State Park; see chapter 2). Drury considered Jedediah Smith the crown jewel of the state's redwood parks: it was the most pristine, its acreage largely virgin growth. In my view and that of the Sierra Club, however, the prospect of a freeway slicing through Prairie Creek was just as bad. Prairie Creek was my personal favorite of the parks, and I refused to see it sacrificed for the sake of expediency.

Of the four proposed routes for the Highway 101 extension, three would wreak havoc in Prairie Creek State Park. The Sierra Club was determined to block any route through Prairie Creek, advocating instead the fourth route, which would bypass the park and pass through cut-over land nearby. The lumber companies opposed this plan because the route included a 1,400-foot elevation gain—a difficult haul for eighteen-wheelers carrying logs.

The Division of Highways scheduled a public hearing for the autumn of 1963, and NPS planner Paul Fritz, who was doing a survey in the area, advised us not to attend. Backlash from our opposition to the highway proposal was mounting, and anger about the burgeoning park campaign was running too high, he said. He literally feared for our lives. Nevertheless, Peggy and I were determined to go. We took along our youngest daughter, Laurie, aged eight, for "protection."

The Eureka auditorium was half full. Peggy and I took seats in the middle section with Paul Fritz. Seated to our left was a crowd of young men wearing hard hats and boots—lumberjacks, I assumed, whom the logging companies had let off for the day to testify in favor of a route through the park. The engineer for the California Division of Highways spoke first, then the mayor of Eureka, each advocating the shortest, most "scenic" road through the park. Most of the crowd welcomed their comments.

I spoke third, as the representative for conservation groups. Walking up to the podium, I felt somewhat apprehensive of the intimidating crew on the left and prepared myself to be heckled. But as I got through the first part of my talk, I heard dappled applause from these men. The latter part drew even greater applause, and at the end of my testimony, they burst into loud cheers. Dumbfounded, I returned to my seat and asked Paul why a group of loggers would cheer me on.

"Those aren't loggers," he said. "That's the Boot and Blister Club from Humboldt State."

The Humboldt State College students, who explored and treasured the redwoods landscape, proved to be a great resource, both providing testimony against the road and later campaigning locally and writing letters in support of a Redwood National Park. Due in part to public protests, we eventually prevailed on the freeway extension, which was routed outside Prairie Creek State Park.

EACH TIME PEGGY and I went back to Washington in the early 1960s, we would visit Secretary of the Interior Stewart Udall, with whom we had forged a cordial relationship. As the Sierra Club's spokespersons for the redwood park campaign, we kept Udall apprised of our evolving plans. The three of us would get down on his office floor and spread out maps of the different proposed park areas. While the details changed according to our latest research, the Club's proposals consistently hovered above the 90,000-acre mark. They combined the total acreage of the state parks we wanted to see transferred to the National Park Service together with the Redwood Creek watershed, which we saw as the ecological heart of the new park.

Udall wanted to see a park established, but he feared that Congress would reject any plan it saw as overly ambitious and expensive. He was also wary of retaliation from the powerful and vocal logging lobby. His difficulties with the recent creation of Canyonlands National Park in Utah would "look like a picnic" compared to the redwoods, he warned. So Udall at first was mildly skeptical of our numbers, claiming that if the Club's proposal were adopted, then half of all the remaining redwoods would be on protected land. How could the government justify such large acquisitions?

Our response was simple: given the current rate of logging, if no national park were established, the only remaining redwoods would be those already in the state parks. The size of our proposed park in the Redwood Creek area was needed to protect the watershed. Perhaps we never allayed all his concerns, but through the early years of our campaign, at any rate, Udall seemed favorable to including the whole Redwood Creek watershed in the park and encouraged us to continue our work. We were sure we'd convinced him.

In December 1963 the Sierra Club released *The Last Redwoods,* written by François Leydet, with photographs by Phillip Hyde—another in the ambitious Exhibit Format series of coffee-table books produced by executive director David Brower. The book's authors had to straddle a fine line: the Club wanted to make a strong statement about the urgency of establishing a premier national park, yet it avoided a too-specific proposal for fear of alienating the Save-the-Redwoods League, which was by then formulating its own national park proposal. We also wanted to guard against the possibility of "vendetta logging" by the lumber companies: deliberately clear-cutting a crucial area to destroy its potential as national park land. Also, Stewart Udall had agreed to write the book's introduction but was unwilling to specifically endorse the Club's Redwood Creek plan.

Some felt that the book's title, *The Last Redwoods,* was misleading. Former Club director Norman "Ike" Livermore Jr.—one-time treasurer of the Pacific Lumber Company and now California's resources secretary under Governor Reagan—cited the many redwoods already saved in state parks. To me, however, the title focused attention on the last redwoods that still could be saved.

In the summer of 1964, at Udall's prompting, President Lyndon Johnson announced his personal commitment to a redwood national park. Public opinion favored the move, and it seemed a natural complement to

First Lady Lady Bird Johnson's self-created mission to "beautify" America. Johnson charged the secretary of the Interior with preparing the administration's official proposal. It was known that Johnson didn't have strong feelings about the park's location or extent—he just wanted his administration to accomplish the project with a minimum of backlash.

Over the next several years, however, the national park campaign would become deeply enmeshed in just those issues of location and extent. To start with, the Save-the-Redwoods League had a very different conception of the park than did the Sierra Club. Essentially the League felt that the finest groves were already protected in the state parks, for which it was principally responsible and which it wanted to see rounded out. As prime targets, it identified fine forests of virgin redwoods above Mill Creek and adjacent to Jedediah Smith Redwood State Park.

The League felt that only the Mill Creek watershed could provide tree specimens of national park caliber, and in the summer of 1964 it went public with its proposal for a 42,000-acre park centered on Mill Creek and including all of Del Norte and Jedediah Smith Redwood State Parks. Its plan also proposed purchasing buffer zones around each of the existing state parks to avoid a repeat of the Bull Creek catastrophe. The League's proposed acquisitions were modest, all bordering on existing state parks; its proposals did not advocate protecting any new acreage not adjacent to state-controlled lands.

There was ample precedent for the League's modest stand. Executive Secretary Newton Drury had rejected the concept of a national park while director of the National Park Service in the 1940s, feeling that the redwood state parks had preserved the finest redwood stands and would suffice. Drury also felt the government would reject the cost of a large park and would consider the League's $60 million proposal reasonable compared to the Club's more costly plan. Forester Gordon Robinson, who conducted an extensive study for the Club, attached a price tag of $92 million to the Redwood Creek proposal. Estimates continued to rise throughout the course of the campaign, however, as the logging industry inflated the value of its holdings to as much as $150 million.

Until the Bull Creek disaster, the Sierra Club had only applauded the efforts of the Save-the-Redwoods League. In an era before state and federal governments agreed to foot the bill for purchasing protected lands, the League promoted the 1928 California State Bond Act to provide matching funds for the acquisition of parklands. Through this system the League had helped secure most of the state's redwood parks—for the most part, superior bottomland groves. Without the League's continued efforts, these stands, themselves scraps of the original great forest, would surely have been cut.

Because the League had worked so hard to protect the redwoods, public criticism of its strategy was a delicate matter. Peggy's article in the *Sierra Club Bulletin* raised tensions in certain Club ranks. Leadership of the League and the Club overlapped, with Club directors Will Colby, Francis Farquhar, and Dick Leonard also serving as councillors for the League. And some Club leaders were concerned about alienating Newton Drury, one of the most important resource managers in the country. Although true enthusiasts of the California landscape, League councillors (as they were called) were schooled in an older style of conservation that relied on their personal influence and contributions from private philanthropy rather than the allocation of public funds. Their game plans grew out of quiet, back-room negotiations with the state's top officials.

While the Sierra Club certainly had similar roots when it was established, by the late 1950s it was quickly becoming a populist organization. The Dinosaur campaign of the 1950s had launched the Club onto the national scene. Differences not only of style but ultimately of visions and priorities for a redwood national park would eventually cause a falling-out between the League and the Club.

A key difference in the two organizations' visions concerned the nature of what might be called the *park experience*. The League's concept was based chiefly on accessibility. Its plan called for extensive roads and campgrounds, short easy trails that allowed visitors to reach the most impressive stands quickly, and scenic groves visible from the highway—all designed to appeal to the broadest range of tourists by making it easy to appreciate the great trees. A further drawback in the League's Mill Creek proposal was the existence of a sawmill complex that would have to be removed if the area became a national park.

For the Club, however, the most critical factors were watershed protection and, consequently, size. The protected area had to be large enough to ensure the redwoods' survival through the ages and permit visitors to escape the blare of car horns and the rush of freeway traffic. While the League's park plan would highlight the finest specimens like masterworks in a museum, the Club wanted the redwoods to be experienced in their ecological context—a park that would include trees of varying ages with other types of flora composing the northern California coastal biome. We envisioned a space large enough that visitors could trek through a variety of climate zones: from the chilly fogbanks at sea level to sun-baked slopes inland. A large area was also needed to accommodate nature's cycles of flood, disease, fire, and drought.

In the fall of 1964, the NPS released *The Redwoods,* the report on its survey with the National Geographic Society, accompanied by several alternative proposals for the national park. Shockingly, the Club's plan was not among them. Club leaders, myself included, had been in frequent contact with Chet Brown and Paul Fritz of the NPS as they conducted their surveys. From these conversations it seemed clear that both NPS landscape architects supported the Club's concept of a large park centered on Redwood Creek. But while all of the plans published with *The Redwoods* advocated some acquisition around Redwood Creek, the largest of the three totaled 53,000 acres—little more than half of the area advocated by the Club.

Because *The Redwoods* was such a clear departure from views previously expressed by the NPS, I called on the agency for some explanation. Where was the fourth plan? I asked—the plan that Brown and Fritz had said they supported, the plan that would make the best park? At first the NPS claimed there was no fourth plan. But a careful reading of the report's text left no question. The agency seemed to tacitly acknowledge the existence of a better alternative in this comment on its largest option, Plan One:

> It should be noted, and clearly, that this plan does not represent the ultimate that might be considered worthwhile, if other interests and feasibility factors were not considered. Certainly in detail it is not the solution that might be suggested if the clock could be turned back a decade or two.

After being pressed on the issue, Brown and Fritz eventually admitted that the word had come from above in the Department of the Interior: our Redwood Creek proposal was too large to be offered publicly. It had been redlined from the report.

I spent the next few months compiling the Sierra Club's response to the NPS report. I questioned not only the agency's integrity but the values of a nation that would spend a billion dollars to put a man on the moon but balked at spending a fraction of that to preserve a magnificent piece of the earth. Most of us in the Club were determined to continue pushing for a 90,000-acre park. But Dick Leonard, who sat on the boards of both the Club and Save-the-Redwoods, and who sought to ally the organizations, did not want my answer to condemn the League's Mill Creek proposal. At his request, my response concluded that both areas were worthy of national preservation status.

By EARLY 1965, the Sierra Club was ready to launch its legislative campaign for the park. Redwoods represented the Club's first large-scale affirmative campaign. In contrast to negative campaigns in which we might seek to block development or legislation at many turns, success here would depend upon favorable progress at every step of the way. Bill Zimmerman, the Club's first Washington representative, began collecting whatever inside information he could on Capitol Hill. In one of his weekly memos, Zimmerman wrote that Secretary Udall had grown "crotchety" over the redwoods. In February, Mike McCloskey became my full-time assistant for the redwoods campaign, bringing his energy and expertise to the effort. Mike joined Bill Zimmerman in Washington that spring.

Also that spring, I went back to Washington for the White House Conference on Natural Beauty and to keep an appointment with Laurence Rockefeller, personal advisor to President Johnson and his appointed chair for the conference. I wanted to show Rockefeller our plans for the Redwood National Park and try to enlist his support. Money, we knew, was becoming an issue with Udall, and our proposal was large and costly. Acting for the Rockefeller Foundation, Rockefeller could provide critical funding, and his opinion would carry great weight with the administration.

Despite his conference responsibilities, Rockefeller was very accommodating and set our appointment for just half an hour before his opening speech. We met in the anteroom of the auditorium where participants had already gathered. As I spoke, Rockefeller became so interested in the Club's proposal that he neglected to watch the time. His assistant, Fred Smith, repeatedly tried to pull him away, but Rockefeller continued to listen even after the conference was scheduled to begin. Finally he came to the point.

"How much will this cost?" he asked.

"One hundred fifty million dollars," I said.

I expected a dismayed reaction but the figure didn't faze him. "That's not a problem. We, the Rockefeller Foundation, could put in fifty million, the Ford Foundation could put in fifty million, and so could the Old Dominion Foundation," he said, as casually as if drumming up pocket change.

If I was hearing him right, one of the wealthiest men in the world was offering to help us. My heart was flying on the ceiling. Smith was anxious to shuffle me out the door, but I didn't want to leave without solidifying the next step.

"Mr. Rockefeller, what can I do for you now?" I asked.

He held up his hand. "I have made no commitment, but when I do make a decision I will be guided by my long-standing advisors, Horace Albright and Newton Drury."

My heart thudded to the floor. I already knew what Albright and Drury thought: they supported the smaller Mill Creek Park. I wondered if they even really wanted a national park at all. Both men had served as director of the National Park Service and had had ample opportunity to recommend a redwood national park if they had wished to.

That summer, while traveling to Wyoming to explore the proposed Bridger Wilderness in Wyoming's Wind River Mountains, I made one of my routine phone calls to Secretary Udall. He did not return it, however, nor any of the follow-up calls I made to his office. I knew then that the jig was up. The political winds had shifted. Sometime that summer Udall abandoned his advocacy of Redwood Creek in favor of the League's smaller 42,000-acre park. I learned further details later, when we returned to the redwood country and Jean Hagood asked, "Are you following Laurence Rockefeller around?"

I said, "No, why?"

"Laurence came through here just three days ago along with Newton Drury."

In July 1965, Laurence Rockefeller wrote to President Johnson, outlining his thoughts on a redwood national park. I later obtained a copy of the letter, which I believe had a strong impact on the administration and therefore on Udall's ultimate stand. Rockefeller wrote:

> We believe that a national park might be created at this time with
> a minimum of opposition and perhaps even with considerable
> local support if a reasonable plan is prepared and put forward in
> an intelligent and constructive way. But we are confident that
> to demand more than this is an unrealistic approach which would
> consolidate all the opposition and eliminate for all time the
> possibility of any national park. . . . The two extremes in this
> controversy are the Sierra Club and the Industry. It is doubtful
> whether the Sierra Club will actively support any but an extremely
> far-reaching plan.

In September, despite the negative rumblings, Senator Lee Metcalf of Montana introduced legislation for the Club's proposed 90,000-acre redwood park. In the House, San Francisco area representative Jeffrey Cohelan was the principal sponsor of an identical bill. Both were introduced on the last day of the session. The Club did not expect deliberation; we simply wanted to register the bills on the docket because Wayne Aspinall, the autocratic longtime chairman of the House Interior Committee, often used chronological order as a criterion in determining the committee's upcoming agenda.

Indeed, Aspinall would prove no friend to our park proposals. But of more immediate concern in 1965 was the defection of Interior Secretary Udall. For four years Udall had pledged his support and encouraged the Club's efforts. Although he was ultimately responsible for the administration's position, he repeatedly rejected our invitations to come and view the redwoods—a bad omen. And the events of that summer—Rockefeller's intervention and the fact that Udall never returned our calls—made it clear that he had switched camps and closed the lines of communication.

Udall's opinion mattered to the uncertain President Johnson; he could have pressed for a larger park and won. Instead, he chose to put aside his personal preferences and those of his assistants, opting for a less controversial proposal that he thought would more easily succeed in Congress. As he once told me, he wanted to "pick a park, not a fight." His speeches continued to urge vision and boldness, yet his actions with regard to the redwoods did not live up to them. Because he knew the score so well, his defection amounted to the biggest disillusionment in my conservation career.

In November 1965, the NPS released an updated proposal for a two-part, noncontiguous park designed to placate both the League and the Club. The southern unit focused on an expanded Prairie Creek State Park and the acquisition of parts of the Redwood Creek watershed, while a northern unit centered on Jedediah Smith and Del Norte State Parks and included the purchase of the Mill Creek watershed. The combined lands totaled 93,000 acres, and while the plan called for less acquisition around Redwood Creek than we sought, the Club would have accepted the NPS proposal.

Udall, however, would not commit even to this plan. The following month, he tried going around me by writing directly to Dave Brower, urging him to compromise and support the administration's final proposal—whatever that might turn out to be—even if the Club did not think the site was optimum. Udall expressed concern that the League and Club disagreements were delaying action, and about the Bureau of the Budget's willingness to cooperate—the concept of the federal government buying private land for park acquisitions was still new. He couldn't count on the Bureau to agree to a large park, he said. Brower replied that the Club would be willing to compromise on the total acreage, though not on the site. Protection of Redwood Creek was nonnegotiable.

The Club continued to wage a very active public campaign. We published fact sheets and pamphlets comparing the various proposals, and on December 17, 1965, we ran a full-page advertisement in several metropolitan newspapers under the headline: "An Open Letter to President Johnson on the last chance to *really* Save the Redwoods." Peggy and I had drafted the original text, which was then edited by Brower and public relations professionals Howard Gossage and Jerry Mander, who worked on the campaign pro bono. While not mentioning Udall by name, the ad criticized the administration's refusal to stand up to the logging industry. "Some . . . would settle for a false-front redwood national park," the copy read, " . . . or an existing state park re-labeled as a national park. Some voices, too, are calling for an easy bargain-basement national park." The ad included a map outlining the Club's plan.

The advertisement was designed to be an event, and it met with heated reaction. Both Udall and Dick Leonard were furious; Udall took it as a personal attack; it appeared the day he called a private fund-raising meeting with Newton Drury and members of the Ford and Kellogg Foundations. Leonard, also present at the meeting, felt that in publishing the ad, the Club had failed to honor its promise not to publicly oppose the League.

The ad may have backfired; in any case, by February 1966, Udall had dropped Redwood Creek from the administration's final plan, which he presented that month. At best, this offered a token park: 43,800 acres, including the state parks, centered on the Mill Creek area. It called for acquiring only 6,000 acres of virgin growth. Although this was less than the Save-the-Redwoods League had proposed, the League pledged its support, while the Club opposed the plan. We wanted the best park, not the one most easily approved.

In June 1966, the Senate Interior Committee held field hearings in Crescent City, a dozen miles south of the Oregon border. Committee chair Henry M. Jackson secured three large army helicopters to fly the senators and their staffs, as well as NPS surveyors Chet Brown and Paul Fritz, over the proposed areas. I sat with Jackson, already a personal friend, in the lead helicopter. But as we approached Redwood Creek, Jackson directed the pilot to turn around. I told Jackson he should really see the area, as it was the basis of our proposal.

"I don't need to see it," he assured me.

I never knew if his comment meant that he had seen enough to trust our judgment or if his staff had already convinced him of the merits of Redwood Creek before he came to California. Either way, Jackson pledged to support the Sierra Club proposal.

Predictably, public testimony at the hearings was heated, with the vast majority of locals opposing the expansion of any government holdings in the region. The federal government was the largest landowner in Del Norte County, they said, claiming that further land acquisitions would not only create layoffs but would reduce the tax base. Confronted with such hostile testimony, congressional representative Don Clausen, a former Crescent City insurance agent, withdrew his support for the administration's less-than-modest plan, which he had introduced in the House just three months earlier.

There has always been a tacit understanding in Congress that a local representative's opinion on legislation affecting his or her area must be honored whenever possible. As a member of the House Interior Committee, Clausen was in a strong position to block park legislation. Flying back to Washington after the hearings, Clausen left his seat in first class to talk. "You know if I oppose this, Ed, you'll never get it through Congress," he said, perching on the edge of my seat in coach.

"Yes, Don—and you know the Sierra Club has two thousand members in your district," I replied.

But while he continued publicly to affirm his intent to protect his constituents, behind the scenes and in committee Clausen was not the intransigent opponent he could have been. Clausen's accommodation may have been linked to how he gained his office: in 1961 he succeeded Congressman Clem Miller, who had defeated him in the previous election but died in a plane crash while campaigning. A liberal Democrat from below the timber belt and an avid conservationist, Miller had been instrumental in promoting the establishment of Point Reyes National Seashore. Had he lived, he would have been among the first to support the Sierra Club's redwood national park proposal. Mike McCloskey and I surmised that Clausen may have felt obliged to respect Miller's legacy.

A far more worrisome opponent was Wayne Aspinall, who chaired the House Interior Committee. I had first encountered Aspinall in 1961, having asked Bill Zimmerman for an introduction. Although I knew he was a strong opponent of all conservation measures—I considered him the tool of Colorado's mining and lumber interests—I felt I had to make his acquaintance. Bill arranged a half-hour appointment, and after waiting some time in the outer office while Aspinall pursued other business, we were finally called in. For the next twenty-five minutes he ranted against David Brower, using a wide range of expletives. Among other sore points, Brower's success in stopping the upper Colorado River project dams still rankled, it was clear. He believed Brower had attacked him personally. At last Aspinall stopped and said to me, "Now, young man, you have five minutes left. What do you want?"

I gave a short outline of the Sierra Club's project priorities. To my surprise, Aspinall listened and then thanked me. When the half hour was up, he pointed at Bill Zimmerman and said, "This man you can bring in any time you want. But don't ever try to bring in that son-of-a-bitch David Brower."

It is doubtful whether Aspinall retained any positive impression of me or the Sierra Club, based on his performance regarding Redwood National Park. Meanwhile, as Congress debated and held hearings, the timber companies stepped in with their own method of shaping the park-to-be. Late in that summer of 1966, the Miller-Rellim Lumber Company clear-cut a strip of virgin redwoods along the southern border of Jedediah Smith Redwood State Park, razing a section tagged for preservation by the administration's proposal. Although Miller-Rellim claimed it had done the logging out of economic necessity, its real motivation for degrading the landscape seemed clear: after the cuts were discovered, the land was deemed substandard and therefore unsuitable for a national park. Photographs of the shaved hillsides sparked public anger, and amid bad press, Georgia-Pacific, Simpson, Arcata, and Miller-Rellim all agreed to a one-year voluntary moratorium on logging in the areas currently under consideration for park status.

Even in the face of mounting public demand for a park, both houses of Congress failed to bring a bill to the floor that year. Aspinall announced that his committee would not review any redwood legislation until the next Congress convened in January 1967. And in the Senate, neither the administration's proposal sponsored by California senator Thomas Kuchel nor the Club's proposal sponsored by Senator Lee Metcalf made it out of committee.

A concerned Senator Kuchel wrote to Dick Leonard that the rift between the League and the Club had erected a legislative roadblock and urged him to ally his two organizations. If conservationists couldn't agree, how were members of Congress supposed to? Leonard in response organized a meeting of Club and League leaders at San Francisco's exclusive Bohemian Club in autumn 1966. At the meeting he argued that I, as chair of the Club's Redwood Task Force, should accede to Drury, who had the most connections and experience from his decades in government agencies. I was disappointed in Leonard, who in the early 1950s had been among the new Club leaders pushing for a stronger conservation platform. Now, while he continued to sit on our board of directors, he always seemed to side with the League. I had never agreed with Newton Drury's park philosophy (keep them small and accessible) on other occasions and saw no reason to compromise now. After two hours, the sides remained deadlocked. No compromise was reached; we could only agree to meet again when the next series of bills went through Congress.

Within weeks of this meeting, the League discovered that Miller-Rellim had violated the moratorium and continued to log and build roads along the eastern boundary of Jedediah Smith State Park—including old-growth stands at the heart of the League's proposal. The League issued a press release mourning the loss of the virgin trees but reiterated its support for national acquisition of the area. To its credit, the League's press release mentioned Redwood Creek as another area worthy of preservation.

Although we had stood adamantly in favor of Redwood Creek, no one at the Club wanted to see Mill Creek logged. The League was right in wanting to save these groves, just as the Club was right in wanting to preserve the Redwood Creek watershed. True responsibility for the delay that led to the cuts at Mill Creek rested with a political system that demanded environmentalists choose between the two locations. The administration and Congress repeatedly complained that lack of unity between the groups was stifling action, yet neither branch of government was willing to pursue a plan large enough to incorporate both areas. The wheels of democracy turn slowly and the public generally benefits from critical debate, but in redwood country the chainsaws did not stop while politicians and bureaucrats argued. The longer the delays, the more likely it became that the lumber industry would define the ultimate boundaries of the park.

That December NPS director George Hartzog and the head of the new Bureau of Outdoor Recreation, Ed Crafts, flew out to California to strong-arm me into supporting the administration's bill. Their reasoning followed lines I'd heard many times before: compromise now or you might not get anything later. My response was the same as ever: if you compromise first, you're guaranteed never to get anything more. We didn't believe that we risked coming up empty-handed, but rather that if we held out, we would get more.

The Club's board of directors met in early January 1967 in the aftermath of the cutting at Mill Creek. Dick Leonard proposed a resolution that the Club publicly support a redwood national park of maximum size containing both the Redwood Creek and Mill Creek lands. The League, he said, was prepared to do the same. For the sake of the park, we would endorse each other's proposals. Both organizations would continue to campaign actively for their areas of choice but would not dispute each other's boundaries nor claim that one area was superior to another. If Congress and the agencies selected the Mill Creek proposal, the Sierra Club would not fight the legislation; neither would the League oppose Redwood Creek if it were the chosen site. The board passed Leonard's resolution, and for the first time since the campaign began, the two groups had reached agreement. Alas, it would be short-lived.

WHEN RONALD REAGAN became governor of California in January 1967, he pledged neither to strongly support nor oppose a redwood national park. Under pressure from the logging industry, however, he questioned the legitimacy of turning over state parks to the federal government, as all the proposals had advocated. He suggested instead that the federal government contribute some of its national forest lands in northern California, thereby avoiding the need to acquire private lands.

During Reagan's campaign he reportedly made the infamous comment, "When you've seen one redwood, you've seen them all." His term as governor, however, was not infrequently marked by solid conservation policies. This was entirely due, I thought, to his secretary for natural resources, Norman B. Livermore Jr. A former Sierra Club director and initiator of the Club's Wilderness Conferences, Ike Livermore was an avid outdoorsman with a passion for the Sierra Nevada. While a student at Stanford University, he wrote a thesis on mule packing in the High Sierra, where he later operated two pack stations. When he became treasurer of the Pacific Lumber Company, he had to forgo his connections with the Club, but he retained an interest in conservation, particularly in the Sierra.

Ike thought that the governor should become better acquainted with the aims of the Sierra Club and arranged for a meeting in Sacramento attended by Peggy and myself, then-president Will Siri, and his wife, Jean. Waiting for Reagan in his office, we ate jelly beans from the large jar he kept on his desk. Then the door opened and the governor rushed in smiling and exclaiming, "Oh, that legislature! They'll be the death of me!" He knew who we were and put out his hand to me.

"Dr. Wayburn, I want you to know I never said it."

As the chief proponent of a redwood national park, I understood his reference.

"Thank you, governor," I replied. After chitchatting for fifteen or twenty minutes, we left. I was pleased that the meeting had been so cordial.

A few months later, I was in Los Angeles on business for the California Medical Association. Thinking I would sandwich in a few conservation matters, I agreed to be interviewed by a pleasant television reporter. As I told him my story about meeting Reagan and how the governor had denied the redwood comment, the reporter, up to that point soft-spoken, suddenly turned purple.

"He's a goddamn liar," he bellowed. "And I've got the tape to prove it!"

But I never saw the tape, and Reagan's remark has since passed into the realm of myth.

The story doesn't quite end there. Years later, when I was a trustee of the Pacific Medical Center, our board held a retreat in Marin County. At a recess, I was chatting with chairman of the board Jacques Hume, and I described my exchange with Reagan. Hume considered himself a conservationist; he also chaired Headlands, Inc., a local organization that facilitated the transfer of surplus Bay Area military land from the Department of Defense into public ownership (later to become part of the GGNRA). When I mentioned Reagan's assertion that he had "never said it," Hume smiled and remarked, "He probably didn't." Then I related the reporter's version, and Hume's face froze. I had forgotten that he had a personal link to Reagan; as the candidate's finance director in his run for governor, Hume was considered part of Reagan's "kitchen cabinet." He remained silent, and as the bell signaled the end of the recess, we walked side by side—though quite separately—into the conference room.

Reagan gave his secretary fairly loose rein, and Ike Livermore proved extremely helpful during Reagan's governorship. He went with Peggy and me to the redwood country and rafted down Redwood Creek with us. I believe that journey and Livermore's ongoing advocacy as the governor's top environmental official were critical in eventually securing the Redwood Creek watershed for the national park. Livermore also was critical in stopping a trans-Sierra highway proposed by the California Department of Highways in the late 1960s (see chapter 3.)

The redwood park debate resumed in Washington in March 1967, when President Johnson proposed his own measure favoring Mill Creek. The president's plan did call for the acquisition of 17,000 acres along Redwood Creek to be purchased through private contributions. Aspinall sponsored the bill in the House and Kuchel in the Senate, but it did not pass out of either committee.

In the Senate, Interior Committee chair Henry M. Jackson and Senator Lee Metcalf reintroduced the Club's proposal for a 90,000-acre park. In the House, fifty-eight representatives sponsored similar bills, a legislative action demonstrating substantial national support for a larger park. At the Sierra Club, we continued an aggressive advertising campaign with headlines appealing directly to President Johnson.

That spring marked another important development in the campaign. A private survey of foresters concluded that there were indeed more virgin redwoods growing in the Redwood Creek watershed than in that of Mill Creek. The study provided corroborating evidence for what we who had explored the lands firsthand already knew. I wrote to Udall demanding that, in light of the study, the Interior Department advocate the Sierra Club proposal originally supported by Brown and Fritz but censored from *The Redwoods*. Interior refused to do so or even to respond.

It was a trying period. Congress remained deadlocked until November, when, in an attempt to find common ground, Senators Thomas Kuchel,

"Scoop" Jackson, and Alan Bible devised and introduced a compromise bill. Jackson, who admired Mike McCloskey's work, gave Mike a desk in his office, where Mike worked helping to prepare the bill. Mike recalled entering Jackson's outer office one day to find Laurence Rockefeller waiting for an appointment with the senator. When Mike strolled right into the inner office without consulting the receptionist, Rockefeller's face dropped. The moment symbolized the changing tide of conservation—the ebbing influence of patrician advisors and the gathering tide of public lobbying and campaigning.

The Jackson-Kuchel plan called for a two-part park totaling 64,000 acres, with new acquisitions along both Mill Creek and Redwood Creek. Approximately half of the land was already contained within three state parks; the other half would be acquired by public funding. Still more lands could be purchased through private contributions. As Governor Reagan had suggested, the Forest Service was to trade its holdings along the Klamath River to Miller-Rellim for the latter's stands along Mill Creek. This bit of barter would save the federal government a substantial amount on the purchase price.

Although nothing short of the Club's proposal would have satisfied me, the Jackson-Kuchel compromise was an acceptable beginning. First, it represented a bipartisan effort. Kuchel and Jackson had aimed to appeal to both the League and the Club's demands. Moreover, we felt we could add acreage through amendments in the House—for example, Redwood Creek's stunning "Emerald Mile" stretching upstream from the Tall Trees, which was not part of the compromise. Relying on Jackson's political savvy, we were confident the bill would move ahead, despite opposition from the Forest Service, which did not want its lands traded away for a national park, and from the president, who disagreed with the whole concept of trading Forest Service lands. In fact, the compromise passed the Senate by a wide margin.

Also that November, the Club issued press releases exposing recent logging by Georgia-Pacific. Clear-cuts had been discovered in the company's holdings near the Emerald Mile. Like Miller-Rellim, Georgia-Pacific had no desire to sell its lands and was dangerously close to marring the landscape permanently. The company claimed that this cutting did not violate the moratorium, which in its view gave protection only to holdings under serious consideration by Congress—in other words, the lands in the Jackson-Kuchel bill.

There followed a vicious exchange between Georgia-Pacific and the Sierra Club. The company ran a series of ads countering our charges and, citing Drury, claiming that all the important redwood groves were already protected in state parks. The Club did not feel it could let such lies stand, or that a company should be able to dictate park boundaries by degrading potential parklands. In countering ads, the Club called such tactics "Legislation by Chainsaw." Georgia-Pacific wrote me a furious letter condemning our ads, accusing the Club of slander, and threatening to sue. We threatened to countersue, citing Georgia-Pacific's attacks as libelous. Although neither suit ever went to court, the tensions spilled over in March 1968 when a San Francisco Bay Area TV station organized a brief televised debate between me and a Georgia-Pacific official.

I recognize a great difference between those who survive on the land and those who seek to profit from it. A handful of industry executives profited greatly from cutting down redwoods. The majority of workers, loggers, and company staff, did not. Most logging employees eked out a meager living, as a quick drive through the lumber towns revealed. Tragically, most residents of Del Norte and Humboldt counties had been persuaded to believe that logging was their only employment option. Already financially strained, the workers and their families were told that if the Sierra Club got its way, they would have nothing. They clung to logging because it was the only way of life they knew, the only sure paycheck in a depressed economy.

We knew that the park would come at the immediate cost of logging jobs, but we also knew that the logging industry—or any industry that depends solely on an exhaustible fragile resource—was bound to fail, and soon. The companies could not go on cutting forever. Studies appearing in the 1960s and later, both private and by the U.S. Forest Service, concluded that the redwood logging industry was nearing its end. The most liberal estimates gave the companies just twelve years before they ran out of trees, and typical estimates fell between six and eight years. Public pressure, voluntary moratoriums, and ecologically minded state forestry reviews might slow the rate of cuts, but such measures could only stave off the inevitable. Despite their dwindling stands, however, the companies held out, often refusing to sell parts of their holdings even to low-profile organizations like the Save-the-Redwoods League, which offered to pay full market value.

The lumber companies in 1967 were poised to harvest the last crop of virgin redwoods. If the cuts weren't abated, ten years down the road there would be no logging jobs. Nor would there be anything to attract tourism in these counties. Who would take their children to see shaved hillsides? In my mind, the choice was clear. The redwoods did not exist for the economic benefit of a few people. Indeed, they would have a right to flourish if no humans existed at all.

On New Year's Eve 1967, Peggy and I flew up to Arcata. A group of us had decided to spend the holiday at Hagood's Motel; most had already arrived and were spending the day hiking in the forests. Peggy and I arrived about 1 P.M. and got a lift to Skunk Cabbage Creek, a tributary of Redwood Creek on Arcata Redwood's land, where we met Martin Litton. Martin suggested that we walk in and catch up with the rest of the group. Peggy and I thought it was late to be starting out, but we soon found our friends.

As we explored Skunk Cabbage Creek, dusk began to fall, and we figured it was time to head back to the hotel. But Martin was persuasive— he'd been over the area by plane and foot. "Oh, I know this country so well," he said. "Let's keep going." His idea was to cross the ridge and get to a road on the far side; we made the mistake of going along, bushwhacking through the roadless forest, sometimes climbing over huge fallen redwood logs. As the last vestiges of light faded, half of the party turned back, but nine of us continued on in the dark with the confident Martin. We had just reached the top of the ridge when a gentle rain began. At that point we admitted we were lost.

The rain continued, the night turned cold, and we collected wood for a fire. Like characters from a Jack London story, we found ourselves with three matches. The first went out, and then the second. The third match took. All night long we kept close to the fire, trying to keep warm.

Between the chill and the damp, no one could sleep, so we told stories and sang every song we knew. Now and then we would spot a light in the distance and hope someone was coming to rescue us. But the lights must have been distant cars.

In the dawn's light we could finally see our way clearly and started down toward the highway. Martin warned us all, "Don't let anyone know that the president of the Sierra Club was caught on Arcata Redwood land in the middle of the night." We were trespassing, it was true. We made a quick descent, however, and soon reached the road and a motel. In fact, we weren't far from our objective, but the dark had completely disoriented us. Martin got on the motel phone to the Hagoods, who he knew would be anxiously looking for us. We overheard him announce: "What do you know—the president of the Sierra Club just spent all night on Skunk Cabbage Creek!" We celebrated the rest of the holiday quietly.

The spring of 1968 was a turning point in the battle for the redwoods. For the first time, Governor Reagan acknowledged that he would cede state lands to a national park and endorsed a park of 58,000 acres—slightly less than the Senate's proposal. Then President Johnson made an about-face, declaring that he preferred a park on Redwood Creek and was willing to trade federal forest lands for private timber holdings. The logging industry as a whole seemed to realize the inevitability of a park and showed signs of being willing to negotiate.

Also that spring, members of the House Interior Committee flew to California to hold field hearings. When Wayne Aspinall took his committee up to the redwoods, he said that they could not afford to hire helicopters as the Senate Committee had done the previous year; instead, members would ride in private cars on logging roads over the cut-over land of Georgia-Pacific down to the Big Trees.

Loath to miss the opportunity to show the committee some of the remote areas in our proposal, the Sierra Club chartered its own helicopter. We flew five congressmen over the area and let them make their way back on foot. Unfortunately, the craft could seat only three, including the pilot, so we had to make five trips in all, with me acting as guide. We made sure to fly over the Emerald Mile, a magnificent stretch of forest that Arcata claimed held only "commercial timber."

We were confident that the combined flyover and hike would make a deep impression, and we were right. Congressman William Fitts Ryan, who represented New York's gentrified upper east side and had never seen a redwood, made the walk back in patent leather shoes. He was visibly stunned on his return, having never imagined a tree could be so majestic. Nothing akin to redwoods grew in his state. Ryan was so impressed that he demanded the Emerald Mile be included in the final bill or he would not sponsor it.

Another committee member was Morris Udall of Arizona, who had been elected to fill his brother's House seat when Stewart Udall was named secretary of the interior in 1961. "You never in your life saw five such angry congressmen," Mo Udall told me later, "when they learned how the lumber companies had lied to us." Udall later became chair of the Interior Committee and one of conservation's strongest supporters in Congress.

Curiously, Representative Aspinall did not demonstrate any interest in taking the helicopter ride until the last group of passengers had returned. Then he chided me, "You didn't have the courtesy to ask the chairman to go up."

"Mr. Chairman," I replied, "you suggested that you didn't want to go." But I did not want to incense him further. "Let's go now," I offered.

"No, it's too late," he snapped.

In June, all the forward momentum of the campaign came to a crashing halt. Mike McCloskey, who had been actively lobbying members of the House Interior Committee, made a disturbing discovery: Aspinall had just introduced his own proposal for a redwood national park of 25,000 acres—less than half of the acreage in the Senate's version and about a quarter of what the Club advocated. Equally alarming, Aspinall was seeking to bring up the bill under a suspension of the rules, a procedure normally reserved for bills of general consensus. This meant that no amendments could be added to Aspinall's bill once it reached the floor. Congressman Ryan moved to overthrow the suspension but lost to the cantankerous and intimidating chair.

McCloskey worked desperately with committee members to push for additions—Skunk Cabbage, Lost Man, and Little Lost Man Creeks—but these attempts were defeated. Disappointingly, although he had enough proxy votes to block the chairman, Mo Udall did not vote in favor of all these additions. Recalling his helicopter ride, Ryan pushed for the Emerald Mile, and Aspinall—perhaps feeling that he'd already achieved his primary aims—allowed this part of Redwood Creek to be included. Even so, the bill passed out of his committee at just 28,500 acres. McCloskey felt betrayed. Just the day before, Representatives Saylor and Udall had pledged to oppose Aspinall's plan, but on the day of the vote Saylor abstained and Udall gave in, giving Aspinall the narrow margin he needed.

The park described by Aspinall's bill was limited to the lands then comprising Prairie Creek and Del Norte Coast state parks, with only 2,000 acres of virgin redwoods added. The original impetus for a park— the need to provide watershed protection—had been lost in the shuffle. That Aspinall had been able to orchestrate a one-man coup d'etat pointed to a dangerous failing in the American legislative process. The bill was an abomination, an insult to conservationists.

Newspapers across the country ran editorials condemning Aspinall's plan, and seventy-three congressmen raised objections to the chairman's tactics. Many feared, however, that if Congress did not act now, there would be no park at all. Johnson's term would end that December. He had chosen not to run again, and the changing political winds pointed to Richard Nixon as his successor. No one knew Nixon's stand on the park. Moreover, the one-year moratorium on logging would expire with the end of this congressional session.

Perhaps in response to press criticism, Aspinall let it be known he would consider additions to the bill in the final House–Senate conference. Many congressmen, just wanting to be done with the issue, saw that as comfort enough, and Aspinall's bill passed almost unanimously. Phil Burton was one of just four representatives who voted against it. He had been one of the park's earliest proponents and a cosponsor with Jeffrey Cohelan of the original legislation in the House three years earlier; he couldn't bring himself to endorse such a watered-down plan.

"It was such a bastard," he told me later.

In the joint conference, the Senate members, particularly Jackson, Kuchel, and Bible, represented the strongest block in favor of expanding the park. Burton, too, pushed for additions, but his House colleagues had turned lukewarm. Fortunately the Senate prevailed, and the conference recommended a final bill of 58,000 acres (the same total advocated by Governor Reagan). The acreage would be split almost equally between existing state parks and new private acquisitions. Although 5,600 acres were to be added to the Mill Creek area, the new park centered on the great old stands of Redwood Creek—the Emerald Mile among them. The final bill also provided that the lands would be instantly condemned and moved into federal ownership when the president signed the bill—meaning that they could longer be logged. President Johnson signed the bill into law on October 12, 1968.

Secretary Udall acclaimed the new park as a victory for conservation. I was less enthusiastic. "You know as well as I do that this bill is a bad compromise," I told him.

It was a bittersweet victory for the Club at best. The park was not con-figured according to ecologically appropriate boundaries, nor was it large enough to provide a sustained wilderness experience. Instead, it comprised a long ribbon of land along the coast from Del Norte Redwoods State Park to Prairie Creek Redwoods State Park, the watershed of Redwood Creek up to the Tall Trees grove, and the upstream strip of Redwood Creek known as the Emerald Mile. Of the new acquisitions, only 10,876 acres represented virgin redwoods, the rest being primarily other species or logged areas. In several places, lumber companies retained control of the ridges, exposing the bottomlands to erosion and flood. The slender width of the corridor along Redwood Creek led conservationists to dub it "the worm."

Representative Cohelan made promises to expand the legislation but was defeated in the next election. Senator Jackson agreed that the park was inadequate but told me that since the Congress had acted, the issue would have to rest for a considerable time. The lessons of Bull Creek had been forgotten or ignored.

The park dedication ceremony featured Lady Bird Johnson, at a grove named for her. Many celebrities as well as park advocates and lumber company executives attended and delivered accolades. But I remained unsatisfied.

From 1969 to 1973, the lumber companies continued to log their remaining holdings on lands immediately adjacent to the national park. Louisiana-Pacific (formerly Georgia-Pacific) razed several sections above the Emerald Mile. If the logging were not stopped, the park soon would be ringed by clear-cuts. Without a buffer zone, even the trees within the park remained in peril.

The new law did have three provisions that could have diffused potential damage, all to be acted upon at the discretion of the secretary of the interior. First, of the 58,000 acres called for, 56,200 had been identified. This left 1,800 acres yet to be acquired. A second provision permitted the purchase of additional lands along Skunk Cabbage Creek to maintain a scenic corridor between the park and logged areas. And the third gave the secretary of the interior authority to acquire more lands if the park's welfare was in question. I continued to write letters and visit Washington to remind the Interior chiefs of their obligation to act, but neither Udall nor his successors, Walter Hickel and Rogers Morton, would exercise their authority to acquire a buffer zone. The response from Interior was always the same: the issue had been dealt with; the redwoods were safe.

Two studies conducted in the early 1970s demonstrated that continued logging around the park was exacerbating conditions that threatened the park's redwoods. Their conclusions were echoed by Richard Curry, special assistant to Secretary Morton, in another study conducted by Interior. Word of the reports leaked out, but the Interior Department refused to publish either study. As his first action, attorney James Moorman, executive director of the newly created Sierra Club Legal Defense Fund, sued the federal government for the release of these reports under the Freedom of Information Act. Jim and I personally delivered the letter he drafted to the Department of the Interior.

Neither Secretary Morton nor Nathaniel Reed, his assistant secretary for fish, wildlife and parks, was in the office, as they were escorting President Nixon on a flight over the future Gateway National Recreation Area in New York. The highest-ranking official we could find was a brand-new deputy assistant secretary, a young man named Curtis (Buff) Bohlen. He looked at the letter and his jaw fell.

"This is my first day on the job. Why are you giving this to me?"

"Because there's no one else to give it to," I said.

Later we took Reed on a flight over the prospective national park additions and areas currently being logged. Reed's plane picked me up at Crissy Field in San Francisco's Presidio, a short walk from my home. (Ours was one of the last flights to take off and land at the now-decommissioned airstrip.) We toured the sky over redwood country, paying particular attention to the Redwood Creek basin with its landscape of primeval forest on one slope and cut-over land on the other side of the creek. The contrast was overwhelming.

On the return journey, Reed had his head in his hands. "Why did you do this to me?"

"Because you're the one who can take action to stop the logging."

The department released the reports before the SCLDF suit came to trial. It refused, however, to include Curry's recommended plan of action. As with NPS's report *The Redwoods*, it was easy to infer the content of Curry's proposal: a buffer zone was needed. At the Club, we decided to press forward with a different legal action: we would sue the Interior Department for failing in its duty to protect the park.

The right of citizen groups to sue a federal agency was not yet firmly established in the courts. The first step was to demonstrate that the Sierra Club had a vested interest in the park; this we accomplished by showing that Club members had enjoyed the forests before and during the park's establishment, and that damage to the park therefore would compromise our ability to use the area. We claimed that, as trustee for the park, the Department of the Interior had failed to act. This was a new concept. While federal agencies had been sued in the past for what they had done, never had an agency been sued for what it had *not* done.

Interior tried to argue that the logging practices were reasonable and that it needed another study before initiating further acquisitions. During the trial, however, it emerged that a previously unreleased report—the department's own Master Plan of 1971—had advocated a 10,000-acre buffer zone around the perimeter of Redwood National Park. Interior had failed to follow its own recommendations. Federal Judge William Sweigert ruled in favor of the Sierra Club and gave Interior until December 1975 to report back to the court on its restorative strategies and actions.

California's State Forestry Board was unwilling to follow Interior's subsequent suggestions for tightening logging practices, going so far as to say that second-growth redwood was preferable to old growth. It called the newer trees more *vigorous* and *healthy*. Interior then tried to persuade the logging companies to implement voluntary restrictions on cutting, but the big three companies made it clear that if the government wanted to restrict logging, it would have to reimburse them for lost revenues. Interior balked, claiming it didn't have the funds to subsidize uncut trees or to purchase new lands. President Gerald Ford would not authorize additional funds, and all the money allocated by the 1968 Redwood National Park Act had been spent.

In the summer of 1976, Judge Sweigert ruled that the Department of the Interior had done all it could do. If the Club wanted land added to the park, it would have to go back to Congress. The time had come for a second legislative campaign. Several congressmen, notably Phil Burton, had attempted to expand Redwood National Park since 1968, but these efforts never made it past Wayne Aspinall or his replacement as chair of the House Interior Committee, James Haley. The National Parks Subcommittee chair, Roy Taylor, a softspoken Democrat from North Carolina, was not interested in pursuing controversial legislation.

In 1976, HOWEVER, the political tide turned again—but this time in the Club's favor. Before the elections that fall, California representative Leo Ryan, who chaired the House Conservation, Energy, and Resource Subcommittee, announced he would hold public hearings on expanding Redwood National Park. Ryan's was an oversight committee without the authority to originate bills, but he hoped the hearings would generate publicity.

I flew to Washington for those hearings to testify about grave dangers to the park. Since 1968, new logging had eroded the hillsides of the watershed, and a mass of sediment and debris five to fourteen feet deep was moving down Redwood Creek. Winter rains could topple the Tall Trees just as they had brought down the great redwoods of Bull Creek in 1955. Complete watershed protection was needed more than ever. According to current estimates, less than 5 percent of the original redwoods belt remained; 90 percent of the original stands had been logged in just the previous twenty-five years.

Happily, the Save-the-Redwoods League seconded my testimony, also advocating for ridgetop-to-ridgetop acquisition. Responding to our testimony, the lumber companies claimed the erosion at Redwood Creek was natural. Geologically unstable hillsides, not logging practices, they argued, were responsible for the sediment buildup in the creek.

Ryan's hearings, as he had hoped, renewed public interest in the park. Many Americans were angry to discover that the trees they believed protected were, in fact, still in danger of being destroyed. Just one day before his election as president, Jimmy Carter pledged his support for protecting the park and called on the lumber companies for a one-year logging moratorium in all border areas.

With Carter's election, Arcata, Simpson, and Louisiana-Pacific agreed to the National Park Service's request to submit harvest plans for federal approval before giving them to the State Forestry Board. Some saw this as enough. I disagreed. While the NPS could make recommendations, it lacked the authority to enforce them. The companies still retained total control of their holdings, and the state board rarely rejected harvest plans.

The shifting political winds that blew Jimmy Carter into office also reached to California, where Edmund G. (Jerry) Brown Jr. succeeded Reagan as governor. The U.S. House of Representatives also saw big changes, with Morris Udall replacing James Haley as chair of the Interior Committee. In the biggest change of all, Phil Burton became chair of the Subcommittee on National Parks and Public Lands. At its first meeting he announced, "Gentlemen, this committee will entertain no legislation until we first act on the expansion of Redwood National Park."

The timing finally seemed right to reshape the park as it ought to be. In February 1977, Burton introduced in the House a bill to expand the park, which I had helped draft. At 132,000 acres, 74,000 more than the original park, Burton's proposal was ambitious, and it met with immediate resistance from the Carter administration for being too costly. Shortly thereafter, the National Park Service submitted its own plan for 21,000 additional acres, and Cecil Andrus, the new secretary of the interior, presented the administration's compromise package: an increase of 48,000 acres focused on acquisitions in the Redwood Creek watershed, especially along Skunk Cabbage Creek and Lack's Creek. All three proposals were referred to the House Subcommittee on National Parks. Burton scheduled hearings for that spring.

Despite pleas by Burton and Andrus for a six-month logging moratorium, the timber companies continued to cut virgin stands being considered for inclusion in the park. They again accused the Club of "big lie" tactics, claiming that the best redwoods had already been saved. While it was quite true that some of the finest stands were on protected lands, the companies missed the point. The question now before Congress was how to save enough additional land to protect the trees already in the park.

In April 1977, Burton's subcommittee met in Eureka amid mass demonstrations and open hostility. The lumber mills had been closed that day to give employees a chance to denounce the park expansion. Mayor Sam Sacco rode through town shouting his opposition through a bullhorn. Tractor-trailers roared around the building where the hearings took place, and the congressmen had to be escorted into the auditorium by police. John Amodio, a Humboldt State College student who had formed the Emerald Creek Committee, testified amidst jeers and hisses. Students like Amodio had proved critical in both the original redwood campaign and the expansion effort. Diligent and dedicated workers, they became on-the-ground experts because of their proximity to the park. Later in the legislative campaign, John joined the Club's Washington office as an assistant to Linda Billings, who replaced Mike McCloskey as the Sierra Club's lobbyist on the redwoods issue. Eventually the Club hired John, but all his work during both redwoods campaigns was as a volunteer.

I testified at a separate hearing in San Francisco, passing through a cordon of lumberjacks and logging trucks to enter the federal building. I concluded that the park must be expanded but expressed great concern for local residents who faced unemployment in an already depressed area. We believed that the loss of jobs would be offset in part by increased tourism drawn by a superior park—just as new jobs had been created when the park was first established.

In May, a caravan of logging trucks left Eureka bound for Washington, D.C. In a misguided attempt to gain sympathetic press and the attention of President Carter, the lead logging truck carried a giant redwood trunk carved into the shape of a peanut. The ploy turned into a fiasco for the logging industry. Carter refused to acknowledge the trucks, and dozens of newspapers condemned their owners for wasting fuel during the energy crisis that gripped the nation. The peanut log became a symbol of the industry's desecration of the nation's most magnificent tree. The Sierra Club organized a massive mailing advocating park expansion, timed to coincide with the caravan's arrival in the nation's capital.

Meanwhile, the Save-the-Redwoods League privately pursued efforts to acquire patches of virgin stands. New League president Dick Leonard, who was acquainted with Arcata's vice president, arranged for himself and Newton Drury to meet with Arcata officials. Leonard told Arcata that the League would pay full market price, $15 million to $20 million, for the remaining stands along Skunk Cabbage Creek, but the company would not respond to the offer. It was no longer a matter of compensating the companies—they simply refused to cooperate.

In July, Phil Burton introduced a modified proposal for park expansion. Burton's new bill used Andrus's target of 48,000 more acres; it also addressed the administration's and local concerns about worker compensation, relocation, and retraining. Under Burton's benefit package, laid-off loggers would receive preferential hiring for jobs to restore the park's harvested slopes. In committee, Burton added a couple of critical measures the Club considered important. First, if state regulatory agencies failed to protect nonfederal lands immediately outside the park, and adjacent logging threatened the park's integrity, the Department of the Interior would have the authority to step in and regulate logging in those areas. Should Interior fail to do so, citizen groups such as the Sierra Club would have the right to sue and, in the case of a favorable judgment, to be reimbursed for litigation costs. That provision would greatly help organizations like the Club, who were turning increasingly to the courts to help enforce conservation measures. In the Senate, Alan Cranston introduced a similar bill. The Club pledged to support both.

Although Burton's proposal provided generous benefits and compensation for displaced loggers (who had no union of their own), other labor interests (the AFL-CIO, representing teamsters, carpenters, et al.) were irritated that they had not been consulted when the legislation was drafted, and labeled the plan anti-union. This was completely unjustified, particularly since Burton had dedicated his congressional career to improving the lot of working men and women. Some members of the Senate objected to giving the Department of the Interior authority to regulate nonfederal land, so both Cranston and Burton removed that language from their bills, substituting a provision granting Interior the right to purchase additional lands needed for the buffer zone. The Sierra Club would have preferred stronger federal authority but recognized the need to compromise on this point. Also dropped from both bills was the citizen groups' right to sue, an omission the Club protested strongly but in vain.

The Senate bill easily passed out of the Interior and Appropriations committees in time for a floor vote in fall of 1977. But California's other senator, S. I. Hayakawa, a pro-industry conservative, was so vocal in his opposition that Cranston's bill was tabled until the next session. In 1978 it passed easily.

Between sessions, Burton worked with union officials to smooth out any labor opposition. Together they created an unprecedented benefits and compensation package. In addition to funds for job relocation and retraining, the new bill stipulated that all loggers and industry workers laid off in the park's expansion would be entitled to full pay and pensions based on their length of service. The terms were generous, allowing many employees to qualify for the maximum period of six years. Estimates put these costs at $40 million.

Despite the administration's cries of extravagance, Burton's bill swept the House 328 to 60 on February 9, 1978. In the final Senate–House conference, the new acreage remained at 48,000, with an additional 30,000-acre buffer zone to be acquired at the Secretary of Interior's discretion. In March, President Carter signed the bill. Ultimately totaling more than $1.3 billion, the Redwood National Park Expansion Act was the most costly land acquisition ever approved by Congress.

THE CAMPAIGN FOR the redwoods was the toughest of my conservation career. It wasn't just about finding enough money to buy the forests or about saving the forests from speculators. While these were factors, our efforts represented much more. Establishing the park meant challenging a way of life long entrenched in northern California. It meant acknowledging that trees—and those who enjoy and respect them—can have rights, even at the immediate cost of some jobs.

Saving the redwoods for posterity also meant challenging the belief that nature exists exclusively for the present generation to exploit—a belief that had gone relatively unquestioned for thousands of years. Our first eight years of travail achieved a park in name but not in the spirit of our original vision. The first national park legislation served human interests. It was the result of a compromise between various groups: the lumber companies, the Johnson administration, the Save-the-Redwoods League, the Sierra Club.

The second redwood legislation a decade later, by contrast, served ecological purposes, primarily by recognizing the need for watershed protection. In expanding Redwood National Park, the nation recognized that great natural legacies are not created simply by reserving small plots of land. Watersheds, not property lines, should determine the extent of an important, enduring park.

During the course of the campaign, all four presidents in office received thousands of pro-park letters, many from individuals who had never touched the bark of a redwood tree. A photograph was all it took for some to recognize that *Sequoia sempervirens* is not just another species of tree.

The establishment of Redwood National Park remains a beacon in the history of our national parks. Twenty-five years after the park expansion, restoring the forest landscape has been an enormous success—perhaps the outstanding example of a restoration project in a national park.

I have had the personal good fortune to walk through many redwood forests: I know the shades of their green-needled boughs, the smell of their wet moss, the cool touch of their morning mist, the dappled sunshine filtering through their branches. These soaring trees invite my gaze upward to the sky, and in this simple gesture there is the recognition of something sacred.

CHAPTER SIX

ALASKA

Encountering the Great Land

❦

Tomorrow to fresh woods and pastures new.

—John Milton, *Lycidas*

The year was 1967. As summer approached, Peggy and I discussed where to spend our vacation; with the children almost grown and dispersed on outings of their own, Peggy and I could choose any destination we liked. Our summer expeditions did double duty, helping us gather background for our conservation vocation. We had spent parts of the last twenty summers exploring and evaluating various parts of the American west—beginning in the Sierra and gradually spiraling outward to encompass much of the geography of the western United States. With each successive exploration, we were preparing ourselves for something larger.

Now, to continue expanding our personal conservation mission, we felt the need to go farther afield. Although it was not a conscious decision at the time, in retrospect I have little doubt that on some level we were looking for a new source of inspiration, a fresh sense of purpose. Our efforts had been personally satisfying and crucial for conservation, but we felt it was time to move on.

The whole of the north country waited. I suggested we join a Sierra Club canoe and camping trip along the Abi Tibi River in northern Ontario. Peggy suggested Alaska.

The state had held a steady fascination for her since her days at Barnard when a classmate, bound for Anchorage at graduation, had described a series of wondrous images: icy shores, roaming animals and wild vistas, limitless space—in sum, the kind of true wilderness long lost in California. Since then, Peggy had read enough about Alaska to sustain her interest. At the 1963 Sierra Club Wilderness Conference, she listened intently as Starker Leopold, the son of Aldo and himself a noted forester and a Sierra Club director, discussed his experiences in Alaska.

Misconceptions of the Great Land (as Alaska natives called it) had run rampant since 1867, when Secretary of State William H. Seward purchased its 375 million acres from Russia for $7.2 million. Dubbing it "Seward's folly," most Americans wondered why anyone would pay a dollar for a land thought to be as barren as a giant ice cube. Geopolitical strategy was the original purpose of the acquisition, and indeed that vision was fulfilled during World War II, when Alaska became a military center of operations because of its proximity to Russia and Japan. Later, the importance of the Arctic in the Cold War solidified the military's presence. Between 1940 and 1960, Alaska's population tripled, with military personnel and their families accounting for a quarter of the increase. In 1959, Alaska became the forty-ninth state. Even with the postwar surge of population, its residents in 1959 totaled fewer than 230,000.

In 1967—exactly one hundred years after Seward bought the land from Russia—I too harbored my fair share of misunderstandings about Alaska. The fact that we decided to spend our vacation there rather than canoeing on the Abi Tibi owed less to my personal interest in the place than to the fact that my wife generally got her way.

In some respects, we followed John Muir himself. In 1879, after a decade of concentrated explorations in California, Muir stepped onto the planks of the steamship *Dakota,* bound for the Alaskan wilds. He returned several times in the 1880s and 1890s, eventually producing *Travels in Alaska,* the chronicle of his journeys by foot and canoe.

Peggy and I agreed that our two-week trip would be primarily for pleasure, but we also intended to investigate some of the important park, forest, and wildlife refuge areas. And we planned to spend as much time in Alaska's cities as in the wild. We said we wanted a change; we had no idea how profound a change it would be.

W E TRAVELED TO Alaska by a circuitous route. Immediately before our journey was to start, I needed to be in New York to represent the Sierra Club at the opening of a photography exhibit sponsored jointly by *Time* and *Life* magazines and the Club. Leaving New York, we flew west, stopping in Chicago. Over Wisconsin and Minnesota, I noticed that we seemed to be circling over the same terrain. The pilot came on the loudspeaker to announce that the plane was having trouble; we should prepare for an emergency landing. During the landing we heard sirens and saw the lights of several ambulances and fire trucks roaring down the runway—but we landed safely, switched to another aircraft, and continued on to Seattle and finally north to Alaska.

Our plane touched down at Fairbanks International Airport at 2 A.M. on a cool early August morning. As it was still summer, the sky never turned black at this latitude; the horizon was streaked with steel blues and grays like a watercolor painting. From the airport, we were bused to the Nordale Hotel. Recommended by friends as one of the remaining traditional old-style Alaskan hotels, the rustic Nordale had few modern conveniences. There was little need. Most of the guests were Alaskan Natives, other Alaskans in from the bush, and prospectors in town for a few days to take care of business. After buying supplies and conducting transactions, they would soon be back out in the country. Sadly, the Nordale burned down several years later.

We caught a few hours of sleep, then took a taxi to the Alaska Railroad station. The friendly driver, eager to show off his city, chauffeured us through the flat streets and along the flanks of the Chena River, pointing out local landmarks, including the fairgrounds where the centennial of Alaska's purchase was celebrated. He charged us only for the ride from the hotel to the station. At nine, in an Alaskan drizzle, we boarded the train for Mt. McKinley National Park. (In 1980 the park became known as Denali National Park and Preserve.) At the time, there was no road from Fairbanks to the park: trains offered the only direct access from the cities. The rain continued as we wound through low-lying terrain, the tracks following the banks of the Tanana River with its streamside forest of spruce, poplar, birch, and aspen. Next came a steady climb up the Nenana River canyon, marked by a succession of cascades.

Meanwhile, the rain in Fairbanks intensified. By the time we reached McKinley Park station, four hours and 120 miles later, we heard that the centennial exhibit halls and fairgrounds shown to us by the taxi driver had been deluged. The "Centennial Flood" was our introduction to Alaska's temperamental weather.

We were met on arrival by Celia Hunter and Ginny Wood, owners of Camp Denali, a set of rustic cabins eighty-five miles from the train station and just outside the park's northwestern boundary. We had no way to realize how close our future alliance with these two vital ladies would be. Climbing into Celia and Ginny's Land Rover, we began the drive, which traversed half the length of the park over the unpaved Wonder Lake Road.

After a dozen miles on paved road through spruce forest, we crossed the Savage River, where the road narrowed then turned to dirt and began climbing up and down hills that elsewhere might have been called mountains. Peggy and I sat entranced as we made our slow way through a vast landscape of tundra, mostly above tree line, past raw, eroded hillsides and alongside weaving glacial rivers. Park buses, too wide to share the route, waited in turnouts as we edged by. Before long, wildlife began to emerge in fantastic display: grazing caribou and moose, trotting foxes, white Dall sheep balanced on high ridges, birds gliding overhead. Travelers had called the park the American Serengeti, and it was easy to see why. We stopped many times in the six-hour trip, once at a picnic spot for dinner but mostly to view the animals. Despite having slept only a few hours, we were more charged by the end of the journey than when we had left McKinley station. Six hours in a Land Rover, and we already knew we had come to a place of superlative wildness. Nothing in all our years of exploring the west could compare.

Celia and Ginny had been pilots in the Women's Air Force during World War II, ferrying U.S. fighter planes from construction sites in the lower forty-eight to bases in Alaska. Since women weren't allowed to fly foreign duty, Russian pilots then took over and flew the planes to Siberia for use in Russian campaigns. Like many service personnel, Celia and Ginny were mesmerized by the Alaskan landscape. After the war, they decided to stay, staking a land claim under the nineteenth-century

Trade and Manufacturing Act. In 1952, they opened Camp Denali. Avid hikers and naturalists, they were also experts on Alaska's land issues and devoted conservationists.

The Wonder Lake Road had its own interesting history, they told us. Like other environmental decisions, it was the result of a compromise between diverse interests. The driving force behind the establishment of Mt. McKinley National Park was the renowned hunter Charles Sheldon, who wanted to see this wondrous animal reserve kept intact. He formed an unusual alliance with gold and silver miners who had staked numerous claims at Kantishna, just outside the northwestern boundary of Sheldon's proposed preserve. At that time the miners had to make a slow, difficult trek over hilly tundra from the railroad to access their claims from the east. They were willing to lend Sheldon their support if in return they could get a road from the station. Mount McKinley was declared a national monument in 1917; the road was completed six years later.

Camp Denali, elevation 3,500 feet, consisted of two communal buildings, a dining hall, and fifteen one-room log cabins, each with its own outhouse, all blending into the landscape. From the front porch of our cabin, we gazed onto a vast scene of rolling hills and U-shaped valleys scooped and smoothed by the prolonged sweep of glaciers. This was subarctic country; the higher slopes spread out in a thick carpet of tundra. Below tree line, patches of resilient spruce—the dominant tree species— striated the landscape. The McKinley River, flat and blue, wound through the broad canyon.

Winters arrived early here. We had come just in time to see the last of the wildflowers. By late August, most of them would have vanished, replaced briefly by blueberries; then the tundra would blaze with rust and amber, and snow would begin to cover the foothills.

Distinguishable in the distance was the Alaska Range itself. The Outer Range (where our campsite was located) consists of a series of peaks between 5,000 and 6,000 feet high. The main range, across the broad valley below, rises in a series of white buttresses from 10,000 to more than 20,000 feet high and is swathed in clouds and covered year-round by snow and ice. The peaks of the Alaska Range possess a stark, almost cruel, beauty: huge mountains whose forms are delineated by serpentine white ridges crossing azure skies. At their feet, the compressed ice of glaciers glows blue under the sun's shadow. If not for their proximity to Mount McKinley, peaks such as Mounts Silverthrone and Foraker would be famous in their own right.

Some twenty miles south of Camp Denali, Mt. McKinley soars to its crest at 20,300 feet. Denali, the Great One, as the Athabascan Indians call the mountain, is the highest point in North America. The mountain is so tall it creates its own weather system, and the day of our arrival it stood invisible behind a thick wall of clouds. Its stark white summit can be seen only a third of the time in most years from Camp Denali and less frequently from other areas of the park. Many visitors leave without ever having seen the mountain that drew them. As we discovered, one takes the view when one can get it.

Nor did Denali appear on our second day. That night, however, we woke to a knock on the door. "The mountain is out," said a voice on the other side. Peggy and I pulled on our parkas and boots and stepped into the cool gray light of 4 A.M. Neither of us was prepared for the sight we beheld. We had grown accustomed to the vista beyond our porch, but the peaks to the south and east, which had loomed in our vision for the past two days, were now dwarfed by Denali's monstrous bulk. Its size was amazing and mesmerizing. One cannot simply *look* at Denali. Peggy and I stood silently gazing, entranced. I followed its rounded hump towards the crest, craning my neck to see its summit. It would take two full days to walk to its base, and yet it was as if the mountain had already come to us, an almost palpable presence.

CELIA AND GINNY proved to be knowledgeable guides, introducing us to the park and its staff and leading us on several hikes. We soon found ourselves engrossed by conservation issues. Of most obvious concern was the damage caused by mining. About three miles northwest of Camp Denali, hydraulic mining at Moose Creek had devastated the landscape. Huge areas of earth had been blasted away and piled high in waste mounds; rain had washed away the tailings onto land downstream. Mining had churned up so much soil that the river, once free running and clear, ran thick with brown mud. The disastrous effects of hydraulic mining were already widely recognized. The practice had been outlawed in California, but in Alaska it was allowed to continue full force.

Even more pressing than the mines at Kantishna was the National Park Service plan to build a new hotel above Wonder Lake, just inside the park's northern boundary. And at the eastern entrance to the park, the NPS was surveying sites to expand the existing hotel there. The park's lone hotel was continuously full in season, and some feared that once the highway from Anchorage to Fairbanks was completed, the park entrance would be flooded with motels unless new lodgings were built inside the park.

Even in a land of superlative beauty, Wonder Lake stands out as one of nature's perfect creations. Celia and Ginny led us on a hike through the tundra-clad hills above the lake, from where we looked down onto its pristine waters, aptly named for the reflection of the Alaska Range on its elliptical blue surface. On rare clear days, Mount McKinley seems to rise directly overhead.

Unfortunately, the NPS found Wonder Lake too perfect to resist. The preceding summer, an NPS team had surveyed the area, accompanied by the famed wolf expert Adolf Murie and the biologist and author Sigurd Olson, then serving as advisor to the secretary of the interior. Although Murie and Olson opposed the idea, the NPS team adamantly declared they would propose a hotel on the ridge overlooking the lake. Peggy and I envisioned bulldozers uprooting the ground, and vowed to do whatever we could to keep that from becoming a reality.

Development around Wonder Lake posed greater concerns than the visual intrusion of a hotel on the ridge. There was the potential for pollution—the NPS site was just above the lake ingress and egress streams, which were very close together—and threats to wildlife. Moose, wolves, and caribou—all migratory creatures, as our guides explained—passed through here to reach their summer ranges. Their route pointed to a larger problem: Sheldon's Mt. McKinley National Park had not been drawn on ecologically meaningful boundaries. The natural range of the park's wildlife extended beyond the northern periphery, outside of which hunting and trapping were permitted. Eventually, if the park boundaries weren't expanded, private development would threaten the wildlife migrations and jeopardize the survival of animal populations.

It hadn't taken us long to fall in love with Alaska. Within days of our arrival, Peggy and I knew we had come to a place with unparalleled possibilities for wilderness and wildlife preservation. A breakdown of the landholdings in the state revealed the potential for establishing parks on a greater scale than would ever be possible in the lower forty-eight. At the time of Alaska's statehood in 1959, fewer than a million of the state's 375 million acres were in private hands. Some 13 percent of the total were lands designated as national parks, national forests, or wildlife refuges and ranges. The huge Arctic Naval Petroleum Reserve accounted for a big chunk, and the military and the Bureau of Indian Affairs each controlled several million acres. Of the remaining lands, 290 million acres were considered unappropriated, falling under the administration of the Bureau of Land Management. The fate of the vast majority of Alaska had yet to be decided.

To the outside world, Alaska's lands did not seem in need of more protection. The state appeared to be almost entirely wilderness. A closer look, however, revealed a precarious future. We knew that any chances for real conservation would disappear quickly if development such as mining, oil production, or even unplanned tourism were allowed to take over lands at will. And there was also the issue of state selection: according to the statehood act, Alaska could choose up to 104 million acres for state owner-ship to promote the economic welfare of its residents. Nine years after its acceptance into the union, however, the state had yet to make most of its choices.

Conservation in Alaska faced not only a perception problem but also a distinct lack of attention on the part of the federal government. As I talked with George Hall, director of the NPS Alaska Region as well as superin-tendent of Mt. McKinley National Park, it became clear that the National Park Service in Alaska was under considerable stress. Hall bemoaned a consistent and massive lack of money and manpower, having only a hand-ful of employees to cover all of Alaska. Glacier Bay National Monument— at 3 million acres the second-largest unit in the entire national park system—employed just three rangers. The senior official at Katmai National Monument, the largest unit, was only a management assistant. Organizationally, the NPS Alaska division was a satellite office, with budget and other major decisions made thousands of miles away in San Francisco; Hall was not even a part of the decision-making team for the Wonder Lake development. The Anchorage office—the only NPS office in the state—consisted of three cramped rooms in the Federal Postal Service building. However many well-intentioned, conservation-minded individuals worked for NPS, there simply weren't enough bodies to properly protect the parklands, let alone to organize to expand them.

Our stay at Camp Denali over, we boarded the train for the eight-hour ride to Anchorage. Construction had begun on the George Parks Highway, which would pass McKinley Station, but it was far from completion. For decades, homesteaders and miners had relied on the train for their transportation, so the conductor was on a first-name basis with many of his passengers. There were few stations—mostly impromptu stops to drop someone off at a homestead. Occasionally the train paused while the conductor coaxed a moose off the track. Moose are relatively gentle creatures until provoked—at which point, nothing, including an oncoming train, can make them back down.

At one point, we stopped for several minutes. Suspecting another moose, Peggy and I looked out the window. Then the conductor came sweeping through the cars on a different mission. One of the locals had overindulged at the bar, passed out in the seats, and missed his stop. The conductor found him curled up in a corner and helped him down the steps.

Thirty miles southeast of the park, near Curry Ridge, we came upon a stunning view of Mount McKinley. It occurred to us that this spot, situated several hundred feet above the railroad track, might offer an alternate site for the proposed hotel at Wonder Lake. Being south of Mount McKinley, the location near Curry Ridge also offered many more clear viewing days than the stormy north side of the mountain. Most important, it was much closer to Anchorage, Alaska's largest city, and on an established route that wouldn't threaten wildlife migration. Others had considered this site as well, it turned out, but to date nothing had been built here.

In the course of the long ride, we passed from tundra and summit country into lower-elevation landscapes of lakes and streams, which grew into large rivers and then forested wetlands profuse with birch and black and white spruce. The land was mostly forest until the last third of the journey, then changed to farmland and wetlands as we followed the Knik River through the town of Eagle River and into Anchorage

Checking the Sierra Club's records before we left, I had discovered that our members in Alaska totaled ninety-nine. We began our campaign to rally Alaska's conservation sympathizers by making contact with as many as possible. In Anchorage, we had dinner with Club members Mark and Gerry Ganopole, Mr. and Mrs. George Dixon, and Mr. and Mrs. Jim Harle. They were interested in forming a local chapter, and I encouraged them to round up the requisite fifty signatures and petition for chapter status. The only notable conservation organization in Alaska at the time was the Alaska Conservation Society. Founded by some university biologists and employees of the U.S. Fish and Wildlife Service and the Alaska Fish and Game Department, and centered on the University of Alaska in Fairbanks, the society's chief concern was preserving wildlife, not the establishment of national parks, refuges, or wilderness areas.

Also in Anchorage, we met with staff of the U.S. Fish and Wildlife Service, who arranged an airplane tour for us of the Kenai Moose Range (now the Kenai National Wildlife Refuge) southwest of the city. We flew over the Kenai Peninsula—often referred to as "Anchorage's playground"— in a four-passenger Beaver amphibian plane piloted by wildlife biologist Charles Evans. Will Troyer, another wildlife biologist, was our guide.

Cruising at low altitude, at times just a few hundred feet above the ground, we saw a matrix of lakes and streams that in season would be lined closely with fishermen casting for sockeye and king salmon. The Fish and Wildlife Service had already set aside several recreational areas. We flew over the Harding Ice Field, one of the largest ice fields in the world—mile after mile of gleaming white ice, mountain peaks looming above its broad surface. At the lower elevations, myriad new willow, alder, and aspen had sprung up after a fire a few years earlier, covering the country in lush vegetation. The moose were unusually plentiful: single bulls or cows with one or two calves.

Oil had been discovered on the Kenai Peninsula a decade earlier, and we witnessed evidence of seismic research conducted by oil companies—

large stretches of denuded land where the trees had been shaved so the companies could put in their seismic lines and test underground for oil reserves. Cook Inlet, which separates the peninsula from the main bulk of Alaska, was dotted with oil rigs and derricks.

Evans, Troyer, and their supervisor, Dave Spencer, were government biologists assigned to Alaska, who, like Celia and Ginny, had fallen in love with the land and stayed. They had become pilots in order to oversee their vast holdings. All were good men who wanted to see much of the Kenai Peninsula classified as wilderness—but also men with too much land to oversee. Their efforts for wilderness would not be realized for another fifteen years.

A DIFFERENT MENTALITY awaited us in Juneau, our next destination. In 1967, the U.S. Forest Service controlled almost all the land in Southeast Alaska, a coastal realm of magnificent forests, fjords, islands, and peaks. During our time there, we met with Howard Johnson, who, as the Forest Service's regional forester for Alaska, held a powerful position. Included in his domain were the Tongass National Forest, at almost 17 million acres the largest unit of the national forest system, and the Chugach National Forest, at 5 million acres the second-largest unit. Unlike the staff at Fish and Wildlife, however, Johnson's priority was not conservation but stimulating the area's depressed economy—a mandate he had inherited from his predecessor (and later territorial governor), Frank Heintzelman.

As we soon came to discover, the Forest Service was so bent on bringing in business and creating jobs in Southeast (as this part of the state is called) that they gave special treatment to lumber companies, at the taxpayers' expense. Leases were granted for absurd lengths of time, up to fifty years, and the timber was sold cheap. The Forest Service hadn't raised lease rates since 1955. Two pulp mills were working full time: Alaska Lumber and Pulp in Sitka and Ketchikan Pulp Company, a subsidiary of Georgia-Pacific (with which I was already familiar from my campaign for the redwoods), in Ketchikan.

Johnson and his staff were professionally cool and polite. Tall and heavyset, Johnson projected an intense seriousness as he explained that he wanted to create a third mill site near Juneau, with Admiralty Island as the chief source of timber. He seemed more than willing to share the Forest Service's upcoming plans for expanded logging, most likely because he was so sure a third mill would be applauded by the local community.

Comprising a million acres, Admiralty Island lies immediately southwest of Juneau across Stephens Passage. The island's stands of spruce and hemlock made it a prime target for the lumber industry; that those forests also contained the world's highest concentration of brown bears and nesting eagles also made it attractive to conservationists. Local groups had been pushing for preservation of the island since the 1930s. As early as 1932 the Sierra Club had urged that Admiralty Island be made a national park to preserve its wildlife.

I was particularly interested in learning of plans for studies that might lead to the establishment of wilderness areas. Since the passage of the Wilderness Act in 1964, wilderness studies were being conducted on national forest lands throughout the lower forty-eight states to determine which should be granted protection. Many forests had already been through this process; once lands were deemed worthy of wilderness status, all logging was forbidden in the designated area. To me, establishing study areas was the first step to preserving wilderness, for all other uses, including timber and pulp production, usually would cease while the land was being evaluated. Despite managing the nation's largest and second-largest national forests, however, Johnson and his staff had failed to initiate any wilderness studies. Establishing wilderness areas seemed a very distant possibility.

When I asked Johnson how many wilderness areas were in his region, he stared hard as if I had just descended from a spaceship. "Wilderness?" he repeated. "Wilderness! Why, man, the whole God damn thing is wilderness!" It was an argument I'd heard many times. A place didn't need protection because it was so clearly wild. Men like Johnson assumed that because Alaska was so huge, there would always be plenty of land to go around. As a conservationist and particularly as a Californian, I'd learned that lesson the hard way.

"Yes, Mr. Johnson, today it is," I replied. "But tomorrow it won't be. I hope you'll see fit to recommend some wilderness areas in your Alaska region."

"We have scenic areas," he said defensively, referring to the strips of shoreline, no more than three hundred feet in elevation, kept verdant for the benefit of the passing ferry tourists.

I wasn't impressed.

Our last stop in Alaska was Glacier Bay, where we spent two days exploring. In the 1920s President Harding had set aside more than 3 million acres of land around the bay as a national monument. We stayed at the brand-new Glacier Bay Lodge, an example of a well-planned, unobtrusive national park accommodation. The NPS superintendent, Bob Howe, detailed one of his rangers, Greg Streveler, to take us out in a small speedboat. We went up the west arm of the bay, traveling a gamut of evolution from two-hundred-year-old spruce forest to glaciers gleaming in the sunlight, and finally up close to the pristine, white Marguerie Glacier side by side with the dirt-covered Grand Pacific, carved from the flank of adjacent mountains. These two contrasting glaciers made an impressive sight: their snouts rising more than two hundred feet from the bay, their backs sloping several miles inland.

We ate lunch on a rocky cliff that had emerged from the Toyatta Glacier only a few years earlier—another sign of the land's constant evolution. Bathed by sunshine, we sat on the freshly birthed bare rock next to a purple blanket of fireweed. Below lay the iridescent surface of the bay, dotted with countless chunks of floating ice, large and small. On the opposite cliff, a hanging glacier dripped a thin cascade into the water. In 1792, when George Vancouver sailed north along the coast of Alaska, there was no bay and his ship was blocked by ice. Only a hundred years later, John Muir, a self-taught glaciologist, would write about the same place, of the glories of blue water surrounded by frozen rivers of ice. Since Muir's time, the glaciers have receded significantly, allowing the bay to continue to expand. The land is still changing.

In the end, all descriptions of Alaska fall short of the mark. Alaska must be experienced, for such perfection cannot be fully conveyed by the limited scope of human expression. The lower forty-eight contain no reference of comparable magnitude. Even the light is different: so far north that it appears diluted.

Perhaps even more important than the spectacular scenic backdrop is the sense of one's relationship to it: contradictory feelings of the infinite and smallness, but also of possibility and adventure. You realize that you could run across the tundra, scream, wave your arms like a madman, and the space would seem no more filled. Transitions from civilization are abrupt: you trek a quarter of a mile from the road and are thrust into complete wilderness. It is thrilling to be in such country, a thrill that arises from a sense of danger. Unlike the gentle wilderness of the Sierra Nevada, Alaska is not a landscape to be entered without precaution. Each year, backpackers freeze to death in snowstorms, climbers fall from cliffs, and pilots disappear into the clouds. I fell in love with Alaska, but grew to fear it as well.

PEGGY AND I left Alaska concerned for its future but hopeful that enough good people were likewise concerned to make real progress in conservation. If we acted quickly there would still be time to save this last great wilderness. In Anchorage, a reporter for the *Anchorage Times* interviewed me as president of the Sierra Club and asked what I thought about future development in Alaska. I replied, "Alaska seems to me one place where good development and good conservation can proceed side by side." Little did I know how difficult that would be.

We returned to San Francisco inspired and transformed by our experience. In just two weeks, Alaska had seduced us. We knew we had to begin our preservation efforts immediately, focusing first on Mt. McKinley National Park, to expand the park boundaries and stop the construction at Wonder Lake. I wrote to the director of the National Park Service, George Hartzog, whom I knew well, informing him that he would build the hotel at Wonder Lake "over my dead body" and suggesting instead a site outside the park at Curry Ridge or nearby. I cannot say if Peggy and I were the first to note that location's potential for a scenic lodge—it was so obvious that it's hard to imagine others failed to see it. I don't recall the specifics of his reply, but no hotel has yet been built inside the park.

Preserving the land around Wonder Lake represented the kind of campaign the Sierra Club had been mounting for nearly two decades—saving a specific area from a specific type of development—and proposing Curry Ridge reflected the Club's tradition of advocating alternative sites. We were already coming to realize, however, that Alaska would require a different, more monumental effort. In addition to our desire to preserve Wonder Lake, we recognized the need for stronger protection of wildlife on the Kenai Peninsula, of the Southeast forests, and of the lands around Glacier Bay. We had as yet no idea of the particulars: acreages, boundaries, even what form the campaign would take. Nor could we foresee what opposition would arise.

The Sierra Club board of directors' September meeting took place shortly after our return, and I reserved a time slot to make my pitch for Alaska. For an hour I described all the places we had seen, comparing Alaska to the American west of the 1830s. My plea was unqualified: there was no comparable place left on the continent. Though few on the board had ever visited the state, the ensuing vote was unanimous: Alaska would be added as a sixth priority to the Club's existing five: completion of the national park system, completion of the wilderness system, establishment of Redwood National Park and North Cascades National Park, and protection of the Grand Canyon. Being the Club's president certainly helped my case.

That winter, a letter was forwarded to me from the Sierra Club office. It was from a man named Jack Calvin, coauthor with biologist Ed Ricketts of the notable book on California marine biology, *Between Pacific Tides*. Calvin lived in Southeast Alaska, in Sitka, where he owned a small boat tour operation. He was also a dedicated conservationist concerned about Forest Service logging on West Chichagof Island—a long, narrow span of forest and low-lying mountains north of Baranof Island (where Sitka is located). Because West Chichagof was unknown to tourists, he feared the agency would begin offering leases to lumber companies. A member of a small local group, the Sitka Conservation Society, Calvin was pushing for West Chichagof to be designated a national wilderness.

He offered a free boat trip to anyone in the Sierra Club willing to come to Sitka and explore the area. That was all I needed to initiate our next Alaska trip, and I arranged for Peggy and me to fly up the following summer. We would be joined by Brock Evans, the Club's Northwest regional representative and the staff person closest to Alaska.

During the overnight stop in Seattle before we flew to Alaska in July 1968, a small, elderly man stood just behind us at the hotel register.

Reading my name in the guest book, he asked if I was president of the Sierra Club. When I said I was, he introduced himself as Senator Ernest Gruening of Alaska. We knew something about Gruening, mainly that he was one of the few senators who voted against the Tonkin Gulf Resolution authorizing the bombing of North Vietnam. Gruening explained he would be in Alaska for several weeks campaigning for re-election and invited us to join him at a luncheon event at the Palmer Chamber of Commerce a few days hence.

"I'm glad the Sierra Club has gotten interested in Alaska," he said. "Keep at it."

We took up Gruening's invitation to the luncheon, where he invited me to speak to the gathering. We also got a chance to tour the Matanuska Valley, of which Palmer was the principal town. During the Great Depression, this valley in south-central Alaska, fairly close to Anchorage, had hosted a federally funded farming project, in which farmers from the drought-stricken Midwest were transplanted there. The extreme length of summer daylight combined with especially rich glacial soil enabled farmers to grow gargantuan cabbages and lettuces up to four and half feet in diameter. We gave our two-and-a-half-pound souvenir cabbage to Ginny Wood and Celia Hunter, who chopped it into a salad of epic proportions.

On a cloudless July day, Jack Calvin raised anchor in the early morning and his boat, the *Ootka,* glided into the shimmering blue waters of Sitka Sound for a five-day journey. Fifteen miles to the west, snow-crowned Mount Edgecumbe rose from the shores of Kruzof Island like a small version of Fujiyama. Numerous islands, some only a few feet wide, dotted the sound. Dark forests of spruce and hemlock grew right up to the water's edge. At times, the islands appeared like platforms raised on steep gray cliffs.

The *Ootka* (a Tlinglit name meaning "duck") was just twenty feet from bow to stern, her single cabin equipped with a pair of narrow bunks. Peggy and I slept along one wall, Brock and his wife Rachel against the other. Calvin slept on deck, and despite the frequent rain seemed to make do with only a sleeping bag. His average height, slender frame, graying hair, and deceptively mild manner camouflaged a rugged outdoorsman and expert boater.

Calvin had come to Alaska more than forty years earlier, a "brash lad" fresh out of high school, to work in a cannery in Little Port Walter. For several years, he returned each summer to take seasonal jobs in the canneries or the lumber mills. Like so many others we met, Calvin was soon smitten and decided to make Alaska his home. He searched for an Alaskan girl, a rare commodity then, and in 1930 married the daughter of the archbishop of Sitka's Russian Orthodox church. For their honeymoon, the couple canoed from Seattle to Juneau. They made their home in Sitka, where Calvin ran a small printing press. By 1968 Calvin had sold his business and returned to his steady passion: the Alaskan waters.

"Any excuse to go out boating is fine," he told us. "If I can get passengers to go along and pay for the grub and gasoline, well, all to the good." But he was worried. In recent years he had noticed increased logging along his routes, especially outside the established shipping and ferry lanes. Few of the locals knew about it. Calvin had read the Forest Service's timber management plan and knew that the agency was supposed to be managing the lands according to the principle of multiple use—but the main use seemed to be generating profits for lumber companies and jobs for the small communities in Southeast.

Calvin wanted to ensure that the western part of Chichagof Island, part of the Tongass National Forest, was saved from pulp logging, and he proposed designating these 450,000 acres as wilderness. (Chichagof Island is so deeply cleaved by water on the north and south that it is nearly two separate islands.) The Sitka Conservation Society had only a few dozen members, however. Sooner or later, he knew, the small group would need the resources of a national organization. He hoped I would secure that support.

Heading north, we soon passed the Nakawasina Peninsula, where, Calvin explained, logging along an inland creek had destroyed valuable bear habitat. While the deer liked to feed on the post-logging scrub, logging would eventually destroy their habitat as well. I told Brock I thought the Forest Service would continue to cater to the timber industry's desires until conservationists began applying enough pressure to be recognized as a counterinterest. In my experience, Forest Service policies tended toward the center.

Brock wasn't so optimistic. "My personal belief is that the Forest Service is not so much in the middle here or in the Northwest, but rather in the timber end of things," he argued. "But Brock, they have to be convinced," I said.

Ten miles north of Sitka, we turned eastward into Nakawasina Sound, where recent clear-cutting had denuded stretches of the steep shoreline. Above the water's edge, four hundred feet of earth had been exposed. No after-scrub had sprouted yet; the cuts had been recent, most likely in the last year. Erosion had caused a landslide. Soon, I predicted, the natural gullies would widen and more slides would follow. It was like a repeat of the clear-cutting in the redwoods. Calvin pointed out that Nakawasina Sound lay well off the ferry and shipping lanes. In such areas, the Forest Service did not even maintain the pretense of a "beauty strip."

Dozens of trees still lay on the ground where they had fallen. Their trunks looked wide and tall, the makings of good timber.

"Why have so many trees been left behind?" I asked Calvin.

He explained that the way loggers were paid was designed only for lumber. If a log had a patch of rot or if the trunk butt was split, the lumber company wouldn't pay for the tree and the logger wouldn't bother hauling it out. Loggers had to calculate this loss into their cuts; as a result, a lot more trees were cut. The system needed to be revised to credit loggers for pulp, Calvin said, so that even damaged trees could be used profitably.

The logging damage grew worse as we rounded Halleck Island, turning westward. This area had been devastated. For five miles, we passed large, denuded patches of shoreline, stretching five hundred feet up the steep hillsides. Here too, the scrub was minimal, indicating recent cuts. Recovery from such annihilation would be slow. We didn't see any loggers but passed the cluster of tents and cabins that made up their camp.

Briefly rejoining the ferry highway, we reached Salisbury Sound by early afternoon. Across the water to the north rose the green coast of West Chichagof. Its southern shore marked the beginning of the 450,000-acre wilderness proposed by the Sitka Conservation Society. Eastward, the ferry route continued toward Peril Sound, Admiralty Island, and eventually Juneau. Calvin steered the *Ootka* northwest, off the ferry lanes and into the open waters of the Gulf of Alaska.

No match for the rough waves, the *Ootka* rocked violently for the next few hours. Peggy said riding in the open sea was a mixture of excitement and endurance—like a roller coaster ride with no end. Rachel became seasick and crawled into her bunk. I alternated between lying down and snapping photographs of the island's great rocky hump. West Chichagof rose from the sea like a wonderland, reminding Peggy of a fantastic Japanese print. The farther north we traveled, the more the landscape seemed magnified. Islands multiplied into the hundreds, some so small that they didn't even appear as specks on our map. Shoreline was replaced by sheer cliffs tufted with emerald meadows and nearly black forests.

Just before 6 P.M., Calvin turned eastward into a narrow passageway. He dropped anchor in the sheltered end, known to locals as Elbow Passage. As far as we could see, we were the only boat around. A pair of excited eagles circled overhead, evidence of a nest nearby. Calvin postponed dinner, brought out the skiff, and rowed us ashore to one of the old Chichagof mines, abandoned for the last thirty years.

As we climbed onto the old wooden pier, a loose door from the watchman's house swung open and shut with the wind. A vein of gold had been discovered here about 1905, and the mine operated through the 1920s and '30s. The owners put all the money they made back into the mine in the hope of finding other veins but eventually gave up, leaving a ghost village behind. Most of the houses had collapsed; those still standing were tilted and rotted. Branches weaved into broken windows; inside we saw peeling wallpaper, plumbing innards, broken sticks of furniture. A grove of alder sprouted from a tailings pile. The town was sinking under the weight of vegetation. Eventually it would revert back to earth, demonstrating the futility of human efforts to master this country. Alaska has been explored, inhabited, even in places ruined, but it has refused to be controlled.

At midnight, Peggy and I were still awake, gazing into the steel-blue sky as icy blue fog crept around the cliffs. This country was like none we had ever encountered, none we had even imagined. We snapped photographs at midnight just because we could. Muted by dusk, the trees appeared in black silhouette while the waters, as if charged from some internal source, remained glassy and bright.

A giant starfish tumbled off the anchor as Calvin pulled it up the next morning, and the *Ootka* slid effortlessly out with the tide. Lone fishermen once frequented Elbow Passage, Calvin told us, where they could fish undisturbed. In winter, they holed up in their boats or built shacks on the island, surviving on flour, coffee, and what they could salvage from the land until spring came and they could fish again. They had little to break up the long, dark days except the company of the mine watchman, who, Calvin claimed, continued to live alone on the island after the mine closed until he died.

The *Ootka* emerged back into the rough, open waters of Khaz Bay, and for two hours Calvin deftly negotiated the rocking boat northward toward the narrow entrance of Ogden Passage. We were headed for Black Bay and the Black River, farther north on the island. The sky had grown overcast, softening the seascape into a dull palette. As we turned for a final view toward Sitka before heading into the passage, a small cloud of smog hovered over the town.

Again the landscape changed to reveal new, more dramatic forms: taller trees, taller cliffs. In the calm waters of the passage, thousands of silver needlefish schooled alongside our boat, and eagles soared overhead before diving into the water. Since Elbow Passage, a mesmerizing display of birds had appeared: ravens, guillemots, murres, gulls, ducks, geese, and swans. An otter surfaced and quickly disappeared. Peggy and I stood on deck, clutching our binoculars in anticipation of each new sighting.

We anchored in Black Bay, its waters nearly encircled by islands. Calvin rowed us toward shore as a light rain began to fall. This area was of particular concern to him, as the island's best timber grew several miles inland. Ashore, we passed the remnants of an abandoned Fish and Wildlife Service cabin, once manned to police fishermen scooping out the fish where the river ran into the bay. For a brief time, Calvin said, the rangers tried hiding in the woods but quickly abandoned this method when the fishermen got wind of the stratagem and began firing shots into the trees. They now patrolled by air.

Seaweed popped beneath our feet, and spruce grew thick along the river like a smaller replica of Redwood Creek. Overhead, water dripped from the canopied branches beneath which a rain forest sprouted. Mosses and green lichen blanketed the trunks; ferns spread out over the sodden ground. We continued to walk until Calvin admitted he didn't know how far back the big trees began. It was a small frustration; we couldn't verify to what extent, if any, logging had begun. As we retraced our steps back to the skiff, we met up with the retreating tide and had to sidestep a pair of giant clams.

Ten miles north, in Goulding Bay, we anchored for the night. The indefatigable Calvin again took out the skiff and rowed us ashore. By this time, it was late afternoon, and high tide had returned; the forest grew right up to the water's edge. We passed a miner's cabin, recently built, said Calvin, by a prospector looking for copper. As we trekked through sparse patches of Sitka spruce and hemlock, a layer of evening fog began to weave through the branches. Star gentians, rain and white orchids, yellow buttercups, and pale, delicate saxifrage sprouted through the muskeg. The going was slow, the trail mossy and wet. My waterproof boots soon reached their limits.

For a mile, the Forest Service trail was paralleled by a rusting set of narrow-gauge tracks, relics of the old mine eight miles in. A tractor had been jerry-rigged as a rudimentary locomotive to haul ore. Continuing to climb, we suddenly came upon a thick wall of water cascading from forty feet above. Following the stream upward, we discovered it was the lowest of a series of falls spilling over from Goulding Lake.

We tightroped across the river on a fallen log and arrived at the lake, its clear waters forming an elliptical bowl surrounded by snowcapped mountains. The shoreline bore signs of a once-thriving village now reduced to rot: collapsed shacks, metal pilings, half-sunken boats. Miners had once labored fiercely to forge out an existence here, only to depart broke and leave everything behind. The scene seemed to encapsulate much of the history of white men in Alaska: tales of adventure and effort, of success and disaster, and always disregard for the land except as a source of wealth.

Exhausted by the long days and short nights, we slept well into the next morning. When I woke, Calvin had already pulled up anchor and the *Ootka* was headed south on its return journey. We used up the day traversing rough waters southward to Salisbury Sound, then cutting northeast to rejoin the shipping lane, emerging into Poison Cove, the patch of water dividing West Chichagof from the eastern part of the island. After twenty miles, we turned off the shipping lanes and anchored in Fick Cove, fifteen miles north of our embarkation point at Sitka.

The next morning we rowed out in the skiff and docked on the eastern shore of West Chichagof. We followed a logging road for several miles in a drizzling rain. The weather cast a somber mood over our group; we walked in silence, each withdrawn in thought. Brock walked in the lead—but suddenly I saw his six-foot frame come barreling past me. He screamed, *"Bear!"*

Instinctively, I took off after Brock. When I reached Calvin, he was standing his ground, waving his arms in the air and swearing profusely. At that point, my instincts told me to follow the native, and I turned to face the bear. It could have been thirty feet away; it could have been ten. As it loomed almost six feet tall, my first thought was that it had reared up on its hind legs; a second look told me it was still standing on all fours. I knew nothing about bears.

"Look big!" Calvin told me.

I launched into jumping jacks. Calvin continued gesticulating and swearing. Then the bear did rear up, to eight feet, and produced a bellowing, terrifying roar. Calvin didn't flinch but continued to berate the animal. Seconds later the bear fell back on all fours and lumbered off into the trees. Calvin and I collapsed on the ground.

As we headed back to Sitka on the fifth day, I encouraged Calvin to keep pushing for his West Chichagof Wilderness proposal and said I would present it to the Sierra Club board of directors for discussion. In my own mind, I had already decided that this splendid wilderness must not fall victim to wholesale logging. As we were coming to discover, there were many Alaskas, each in need of protection.

WE FLEW FROM Sitka to Juneau in a PBY World War II flying patrol boat. Peggy and I sat around the central bomb bay. Also on the plane was a dark-haired young man, handsome in a slick sort of way, passing out cigars. Next to him sat his stout manager, smoking one of the cigars.

"I'm Mike Gravel," said the young man, holding out his hand. "I'm running for U.S. Senate." A Democrat, Gravel was challenging Ernest

Gruening for their party's nomination. In less than a week, we had encountered both of the Democratic candidates for the U.S. Senate; we'd been told that Alaskan circles of power were small, and this proved it. Gravel invited us to a spaghetti feed that night in Juneau. We thanked him but never went. That fall, due largely to Native support, Gravel ousted Gruening and later won the general election.

Sigurd Olson Jr., the only biologist in the Forest Service's Alaska Region, met us at the airport. We had arranged a slew of appointments in Juneau, and first on the list was Howard Johnson. Johnson smiled as we stepped into the meeting room. "Well, welcome. We've been expecting you," he said, almost as if looking forward to our reunion. He proceeded to tell us that since our last visit, he had called two major meetings with all his resource managers and forest supervisors. "We now have four wilderness study areas," he announced proudly.

"Well, good, Mr. Johnson," I replied. "How many wilderness areas have you proposed?"

"Oh, we haven't proposed any as of yet." Although unwilling to share particulars of all the proposals before the official deadline in July 1970, Johnson did say that he had proposed two national recreation areas in the Chugach Forest. One of them, the proposed Kenai Recreation Area, included the Harding Ice Field. While I was pleased that the agency was considering the need for protected areas, it soon became clear that Johnson's criteria for "land disposal" were based not on concern for protecting exceptional places but on which lands could be given up without losing timber.

"The Chugach does not have much commercial timber, frankly," Johnson noted.

"What about classifying areas where there is a good stand of timber?" I asked.

"I'm not personally inclined to put on ice considerable areas of commercial timber."

Putting on ice, freezing—these seemed to be the favored metaphors of Alaska's Forest Service bureaucrats. They used the terms frequently, as if to suggest that keeping trees in their natural state reduced their worth. In fact, the opposite was true. Once a forest had been committed to lumber, it served only short-term private interests. What could be more permanent than cutting down an ancient tree?

In the end, the Forest Service's recommendations for land use were made on the basis of economics. Furthermore, the service had no plans to "withhold activity" in any of the areas proposed while the studies were being conducted. And the "recreation area" designation, which allowed roads, campsites, and other facilities, afforded much less protection than wilderness. In effect, little protection was established or planned.

When I asked about the Sitka Conservation Society's Chichagof Wilderness proposal, Johnson said the area had already been committed to a cutting contract with Alaska Lumber and Pulp. "You see, I've always tried for a mix in my operations," he added.

I assumed, I said, that by "mix" he meant multiple uses as defined in the Classification and Multiple Use Act of 1964, of which cutting timber was one. The others included fish and wildlife conservation, mineral production, outdoor recreation, occupancy, wilderness, grazing, and water-shed protection. "Oh no," Johnson said. "I mean a mix of operations: plywood, lumber, pulp."

Of all the lands in Southeast needing protection, the most pressing in my mind was Admiralty, the great island of a million acres just south and west of Juneau. Johnson wanted to include Admiralty in a massive logging sale, the third such in Southeast. In the years since 1955, both the Georgia-Pacific and St. Regis companies had optioned the sale, only to turn down the leases after their experts deemed them unprofitable. Now, U.S. Plywood–Champion Paper had an option until July 31—less than two weeks away. Under the same sale, the entire west side of the island, with its highly desirable old-growth spruce and hemlock, was slated for logging, as were stands at Yakutat and Sumdum Bay on the mainland. Champion had yet to complete its feasibility study, and Johnson expected his office to extend the deadline to accommodate the company. Moreover, the lease price was the same as the agency had offered to St. Regis in 1955.

Faced with these far-advanced plans, I nonetheless suggested turning Admiralty Island into a wilderness area. Admiralty would be unique in the world—not only was it large, but as an island it contained a complete ecosystem isolated by water. Designating it as wilderness would safeguard the eagle and bear populations. Johnson listened intently as I spoke, and I naively believed that he was actually considering my proposal.

The next day Peggy and I met with Tom Kelly, the state commissioner of natural resources. Young, attractive, and bright, Kelly had done his homework. He was familiar with the Sierra Club and its burgeoning support in Alaska and was eager to sit down and discuss issues "rationally, before problems arise." But Kelly, who was married to a Texas oil heiress, was no conservationist. Eventually, he said, oil was going to have its way in Alaska. He predicted that oil would soon surpass the fishing and lumber industries to lead Alaska's exports for the next fifteen to twenty-five years.

Despite admitting that there were potentially serious problems in transporting oil and preventing spills, he was adamant that oil development on the Arctic slope, or North Slope—the vast sweep of tundra in Alaska's far north, bordered by the Arctic Ocean—should continue unabated. The Arctic Wildlife Range, which occupied quite a bit of this region, was "too big" anyway. Kelly also predicted that the wells in the Kenai Peninsula would play a close second to the North Slope's oil. I asked what would become of the Moose Range on the Kenai Peninsula. Kelly thought the BLM had been shortsighted in reserving that land "before its full importance and significance was well understood." Too much emphasis had already been placed on preserving moose, he thought.

"It's a question of moose versus man," he said simply. "On the peninsula, you drive around a corner, and bang! There's a moose."

IF MANY OF our encounters with land officials in Alaska were discouraging, there were some pleasant surprises, too. Our 1968 trip marked the start of a good working relationship with Burt Silcock, director of the Bureau of Land Management in Alaska. We had met briefly with Silcock in Anchorage the preceding year, when we were trying to contact the gamut of agency managers. At the time, he had expressed great interest in preserving some BLM holdings, particularly in the Wrangell Mountains bordering Canada and in the Brooks Range—regions still unknown to us.

Peggy and I were somewhat leery of Silcock's talk: we had met many bureaucrats who talked the conservation game but never followed through.

But at the end of our first meeting Silcock invited us to come back and fly with him and staff members around the Wrangells and the Brooks Range. It was an attractive offer—aside from the Mount McKinley area, the Kenai Peninsula, and Glacier Bay, the vast bulk of Alaska awaited us. When we returned in 1968, we took him up on his offer.

We quickly discovered that Silcock was not the typical agency bureaucrat. A man of considerable ability, he'd worked his way up through the ranks, one of the first career men in the BLM. Large and powerful looking, he talked thoughtfully of the vast empire over which he now presided. Later he would become the Bureau's national director.

In Alaska alone, the BLM was responsible for a staggering amount of land: 290 million acres, more than three-quarters of the state's total land. Silcock's domain was larger than all the BLM's combined holdings in the lower forty-eight. Because of this vast responsibility, the Bureau suffered from a lack of manpower to an even greater extent than the National Park Service; Silcock had two deputies for the entire state.

Using the criteria of the Classification and Multiple Use Act, Silcock wanted to establish a series of classifications for the BLM's holdings in Alaska. Not only did he have too few employees for too much land, but he was also up against the clock: the deadline for classifications under the act was December 31, 1971. It was a daunting task. Each proposed classification would require surveys, written proposals, public hearings, and approval from the Department of the Interior. Classifying the whole 290 million acres was out of the question. Silcock and his staff had to make tough decisions, and they had to make them quickly. He needed all the advice and support he could get, and I was more than willing to give it.

It was a symbiotic relationship. In exchange, Peggy and I were able to fly and camp all over the Wrangell and Chugach Mountains as well as the Brooks Range. Previous campaigns had taught me this simple truth: there's no substitute for firsthand knowledge of the terrain. If I wanted to save the land, I needed to know it.

In 1968, Silcock arranged for Peggy and me to see the two areas he most wanted to protect. The first trip centered on the Copper River Basin, a 23-million-acre region that included the Wrangell Mountains. In Anchorage, we boarded a Grumman Goose with Silcock and Jim Scott, the BLM manager for southern Alaska. Equipped with two turbojet engines, the modified Grumman could set down and take off on either land or water.

The Wrangells were as majestic as the Alaska Range around Denali. Peggy and I were stunned to realize that Alaska contained not just one magnificent range, but several. These mountains, though, were volcanic, rising some 12,000 to 16,000 feet. Because they were inland, the weather was sunny more often than in the coastal regions. Our air tour took us over the floodplain of the Nizina Valley just south of Mount Blackburn, tallest of the Wrangells. Larger than Yosemite Valley, the Nizina was awash with green lichen and scrub and dotted with sapphire lakes. Farther on, a matrix of ice fields, spruce-banked glaciers, and turbid glacial streams seemed to defy gravity and flow in several directions. Scott, a self-taught ecologist who had not completed high school, explained that such a proliferation of waterways was the sign of a postglacial period. We spotted the brown bulks of half a dozen moose grazing on the tundra below.

Across the broad valley of the Chitina River rose the ice-covered Chugach Mountains. North and east of the main peaks, the Tebay Lakes chain stretched for four miles in placid blue ellipses and quietly emptied into a small stream. The Grumman touched down near the shore, sending a wave of ripples across the lake. Peggy and I piggybacked on Silcock and Scott's shoulders to dry land.

Around us rose a spaciousness and absolute silence that sucked the breath from our lungs. Alaska does not simply afford pretty vistas; it enfolds you into the experience of its size and the knowledge, often forgotten in the city, that as humans we are but small animals and one of the least equipped to survive. Ducks and geese floated on the surface of the lake, while loons and terns rustled near the water's edge. The tundra, baked crisp in the sun, crackled under our feet. Fifty miles to the northeast, Mt. Blackburn, at over 16,000 feet the Wrangells' highest peak, reared dramatically upward from the flat plains. Its surface was patched with glaciers, threaded with suspended strands of ice falls. Clouds gathered, swirled, and dissipated around its snow-crowned peak.

"When you have administration over this, you don't need Mount McKinley," I told Scott.

Inroads had been made into this wilderness, however. Our flight route had passed over the remnants of the Kennecott Copper Mine complex. Defunct for thirty years, it had left indelible marks on the landscape: two towns, Kennicott and McCarthy, and a narrow-gauge railway running from the mines to the town of Cordova almost two hundred miles away. Throughout the Copper River Basin we came upon abandoned sites with piled logs, sometimes houses or trailers, the traces of homesteaders who had attempted to clear the land but found it too inhospitable or unfarmable. The Homestead Act had been designed for farming in the lower forty-eight; it was problematic in Alaska.

Near our camp at Tebay Lakes, three abandoned school buses were slowly turning to rust. Miners had filed a claim and later drove the buses out there in winter, across the frozen lake. Restoring this landscape wasn't just a matter of removing the buses—the land still belonged to those who owned the claim. Even if the BLM classified it as a protected zone, it would have to be bought back. Each of the claims we had seen would likewise have to be acquired; implementing the various classifications for conservation purposes would be expensive.

Scott and Silcock hoped to classify the land around the lakes as recreation areas and other parts of the basin as roadless areas, but they admitted that, given the BLM's limited authority, acquisition would be difficult. The Homestead and Mining acts, which most people associate with the nineteenth century and Manifest Destiny, were still being used with full force in one of the earth's superlative wilderness regions.

We spent the night at Tebay Lakes, the chill seeping through the blankets and waking us in the dark cold. The next day we headed toward Fairbanks, stopping to refuel in Gulkana, where the airport consisted of a strip of tarmac and a solitary hangar. Peggy waited on the only seat available—a log surrounded by cigarette butts, tin cans, old tires, and torn car seats—while Silcock, Scott, and I filtered the contaminated fuel through a chamois cloth.

In Fairbanks, we bid farewell to Silcock and Scott, then set off again—this time with Silcock's other lieutenant, BLM deputy director Bob Krumm, who oversaw 190 million acres of northern Alaska. Our destination was the Brooks Range, a tremendous sweep of Arctic mountains and the farthest north we had ever been. We flew north over the enormous Yukon River Valley, soaring over mounting hills, then following the Koyukuk River and its tributaries, the north fork and the Dietrich.

Gradually the hills grew into mountains. The north fork of the Koyukuk was a blue pathway beckoning us forward as the Grumman Goose cruised through the Gates of the Arctic: Boreal and Frigid Crags, two peaks that stand like sentries guarding the portal to the great northern wilderness. The Gates had been named by Robert Marshall, cofounder of The Wilderness Society, whose epic explorations in the range are recorded in *Alaska Wilderness*. Marshall dedicated himself to preserving this land, and his accounts supplied critical recommendations to the BLM and us.

Although it is Alaska's northernmost mountain system, the Brooks Range is not a land only of ice and snow. These are old mountains, worn and rounded, rising only some 6,000 to 9,000 feet—half the height of the Wrangells and relatively low in a land of giants. The colors here were softer than in the volcanic Wrangells: muted tones of gray and taupe; at times the mountains appeared to have been dusted with ash. Talus collected in beds between peaks, the crumbs of millions of years of erosion. The snow remaining from that winter's snowfall nestled in the narrow sweeps of the upper elevations.

We headed west at Anaktuvik Pass, at the crest of the Brooks Range, home to an Inuit village of the same name (it translates to "Place of Caribou Droppings"). From this crest rise several streams flowing south, including the middle fork of the Koyukuk, the John, and the Alatna rivers. Turning southwest, we headed for the Arrigetch Peaks, also named by the Inuit, meaning "Fingers of an Outstretched Hand." The Arrigetch seemed like another world, their spiked crests barren of green and encrusted with ground rock. Their aptly named digits pointed skyward as if warning travelers not to come near.

Ironically, in these remote mountains nature had seen fit to exaggerate the designs of civilization. From the Grumman I spotted arches and turrets, spires and cornices, the rude forms of medieval castles recast in natural stone. Some of the peaks were topped like the tip of a gnome's hat. On Mount Igikpak white striations dripped down a dark cliff face. Even in the sunshine, the Arrigetch were eerie; in a storm, I imagined they would be the stuff of Grimms' fairy tales.

We camped at Walker Lake, a place as close to perfection as this world offers and one of the few wilderness areas that Silcock was proposing. After another two days, we returned to Anchorage. Peggy and I were overwhelmed by the vastness and splendor of northern Alaska and determined to protect as much of it as possible. It was clear from the start that Silcock and his assistants favored more development than we did—not surprising given the BLM's mandate to develop unreserved public land. Silcock was a reasonable man, however, and open to suggestions. We quickly agreed that we would return the following year to help him with his classifications in any way we could.

Back in Fairbanks, the headlines blazed with news of the oil strike at Prudhoe Bay. The Atlantic Richfield Oil Company (ARCO) had unearthed a tremendous oil reserve on the Arctic slope, and the Tom Kellys of Alaska were celebrating. As an insider, Kelly may very well have already been in the know. Our meeting with him preceded news of the strike by just a matter of days.

The city was charged, and local reaction was mainly upbeat. The *Anchorage Times* trumpeted the discovery as the fix for the state's economic slump. Others, such as Peggy and myself, were deeply worried. What we had hoped would be a relatively short campaign to enlarge park and wilderness areas had suddenly become complicated. The oil would have to be transported south, perhaps to the Kenai Peninsula, and shipped out; billions of dollars were now at stake. Ultimately, we would have to cross paths with the oil companies. While we felt pressure to act quickly, we understood the power of the oil companies and the state's desire to generate revenue and jobs. We were in Alaska for the long haul and knew we had to plan and time our efforts wisely.

OUR 1968 TRIP continued with a return visit to Mt. McKinley National Park. There we met a young biologist named Gordon Haber, a student of the distinguished wolf expert Adolph Murie. Haber had taken over Murie's field research and volunteered to show us a wolf den on the east fork of the Toklat River. We would be joined by Sigurd Olson, National

Park Service associate director Bill Everhart, and Ted Swem, NPS director for new areas.

Rising at 3 A.M., we headed out in two cars. From the park's eastern boundary we drove the twelve paved miles along Wonder Lake Road to the Savage River, then another thirty miles on dirt and gravel to the east fork of the Toklat. We parked near the river and stepped into a dim drizzle. Haber said the wolf den was about five miles downriver.

We crossed and recrossed the braided stream of the Toklat as it wound through the broad valley, whose telltale U shape gave evidence of glacial carving. The rain continued to fall steadily all morning, blurring our views. We stopped to build a small fire, ate some sandwiches, and then continued downstream. Someone pointed and said, "I see a wolf!" Haber said we were close. I climbed up a hillock, took out my binoculars, and focused downstream. Through the misty lens, I thought I saw the silhouette of a wolf—a solitary figure standing atop what must have been the den. I came down to tell the group.

A mile farther on, we came to the den. A half-dozen openings perforated the hillside. Haber said he could get close to the wolves, as they had come to trust him. These wolves were among those whose migrations transcended the park's boundaries. He crawled in first and reported the den empty.

Silently, the rest of us crawled inside on our knees. The den covered at least a thousand square feet with the roof, three feet high, rising into a shallow dome. While much of the interior had been formed from a natural cave, the wolves had dug out the rest. We moved around on our knees, finding traces of bones and excrement that delineated separate chambers where the wolves—very particular creatures—slept, ate, and defecated. The den, however, was absolutely vacant. Haber estimated that there hadn't been any wolves for three to five weeks. My vision had been a hallucination.

We started back upstream, but in the six hours since we had left the car, the Toklat had risen significantly, the persistent rain combining with glacial melt from the recent warm weather. The river now ran high and fast; what had been an ankle-deep stream that morning now reached to our thighs. Against the swift current, we crossed the river in three pairs, hands on shoulders: first Swem and Everhart, then Olson and myself, and last, Haber, the largest and strongest, with Peggy. As we approached the bank, I looked over my shoulder and saw Peggy fall into the water. Haber quickly lifted her up and they continued to wade. Safely across, I turned to see Peggy fall again, this time drifting several feet before Haber could grab her. I realized that her poncho was the culprit. Wide and long like an apron, it was filling with water, sinking her. I shouted to Haber who rustled it over her head.

Peggy reached the bank drenched and freezing. It was almost five more miles to the car, and we alternated between walking and jogging to keep her warm. By the final crossing at the east fork, we were nearly swimming against chest-high water. Peggy emerged exhausted and in the first stages of hypothermia. She slowed down and grew sleepy. I ran behind her, slapping her as I would a horse, just to keep her going.

Fortunately, there was an NPS ranger cabin near the river. We burst in, taking the ranger's wife by surprise. She took Peggy into the bedroom, stripped her down and gave her dry clothes, then we bundled her in blankets and put her in front of the fire. With the aid of a few swigs of whiskey from Everhart's flask, Peggy recovered completely within the hour. With each foray into the wild, we were coming more and more to understand the frightening underside of Alaska's magnificence.

The preceding year, Ted Swem had offered to take us out to the Wood River–Tikchik Lakes. The park service considered this area, west of Anchorage and near the coastal town of Dillingham, as potentially one of the world's greatest national parks. But in the summer of 1968, Swem had to withdraw the offer. The state had selected the land as part of its quota and wasn't allowing NPS staff to go in. I was furious, both at the state and at the NPS for losing its chance, and still determined to see the area. I wasn't sure what I would be able to accomplish, but if I wanted to be an effective advocate, I needed firsthand knowledge of the place. Peggy and I did a little impromptu research and made reservations at a fishing lodge on River Bay between Lake Nerka and Lake Aleknagik—all part of the Wood River–Tikchik Lakes system.

The lodge owner, John Pearson, had agreed to pick us up in Dillingham. We flew there in an old F-27 propeller plane whose entire front half was loaded with whiskey and beer crates, leaving less than a third of its capacity for passengers. It was enough, as the only other passenger was an Alaska state trooper, resplendent in his gold-and-blue uniform. A large crowd was gathered on the tarmac as the plane touched down in Dillingham and cheered as we exited the plane. Facetiously, I wondered if they had come to meet the president of the Sierra Club, but we soon realized the accolade was for the whiskey, not us. Those waiting were cannery workers who had worked themselves ragged for the salmon season and were ready to celebrate. The trooper, who had been sent to keep the peace, stood at attention while ground crews unloaded the precious cargo.

A lone figure emerged from the crowd and introduced himself as our host, John Pearson. White-haired and distinguished looking, Pearson appeared to be well into his seventies. He drove us twenty-five miles outside of Dillingham to Aleknagik Lake, second lowest of the Wood River–Tikchik Lakes. There we had lunch and proceeded via motorboat up the lake and into the River Bay passageway leading to his lodge.

For three days we were entertained royally. Pearson took me out fishing in a rowboat, and within an hour he had caught enough fish for everyone's dinner. Through the crystal waters, I could see three distinct layers of fish: a top layer of trout, grayling below, and finally salmon along the bottom. It was clear why the NPS had wanted this land, which contained a stupendous array of fjordlike lakes and glacial rivers set against the Togiak Mountains that rise 5,000 feet from the sea. Eastward, flat plains spread out in an endless vista.

On the last evening of our stay, Pearson turned to me at dinner and shot me a knowing look. "Now, Dr. Wayburn, let's talk business."

I had no idea what he meant. "Look at these hands," he said, lifting up his swollen, gnarled fingers. "I've lived here for forty years and loved it, but I'm seventy-five and my wife and I have arthritis. I can't take it anymore."

We stared at each other. I remained silent, unsure of what to say.

"I'll sell you this place for $35,000," he announced.

I was caught totally by surprise. "Thank you very much for your offer; I'm sure it's a fair price, but I don't have the $35,000 to buy it."

"Thirty thousand, then," he said. "It's the only legitimate private property in the area."

"I don't have the $30,000."

"I didn't mean for you to buy it personally," he explained. "I mean your organization."

I couldn't fathom how my intentions had been so misread. In 1968 the Sierra Club was in financial straits, entangled in its overly ambitious publishing program. "The Club is not a wealthy organization, Mr. Pearson. We don't have that kind of funds at our disposal."

"Oh come on, Dr. Wayburn," Pearson protested, throwing his hands in the air. "Everybody knows the Sahara Club is the richest gambling outfit in Reno!" He was disappointed when I set him straight, but we parted cordially.

The next morning a small bush plane came to pick us up. Before returning to Anchorage, Peggy and I wanted to fly west over the Togiak Mountains and off the coast to Round Island, where thousands of walrus gathered. But as our pilot headed toward the mountains, the weather began to turn and the clouds lowered. From the cockpit, I watched them thicken minute by minute; soon there wasn't much space between the clouds and the ground. Visibility was rapidly diminishing; within minutes, it would be impossible to see at all. I became alarmed. We could fly right into the mountain.

"I think we should turn the plane around and just head to Dillingham," I said. I didn't want to risk missing the flight from Dillingham back to Anchorage.

Our pilot shrugged. "Oh, don't worry," he said. "I know this country like the back of my hand."

I was not convinced. "This is suicide. We're not going any farther," I declared.

The pilot tried to reassure me, but I was adamant, and he reluctantly turned the plane around. We arrived safely in Dillingham. A few years later, we learned the same pilot had died in a crash; his plane had hit the side of a mountain during a storm.

Back in Anchorage, I asked Roscoe Bell, chief of the State Lands Division in Anchorage, why the state had selected the Wood River–Tikchik Lakes area.

"Frankly, to keep the feds from making a national park of it," he said.

His comment revealed the underlying competition between state bureaucrats and the federal agencies. The state retained the Wood River–Tikchik Lakes. Unlike other areas, chosen to boost the state's failing economy, the Tikchiks were without logging or mineral resources. Instead, they were considered natural jewels—a vanity choice, so the state could have something as beautiful as the federal parks. Originally the state planned to convert the land into 120-acre estates and sell it to developers. Today half of it is a state park and the other half private property.

FLYING HOME FROM our second Alaska trip, we were already planning to return the following summer. The discovery of oil in Prudhoe Bay mandated quick action. We knew the oil companies would not wait; neither could we. Almost immediately after the oil discovery, the three companies leasing lands on the North Slope (Atlantic Richfield, British Petroleum, and Humble, now Exxon-Mobil) had formed a consortium to build the Trans-Alaska Pipeline System from Prudhoe Bay south to Valdez, an ice-free port on Prince William Sound. Despite the fact that they neither owned the land nor had a permit to construct a pipeline, the consortium ordered eight hundred miles of pipe—the distance from the North Slope to the port. Governor Walter Hickel, in one of his last acts before becoming secretary of the interior, pushed through the construction of a winter road, a truck route to transport pipeline materials from Fairbanks to the North Slope.

Three initial wells were drilled during the summer of 1968, and we soon heard rumors that as many as twenty had been drilled in the next few months. Meanwhile, our own plans for Alaska in 1969 were firming up. I was invited to speak at an August meeting of the American Association for the Advancement of Science in Fairbanks, to present conservation concerns about North Slope development. From Fairbanks, we planned to visit the Arctic slope and see firsthand the extent of the drilling.

In addition to participating in the conference, we would continue meeting with federal and state bureaucrats, including the Forest Service's Howard Johnson and his staff and the BLM's Burt Silcock. With mounting excitement, we counted the weeks, then the days until our return. Last-minute preparations were made—our three weeks in Alaska would be another whirlwind tour. Suddenly the trip was upon us.

The clouds that had steadily obstructed the view since Seattle broke just as our plane passed over Baranof Island, revealing the green island below with its blue lakes and fjords and the pointed tops of peaks rising thousands of feet from the sea. We were met at the Sitka Airport by Dave Gangle, a local bus driver whom we had encouraged to join the Club. That evening over dinner, we watched the twenty-eight-foot *Arrow Maker* sail up the channel to dock. Owned by Dr. George Longenbough, president of the Sitka Conservation Society, the boat was just returning from a nine-person Sierra Club tour of the proposed West Chichagof Wilderness Area. Longenbough had offered his boat to replace Jack Calvin's *Ootka*, destroyed when its gasoline engine ignited and exploded. After dinner, we went down to the docks to help unload and meet the travelers. In just two years, the Club's Alaska membership had grown from 99 to more than 350.

The next morning, we met Jack Calvin, who had offered to show us around Sitka, to explore his concerns about Chichagof Island. The rains returned as he drove us north of Sitka to Harbor Mountain, where we climbed up 2,000 feet among scrub spruce and hemlock to high meadows, their deep greens reminiscent of the Washington Cascades. Even obscured by fog and rain, the views of Sitka Sound were spectacular, a dreamlike landscape. I imagined fantastic possibilities waiting just behind the veil of mist.

Driving southeast of Sitka, Calvin showed us the Alaska Lumber and Pulp mill on Silver Bay. Japanese-owned Alaska Lumber and Pulp was ten years into a fifty-year USFS logging contract for allotments covering most of Baranof and Chichagof Islands. That contract was also, according to Howard Johnson, the main barrier to the Sitka Conservation Society's wilderness area proposal. Despite the smokestacks and swarms of bees drawn to their smell, the beauty of the bay was still apparent. Invisible to the casual observer, however, was the absence of abalone. Once abundant in these waters, they were now extinct due to water pollution.

The Calvins' house sat near the entrance to Silver Bay, close to the beach. A quarter-mile walk from the garage on the road led through patches of forest and berry bushes as pristine as a New England pilgrim's settlement, and the house itself offered broad views of Sitka Bay and tree-covered hillsides. Trekking along the little path, I was seized with a desire to move to Alaska. It was the first time in thirty-five years I considered leaving San Francisco.

While we were out at dinner, local attorney Roger DuBock stopped by our table to discuss the possibility of a lawsuit against the Forest Service for issuing the contract to Champion Paper Company. Champion had accepted the agency's lease offer in December 1968, so in all likelihood Johnson had already been in final negotiations when we had met the previous August. He had never considered my wilderness proposal seriously. If we went forward with the suit, it would be the first time the Sierra Club had sued a federal agency.

The next day we set off early with Chuck Johnstone and Jack Calvin to tour Willis Hoolis Cove, one of two proposed Champion mill sites. This area had once been logged selectively then clear-cut in the last several years. The alders—usually the first vegetation after logging—grew thick, knee- to waist-high. As we had seen before, tremendous numbers of logs had been left lying on the ground instead of being put through a chopper. We walked two miles before coming to a washed-out bridge, one of many signs of erosion. Much of the old stands had been logged during previous leases.

The traffic at Sitka Airport seemed noticeably heavier than just a year earlier as we boarded a 727 jet for Juneau—the first large plane we had flown on within Alaska. The flight, only twenty-five minutes, lacked the intimacy of low-flying small planes, and the high altitude made detailed ground views impossible.

In Juneau we met briefly with Keith Miller, who succeeded Hickel as governor. When we had met Miller the previous year—he was then Alaska's secretary of state—I had found him amiable and willing to answer questions, if unlikely to volunteer information. The visit had been marked by silences during which we sipped our tea and looked out the window. Our 1969 meeting was not as difficult. The conversation focused on the Wood River–Tikchik area; I suggested that the state re-cede the land as California had done with Yosemite Valley in 1893. Miller seemed to nod in agreement with everything I said, but left me the impression that he wasn't about to push for any of it.

That afternoon brought a tense two-and-a-half-hour meeting with Howard Johnson and assistant foresters Bruce Lockhart and George Roskie. The West Chichagof and Admiralty Island proposals had raised the issue of Forest Service classifications as a whole. Like Miller, Johnson and his staff seemed amenable to the concept of wilderness in theory but resisted any discussion of specifics.

"There are problems with setting aside wilderness," he said. Mineral studies would need to be conducted before any proposals could be made. As we had discovered the previous year, Johnson wasn't willing to commit any lands except on an economic basis. The meeting carried an undercurrent of hostility. We had become the outsiders coming in and telling the locals what to do in their state.

"The Alaska Wilderness Council is the organization of conservationists that should be putting up proposals," Johnson said. "The local groups should propose each area." At the time, the Sitka Conservation Society was the only group that had offered such a proposal, and with only a few dozen members, it had been their idea to enlist the Sierra Club's aid. The conversation then turned to Johnson's Kenai Recreation Area proposal. As I had feared, the recreation designation would offer little protection. While there would remain some undeveloped pockets, most of the region would have roads and, most likely, logging.

Most pressing to my mind was the fate of Admiralty Island and Yakutat. I waited until the end of the meeting for Johnson to volunteer information about the Champion contract, but he did not. Finally I raised the issue, but he refused to divulge any details. Had I not asked him point-blank, I doubt he would have offered any information on the subject. Inwardly I was outraged by what I considered the Forest Service's deceit, though I did not let my feelings emerge in words. Erupting at Johnson would get me nowhere.

IN ANOTHER SERIES of meetings in 1969, BLM officials and I began hashing out boundaries and classifications on lands administered by that agency. Silcock and Bob Krumm had divided the BLM's 24 million acres in the Brooks Range into several blocks. While uses such as homesteading, mining, and trade would be prohibited in many of these areas, in others the proposals still allowed for state selection, homesteading (on parcels up to five acres), and Native allotments (up to 160 acres). Of Krumm's 190 million acres, however, only the 2.5 million acres surrounding Walker Lake would be declared a wilderness area. And even in the most protected zone, under Silcock's proposals, there was nothing to stop an Alaska Native from making a claim for 160 acres, occupying the site for three years, and then selling it to an outside developer at market value.

"You have people in Los Angeles who are just dying for this kind of area," Peggy told him. "They'll fly in by the hundreds."

The crux of Silcock's dilemma and frustration was the BLM's undefined role in land protection. Unlike the NPS and the Forest Service, the BLM in 1969 had no specific legislation outlining its responsibilities and authority in differentiating among its holdings—and would not until the mid-1970s. The BLM was charged with managing "unreserved public land"—in other words lands that had not been designated for any particular purpose. In practice, this authority usually had been interpreted as overseeing development and destruction through logging, mining, and homesteading. The agency had not used its powers for protection and preservation. Silcock wanted to change that but so far lacked a vocabulary, a lexicon of designations. We found ourselves using phrases like "wilderness-type area" or "conservation-type area."

Specifically, his agency did not have the ability, Silcock believed, to recommend the establishment of wilderness areas by Congress. Yet without such protection, the places he wanted to see protected could eventually be taken over by private interests. Already the oil consortium was dispatching survey crews to the Brooks Range for groundwork on the oil pipeline. When we flew with Bob Krumm to the Brooks Range this year, we passed over eroded, muddy tracks in the tundra—the remnants of the "Hickel Highway." We also passed over construction camps. The BLM had granted permission for eight such camps to be built. While the crews were supposedly still "making surveys" for pipeline construction, the pipeline's eventual route followed the camps' configuration to a T. The companies knew where they wanted to put the pipe and were really just getting the infrastructure in place to save time.

"Why did you grant permission?" I asked Krumm.

"I was told to," he said.

Nor did the BLM feel it could do much to restrict state selections. Withdrawing any land for wilderness designation might be interpreted as the BLM flexing its muscle against the state. How strong that muscle might be, nobody knew. I suggested that the BLM at least initiate study areas as provided by the Classification and Multiple Use Act, to temporarily keep the state from selecting those lands, but Silcock didn't think he could "lock up" the lands like that. The BLM either had to withdraw an area or not.

He also feared that if the BLM asked for too much, a backlash would develop and the BLM might lose everything it had asked for. As Bob Krumm explained it, "There is one area in the Brooks Range that deserves our thumbing our nose at the state and saying we don't trust you enough," adding, "I have serious reservations about whether we are even going to have the muscle to get this, let alone a larger area."

I'd heard this line of thinking from almost every land bureaucrat I'd ever encountered. In contrast, I saw the BLM classifications as an opportunity to turn things around. "We see an extremely significant step in changing the BLM's role from one of custodial care, which allows individuals or groups to go in at will," I told Silcock, "to one that tries to identify different parts of its domain as suitable for different uses."

As BLM director for Alaska, Silcock was charged with developing the land in the public interest. Just what constituted the "public interest" was at the center of our debate. Krumm repeatedly explained they couldn't serve one group's special interest. However, I have never considered conservationists a special interest group, but rather as representing the public interest and its right to enjoy land for centuries. Conversely, "special interest" to me better describes the private individuals and businesses that might profit from development of the land. Indeed, it is those interests that "lock up" resources, since the land becomes designated for one use only: creating profit.

"I agree with what you are saying: that you can't reserve it all for wilderness," I argued, "but you can reserve it for public use and enjoyment. These other areas—these other uses you are proposing—are not for public use and enjoyment; they're zones of private interest. When the Kennecott Mining company says it is interested in making money for its stockholders, this is a perfectly proper interest, but it should be balanced."

The BLM proposals provided a degree of short-term protection. Silcock was right that in the immediate future not many private interests would try to stake a claim in the Brooks Range. But for the long term, I doubted the lands would be protected at all. Silcock was willing to consider more protection but not without specific plans, and in 1969 neither Peggy nor I knew enough to supply those specifics. We parted from Silcock on very amiable terms, grateful that he and his deputies had shown us more of Alaska's great lands and hopeful that they would step up efforts to protect these places.

In AUGUST 1969, the twentieth conference of the American Association for the Advancement of Science convened in Alaska. The list of attendees read like a Who's Who in Alaska: politicians, bureaucrats, professors, conservationists, and oil men all converged on the University of Alaska campus in Fairbanks to discuss the future of the North Slope. Of course, the dominant question was the future of oil. Only a few days after the end of the conference, oil and gas leases for 430,000 acres on the Arctic slope were to be sold. Talk ran wild of a billion dollars in state revenue from the leases, a staggering figure in the minds of most Alaskans.

An imbroglio of money and power and land was shaping up in Alaska, with the Arctic slope as the main stage. To the industry, the North Slope represented unparalleled potential for profit. To politicians and bureaucrats, it represented state revenue, new jobs, and the chance to establish Alaska as an economic power. For academics and scientists, the North Slope would be a laboratory to test theories. Conservationists, for their part, saw mainly the potential for desecration and massive pollution of the Arctic landscape. Oddly underrepresented at the conference were the Alaska Natives, who in the next few years would become a force that few at the conference could predict.

Though opinions on the state's future covered a wide spectrum, everyone agreed that Alaska had reached the point of no return. The state was about to shed its bushman's clothing for a three-piece suit.

Much of the debate at the conference centered on the route of the proposed pipeline—known as the Trans-Alaska Pipeline System (TAPS)—

from Prudhoe Bay to Valdez. The three giants—ARCO, Humble, and British Petroleum—had already filed that spring for a right-of-way from the Department of the Interior. The companies claimed that mounting tensions in the Middle East, which supplied most U.S. oil, warranted immediate action. Pressed by a self-imposed deadline, they had already contracted with three Japanese firms to supply the forty-eight-inch pipe, much to the chagrin of American steel companies and Pennsylvania representative John Saylor.

Representing conservation interests at the conference, I outlined a variety of concerns about development in Alaska's far north. To start with, the debacle precipitated by building a "winter road" from Fairbanks to the North Slope in 1968–69 raised serious doubts about the state's ability carry out a project like the proposed pipeline. Governor Hickel had pushed the road through after truckers in Fairbanks complained that the airlines were making all the money flying freight to the Arctic, but from start to finish, the project was a disaster. Open for just one month and costing twice the estimated expense, the road carried only a fraction of what the airlines transported. And its planning and construction defied the realities of Alaska's climate and landscape. Instead of building on top of the tundra, the state highway department removed the blanketing layer, exposing the frozen soil. When the warm spring rains came, the soil melted, turning the area into a purposeless swamp and a blight on the landscape. Secretary Hickel was humiliated, and many became distrustful of the state's ability to develop its lands properly.

Now the state wanted the federal government to grant access for another road and an eight-hundred-mile pipeline—a much more complicated technological feat. I didn't want a pipeline built. I didn't believe anyone knew how. Despite all the presentations and materials provided by the oil companies, there were simply too many unanswered questions. The companies maintained that nearly all of the pipeline would be underground, but it seemed unlikely that the research for such construction had been completed in the year since the oil strike.

In the winter of 1968–69, the companies were still considering transporting the oil via tanker. Eight months later, at the time of the conference, they had settled definitively on the pipeline. To prevent the oil from congealing into tar on its long journey, it would have to be kept hot while being pumped through arctic conditions, while passing through several ecological zones. Issues of permafrost, fault zones, and extreme seasonal temperature variations would have to be resolved. Alternative routes had not been fully explored, nor had research been conducted to assess the pipeline's impact on Arctic wildlife. Furthermore, the U.S. Geological Survey had concluded that no pipeline could safely be laid below ground north of the Brooks Range.

Throughout the discussions the oil companies presented themselves as concerned people who were just trying to help Alaska, and they promised to take every precaution to minimize the project's effects on the landscape and wildlife. British Petroleum even offered interested conference attendees a one-day flight and field tour of its facilities on the North Slope—an excursion similar to dozens of "show-me" trips I'd been on. Playing into old myths of the Alaska wilds, BP spokesmen referred to the North Slope as a barren land of ice and snow, intimating that drilling wells would bring little change. It was true that there was little development in 1969—just a few lone wells pumping in a vast sweep of tundra. However, only the shortsighted could be fooled into thinking the North Slope would remain undeveloped. Indeed, the same area today is nearly unrecognizable thanks to large-scale industrial development. Of course, many of those on the trip didn't care what happened to the North Slope as long as it generated state revenue.

Since the start of the conference, I had been anticipating the key luncheon speaker, Alaska's senator Ted Stevens, recently appointed to replace the deceased Senator Bartlett. A Harvard law graduate, Stevens had spent four years as assistant solicitor for the Department of the Interior. We conservationists had lauded his selection and anticipated that Stevens would be a strong voice for conservation in Alaska; we also hoped to tap his expertise and connections within Interior and its management agencies, including the BLM and Fish and Wildlife.

Stevens's lunchtime address, however, delivered a stunning blow. The senator personally was going to see to it that the pipeline went through as fast as possible. He railed against outsiders intruding in the affairs of his state. Referring to the difficulties in campaigning for statehood a decade earlier, Stevens bellowed, "Where were all you termites when we needed you?" The assembled group of distinguished academics and scientists sat speechless over their dessert plates. The speech surpassed provincialism; Stevens came off sounding like a complete redneck. When he had finished, a flabbergasted Richard Cooley—chair of the luncheon and author of several books on Alaska—offered me several minutes to respond to the senator. I replied that there was no need for a rebuttal; Stevens had already taken care of that himself.

A few voices, at least, cautioned against moving ahead full speed on the pipeline. Former governor Walter Hickel, now secretary of the interior, and his undersecretary, Russell Train, demanded that public hearings take place before any lifting of the land freeze established in 1966 by former interior secretary Udall to prevent premature transfers of federal land. Train scheduled the hearings for immediately after the conference, and Brock Evans (the Sierra Club's Northwest representative) and I spent much of the intervening time forming a conservation coalition to testify against the pipeline.

Two days after the end of the AAAS conference, the Interior Department hearings convened in Fairbanks on whether or not the oil companies should be granted a permit to construct a Trans-Alaska pipeline. Brock Evans and I succeeded in our efforts to bring together a conservationist block, with the Sierra Club speaking up first to oppose the pipeline and several local organizations supporting that position. Particularly outspoken was Gordon Wright, a Club member who chaired the University of Alaska's Music Department and also conducted the Fairbanks Symphony. Years later, I learned that after Wright testified, some symphony patrons wrote to the university asking for his dismissal. Wright must have been told to tone down his anti-oil views, for he later allied himself with the more moderate, university-centered Alaska Conservation Society.

But the forces aligned in support of the pipeline were too strong. After considerable improvement in the oil companies' plans, the Interior Department allowed the consortium—soon to be known as the Alyeska Pipeline and Service Company—to move forward with its proposals. Meanwhile, the Sierra Club board of directors discussed bringing a lawsuit against the Interior Department. Lowell Tupling, the Club's Washington, D.C., representative, did the principal research to determine if the Club wanted to pursue such action. The suit would claim that TAPS violated the 1920 Mineral Leasing Act (which granted a fifty-four-foot right-of-way, not one hundred feet as TAPS was proposing) and the newly passed National Environmental Protection Act of 1969, which mandated environmental impact statements for all proposed developments on federal land. TAPS had not filed such a statement.

Along with the Wilderness Society, Friends of the Earth, and the Environmental Defense Fund, the Sierra Club engaged the nonprofit Center for Law in the Public Interest to represent us. James Moorman was the firm's lead attorney on the case. As the filing date approached, however, I received a telephone message from the Alaska chapter that a lawsuit at this time could kill the chapter's current major project: lobbying the state legislature to establish a 500,000-acre state park in the Chugach Mountains. They were making good headway, which they felt would be lost when the Club's role in such a lawsuit became public, and asked us to wait until after the legislative session adjourned.

The board had a tacit policy of deferring to local chapters on local issues, and we agreed to postpone filing. But Moorman and Lloyd Tupling, who was also working hard on the case, maintained that time was of the essence: Secretary Hickel was expected to issue a decision on TAPS in fall 1970. Moorman insisted the case go forward promptly, and the suit was filed—on behalf of the other three conservation groups. Even though the Sierra Club's name did not appear, for years most people believed the Club had brought the suit.

The Club and its allies would continue to fight the Trans-Alaska Pipeline for another five years, in the courts and in Congress. Ultimately, Congress approved the project in 1973, with then vice president Spiro Agnew casting the deciding vote in the Senate, and construction began in 1974. Many issues involving Native claims, routing of the pipeline, and environmental safeguards were brought forward and settled along the way—some favorably and others not. Undoubtedly the project as built was safer, due to our efforts, than it might otherwise have been, but its future safety remains uncertain. And it set a precedent for development in the remote Arctic that will pose a constant challenge to environmentalists as far ahead as we can see.

CHAPTER SEVEN

ALASKA

Litigation and Legislation, 1970–1975

❦

The Alaskan land is alive with change.
It is being continuously worked on by glaciers,
chiseled by rivers, beaten and drenched by storms,
shattered and remodeled by alternate freezing and
thawing, showered with incandescent dust, and
jarred and upthrust in massive earthquakes.

—Peggy Wayburn, *Alaska: The Great Land*

THE NATIVE TLINGITS call it Kootznoowoo, "Fortress of the Bears." The name is fitting: Admiralty Island's forests and mountains contain the world's highest concentration of brown bears. The island is also a superb nesting place for eagles and a range for the black-tailed Sitka deer. In its only town, Angoon, five hundred Tlingits continue a largely traditional existence; otherwise the island is uninhabited save for a few fishing bays scattered along the shores. There are few private holdings. Surrounded by the Inside Passage on all sides, the island is a complete ecosystem unto itself, a living, evolving history. Life there has continued undisturbed for thousands of years. There is no comparable island of forest wilderness left in the world.

But in the early 1970s, the island and all its peerless wilderness values were on the brink of being sacrificed to purely economic needs. In 1968, the U.S. Forest Service had contracted with U.S. Plywood–Champion Paper, Inc., to lease half of Admiralty Island for logging—part of a multimillion-dollar timber sale in the Tongass National Forest, the third such in the years since 1955. It was the largest single attempted act of natural destruction ever in the United States: the clear-cutting of a million acres of wilderness spread over the western half of Admiralty, the mainland forest across Stephens Passage, and the Yakutat forelands, 150 miles northwest of Juneau on the Gulf of Alaska.

The Forest Service's decision to lease was confirmed to me by Regional Forester Howard Johnson in late summer of 1969. Johnson didn't share the particulars then; it would be several months before details surfaced. Of the approximately 8.75 billion board feet of commercial timber in these areas, the Forest Service had committed all. The numbers spoke for themselves: if Champion were allowed to log, virtually every virgin tree on Admiralty's western side would be cut in the next fifty years. Experts agreed that it would take 120 to 130 years for the forest to regenerate fully. If the Forest Service had thought about the fate of the local wildlife—including the bears, eagles, and Sitka deer—thinking was all it did. No special provisions had been taken to ensure the animals' survival. Johnson's all-encompassing priority was boosting the local economy.

Although the logging would be on federal land, the harvested logs and pulp were not even destined for the American lumber business. Champion had dedicated the first fifteen years' worth of cuts for distribution among several Japanese companies. Having overcut its own stands during World War II, Japan was now in desperate need of foreign timber. So while the Forest Service's own charter explicitly states that national forests may be logged to provide for *American* needs, the Champion sale clearly was fulfilling a foreign demand.

The terms of the sale also stipulated that Champion build a pulp mill to stimulate the local economy. The decision on where to locate it had been narrowed to two sites: Berner's Bay, thirty miles north of Juneau on the mainland, and Katlian Bay, just north of Sitka.

My determination to push for a national monument on Admiralty did not at first stem from a deep personal connection with the land. That would come later. But it didn't take such familiarity to recognize that Admiralty represented a unique opportunity for conservation in Southeast. Whereas Forest Service logging had already scarred vast patches of the Tongass National Forest, Admiralty had remained virtually untouched:

a million acres of virgin Sitka spruce dotted with hemlock. Flying over its shores, I had been struck by its grandeur: a vast, unbroken canopy of primeval forest giving way to great humps of open and snow-streaked mountains at the higher elevations.

Aside from the potential desecration of critical habitat, the Champion contract represented everything that was wrong with Forest Service logging policies in the Tongass: the exchange of irreplaceable natural resources for short-term economic gain. Instead of concerning itself with the stewardship and responsible logging of its stands, the Forest Service was acting as an employment agency. There were two mills already in existence: one at Ketchikan, the other in Sitka. A third mill threatened to alter the Southeast landscape—and its air and water quality—irrevocably.

Several events during my summer 1969 visit convinced me, and ultimately the Sierra Club, that we had to take legal action on Admiralty. The day after meeting with Howard Johnson of the Forest Service, I met with Gerald Jackson, vice president of U.S. Plywood–Champion Paper and its director for the Alaska area. Jackson said he was determined to cut the forest "right" or not at all. To show the company's good intentions, Champion had assembled a team of seven independent ecological experts. My heart sank as Jackson produced the list. Two of the seven were friends: Stanley Cain, with whom I had worked during his tenure as assistant secretary of the interior for fish, wildlife, and parks under Presidents Kennedy and Johnson, and Starker Leopold, the dedicated forester whose descriptions of Alaska had enraptured Peggy at the 1963 Wilderness Conference. I found it hard to swallow that two avowed conservationists could be on the payroll of the lumber company.

That night we went with Sierra Club members Isabelle and Joe McLean to Mike's, a popular restaurant across the bay from Juneau. On the other side of the dining room sat Leopold, Cain, and the other expert consultants. Running into them was a coincidence but not a great surprise. Alaska's population was still small, its circle of decision makers— bureaucrats, politicians, academics, and businessmen—even smaller. The two tables at first stared at each other without saying anything. I felt betrayed, too disappointed to speak.

Halfway through the meal, Leopold and Cain came over. "Ed, I want you to know I'm not selling out," Leopold said. "We're going to do a fair job. I have my integrity."

They argued that it was better to have allies as experts rather than timber insiders. This way, I could be assured the study would be accurate. I had to agree. Although I was loath to entertain the idea of conservationists accepting money from logging interests, deep down there was no question of Leopold's or Cain's integrity. Leopold assured me that the results of the study would be made public. He had personally seen to it that Champion included public disclosure of the study's results as one of the terms of his contract.

I believed Leopold, but I was still furious with the Forest Service. The next morning, I called a meeting in our room at the Baranof Hotel. Attending were George Collins, a former NPS land planner, and Dick and Doris Leonard, who happened to be in Alaska at the same time. Doris Leonard and Collins were two of the three members of the Conservation Associates, formed to be a liaison between industry and environmental groups. I proposed to them—as conservationists and Club leaders—that Sierra Club bring a lawsuit. Dick Leonard, who was sympathetic to big business, said he didn't think we should sue Champion since the study was being conducted through outside experts.

Champion would not be the target, I explained. Given everything I'd heard, they were proceeding reasonably; besides, they were a business and expected to pursue a profit. My complaint lay with the U.S. Forest Service, a federal agency charged with the care of our country's forests. The agency was failing its own charter, failing to protect and perpetuate the national forests. In its self-conceived mission to boost the area's faltering economy, it was putting private interests over public.

I felt strongly that this was our last chance to save a great wilderness and to set a precedent for land protection based on true ecologically sensible boundaries. The entire west side of Admiralty Island was slated for logging, with a paved road through the middle of the island. I believed we had reached a point of no return in Alaska: between the oil strike and state selections, the Great Land was being sliced up for private economic purposes. In addition, Native Alaskans, who for decades had sought compensation for lands lost to white settlers, had finally formed a powerful alliance and were beginning to press hard for land selection legislation in Congress. We had to push now. In a few years, there wouldn't be anything left to push for.

It was against this backdrop that we decided to proceed with a lawsuit against the Forest Service. The Sierra Club was not eager to take this historic action. Our experience with litigation had been extremely limited; the Legal Defense Fund had yet to be formed. Financially, the Club was still recovering from Brower's ambitious publishing program. And there were still some conservative directors, such as Dick Leonard, who believed that the Forest Service's panel of independent experts would provide an adequate safety net against overlogging.

We weren't even sure to what extent we had standing to sue. The right of the Sierra Club (or of any conservation organization) to sue a federal management agency remained untested. Environmental law was still in its infancy, and in 1970 a legal precedent for the Champion case simply didn't exist. The Supreme Court's now-famous decision in the case of *Sierra Club v. Morton*—the Club's bid to keep the Disney Company from developing California's Mineral King Valley into a ski resort—occurred *after* we had filed our case for Admiralty. Although the court initially denied Sierra Club standing in that case, it liberalized the rules of standing by thereafter permitting suits to be brought by those who did not have a pecuniary interest in the matter at hand, but only a recreation interest. (See chapter 4.) This decision was not in place, however, at the time the Club was considering a suit over Admiralty.

Nevertheless, I felt we had little choice. Despite the myriad arguments against it, the fact remained that if we did not sue, Admiralty would be logged. My attempts to negotiate with Johnson had failed; legal action was our last resort. And even a lawsuit represented only a temporary fix. Even if we could halt the sale to Champion, the Forest Service eventually would rework the lease and find another buyer. Only a presidential decree or an act of Congress could save Admiralty permanently.

Like the Dinosaur campaign, the USFS Champion suit would push the Club into a new arena of conservation tactics. Long gone were the days when Sierra Club members, as friendly advisors, were prohibited from criticizing the policies of the management agencies. The case would also have a lasting effect on the Club, establishing litigation as a useful, sometimes even necessary, strategy.

In December 1969, Champion announced its decision to build the new mill at Berner's Bay. Several weeks later, *Industry Week* carried a brief news item about the sale titled "Placate Conservationist by Getting Him Involved." The article boasted of how Champion executives had averted a potential snafu with environmentalists by creating an ecologically minded panel of experts to help with its planning. Champion had in fact established such a panel, and the article implied that it aided the two sides in reaching a mutual understanding: "The site and construction recommendations were acceptable to the company, and the conservation groups were pleased with the final plan." No one at the Sierra Club, however, had received copies of or been consulted about the mill plans; nor had the panel experts, including Starker Leopold, yet begun their research.

Two weeks after the *Industry Week* article appeared, Donald Harris, chair of the Club's Legal Committee, announced that the Alaska Chapter of the Sierra Club, the Sitka Conservation Society, and master guide Karl Lane were filing a complaint against the secretary of agriculture, the chief of the U.S. Forest Service, and Regional Forester Howard Johnson. The basis of the suit was twofold. First, the Forest Service was failing in its chartered purpose to provide a continuous supply of timber for the use of and necessities of American citizens. Second, the Champion contract violated the Multiple Use and Sustained Yield Act of 1960, which mandated that uses other than logging—such as recreation, watershed, wildlife, and fishing—be balanced in the use of national forests.

The suit was not against Champion. As a private business, Champion could not be held to the same standards as the Forest Service. Like any company, Champion was simply trying to make a profit. Its president, Karl Bendetson, thought he was getting a good deal.

We tried to cover our bases. In 1970, the Sierra Club was recognized as a national organization; the Sitka Conservation Society represented regional interests. Of prime importance, too, was the need to establish our suit as a response to local economic concerns, to counter the Forest

Service's own justification for the lease. Although Admiralty Island was part of the Tongass National Forest, many Alaskans considered the stands "theirs" and viewed any attempt at federal preservation as encroaching on their turf. The case would be tried in an Alaska courtroom and ruled on by a federal judge who was a longtime Alaskan. We needed to look as close to home as possible, so we searched for a local individual to join the suit. Fortunately, Karl Lane stepped forward. A master guide, Lane was one of a privileged few granted the right to lead big game hunting and photographic expeditions to Admiralty Island. If the sale were enforced, Lane contended, his business would suffer irreparable damage.

Soon after the suit was filed, Champion (now named Champion International Corporation) and the State of Alaska, which felt it too had a vested economic interest in the sale, joined the Forest Service as codefendants. The trial date was set for November 1970. When Peggy and I stopped in to meet with Howard Johnson that summer, he said that he was so busy with the lawsuit, he hadn't had time to follow up on any of our other recommendations. Our discussions thereupon came to an end; within a couple of years, Johnson would be replaced.

While preparing our case, the Sierra Club sent forester Gordon Robinson to Alaska to assess the feasibility and pricing of the Champion lease. Some years earlier, Robinson, who had been chief forester for Southern Pacific Land Company, left his job because of what he viewed as overly aggressive cutting of the company's stands. Now he worked as an independent consultant and as a forest researcher for the Club; we had hired him on several projects before, including our proposal for Redwood National Park. We hoped he would provide expert testimony at the trial.

When it came to hiring a lawyer, again we needed someone local. For advice we turned to Donald Harris and Fred Fisher, who had done pro bono work for the Club and who would soon form the Sierra Club Legal Defense Fund. When their first suggestion, an experienced Alaska lawyer, was unavailable to take the case, they suggested Warren ("Skip") Mathews. Then just two years out of Harvard Law School, Mathews had impressed Harris and Fisher when he had clerked several summers earlier at their San Francisco firm. After graduating, Mathews had returned to Alaska, his home state, to open a practice in Anchorage. There was no doubt that Mathews was green—the Champion suit would be his first major case—but the Club was impressed enough to hire him.

Although we talked considerably on the telephone that summer and fall, I didn't meet Mathews until the trial began in November. On a gray November day, I sat in a courtroom of the Juneau federal courthouse. A fair number of the public seats were filled, and the spectators were clearly divided. I sat on the left side with a dozen Sierra Club members and a few local sympathizers. On the right were several witnesses for the defense, and members of the Forest Service. An impressive crew of half a dozen lawyers was assembled at the defense table: Champion, the Forest Service, and the state each had independent counsel. They spoke in low voices, compared notes. On the left stood the solitary figure of Skip Mathews. Of medium build and thirty years old at most, Mathews did not project the same formidable image as the defense team.

Of greater concern than the disparity in legal counsel, however, was the black-robed man who sat between the two sides, who would decide the fate of Admiralty Island—Federal Judge Raymond Plummer. Now in his sixties, Judge Plummer was an old-time Alaska judge who, from what we gathered, favored industry over preservation, state control over federal regulation. I never doubted that our side was in the right, but I knew trials weren't always decided on that basis. Howard Johnson and his predecessor, Frank Heintzelman, had left a legacy in Southeast. The Forest Service was highly regarded locally as a source of employment and economic aid to a troubled region—and we suspected its admirers included Plummer.

Mathews knew he had his work cut out for him, but from the very beginning he proved an able litigator. Composed, prepared, articulate, Mathews may have been young, but he was no amateur. I was the first witness, called to testify on the issues of *laches*—why the Club had waited so long to file suit. I explained that while the Forest Service may have negotiated the contract months earlier, we had learned of the lease only in the summer of 1969. I felt my testimony went smoothly.

Although I had intended to stay for the duration of the trial, my aunt Maude, with whom I had stayed when I first came to San Francisco, died shortly after its start. I returned to San Francisco immediately.

▲ ▲ Celebration for the tenth anniversary of the establishment of the Golden Gate National Recreation Area, 1982. Left to right: San Francisco assemblyman Frank Foran; then-superintendent of the GGNRA Jack Davis; Bill Whelan, first superintendent of the GGNRA; Amy Meyer; Ed Wayburn; Congressman Phil Burton; and Congressman William Mailliard. NATIONAL PARK SERVICE PHOTOGRAPH COURTESY THE GGNRA ARCHIVE.

◄ Archivist Ann Lage presents Ed Wayburn with the first volume of his Oral History at a Sierra Club banquet in 1985. PHOTOGRAPH COURTESY THE SIERRA CLUB. ► Ed Wayburn presents the Sierra Club's John Muir Award to Wallace Stegner at a Sierra Club banquet in 1982. PHOTOGRAPH COURTESY THE SIERRA CLUB.

▲▲ Ed Wayburn introduces Senator Alan Cranston at the 1985 California Wilderness Conference, where Senator Cranston announced that he was about to introduce a major protection bill for the California desert. PHOTOGRAPH COURTESY THE SIERRA CLUB.

▲ Ed Wayburn with Congresswoman Barbara Boxer at the Wayburns' Bolinas home during a fund-raiser for the Sierra Club San Francisco Bay Chapter political committee, ca. 1987. PHOTOGRAPH COURTESY THE WAYBURN FAMILY.

▲▲ Ed and Peggy Wayburn at Milford Sound in Fiordland National Park on the South Island, New Zealand, December 1988. PHOTOGRAPH COURTESY THE WAYBURN FAMILY. ◀ Ed and Peggy visiting nature parks in Italian Tyrol, May 1989. PHOTOGRAPH COURTESY THE WAYBURN FAMILY. ▶ The Wayburns at their Anniversary Redwood Grove in Redwood National Park, 1994. PHOTOGRAPH COURTESY THE NATIONAL PARK SERVICE.

▲ ▲ Peggy and Ed picketing with the Sierra Student Coalition at the U.S. Capitol in March 1995. PHOTOGRAPH COURTESY THE SIERRA CLUB. ▲ The Wayburn family after the ceremony honoring Ed with the Albert Schweitzer Prize for humanitarianism in April 1995. Left to right: Diana, Cynthia, Peggy, Ed, Laurie, and William. PHOTOGRAPH BY ROBERT J. SMITH JR. COURTESY THE WAYBURN FAMILY.

▲ ▲ Ed and Peggy Wayburn with their host, Andreas Grauel, arriving at his home in Southeast Alaska in July 1995. PHOTOGRAPH BY LOU GRAUEL COURTESY THE WAYBURN FAMILY. ◀ Ed and Peggy on the 1998 Sierra Club John Muir Society outing to Southeast Alaska. PHOTOGRAPH BY NANCY KITTLE COURTESY THE SIERRA CLUB. ▶ At Ed's ninetieth birthday party at his Bolinas home, in September 1996, Congresswoman Nancy Pelosi reads a congratulatory message from President Clinton. PHOTOGRAPH BY MARK FRASER COURTESY THE WAYBURN FAMILY.

▲ ▲ Ed and Peggy with President Bill Clinton during a 1998 presidential visit to San Francisco. PHOTOGRAPH BY PAUL PELOSI COURTESY THE WAYBURN FAMILY. ▲ Ed Wayburn with Congressman George Miller at a February 1999 press event in San Francisco. PHOTOGRAPH COURTESY THE WAYBURN FAMILY.

▲ ▲ President Bill Clinton awards Ed Wayburn the Presidential Medal of Freedom, the highest award bestowed by the nation on a civilian, August 1999. PHOTOGRAPH COURTESY THE WHITE HOUSE. ▲ At an Alaska Conservation Foundation dinner in February 2000 honoring the Wayburns, David Rockefeller presents Ed and Peggy with a plaque. PHOTOGRAPH COURTESY THE ALASKA CONSERVATION FOUNDATION.

▲ Ed with Michael Adams at the Sierra Club's historic LeConte Memorial Lodge in Yosemite Valley, September 2002. PHOTOGRAPH COURTESY JEANNE ADAMS.

The trial continued for a week after I left. Forester Gordon Robinson testified on several matters. His research had proved the Champion contract to be highly problematic and the lease fundamentally flawed. First, it called for excessive cutting. By inflating the number of commercial-quality trees in its stands, the Forest Service was able to likewise inflate the allowable cut. In truth, there wasn't enough timber to fulfill the Champion contract under a plan of sustained yield management as mandated by Forest Service guidelines. Second, the lease encouraged destructive logging practices such as clear-cutting, which would remove the humus and topsoil. These layers would take hundreds of years to regenerate, even longer in tracts where 50 percent or more of the slopes were clear-cut. Nearly a third of the Admiralty Island tracts fell into this category.

Finally, Robinson concluded, the Forest Service was leasing the timber at well below market value. He reviewed fifty timber sales in Southeast Alaska and the Pacific Northwest over the previous decade, calculating an average price of $33 per thousand board feet for spruce and $8.50 per thousand board feet of hemlock. Conceivably Alaska's spruce could have gone for even more, considering that it was the world's finest old-growth softwood for pulp. Despite this, prices for the Champion lease averaged $6.54 per thousand board feet of spruce and $5.10 for the same measure of hemlock.

Plummer did not rule until May 1971, several months after the close of trial. He agreed that the Forest Service had made an "overwhelming commitment of the Tongass National Forest to timber and harvest objectives in preference to other multiple use values." Yet despite Robinson's testimony and the lack of any published findings by Champion's own panel of experts, Plummer found no evidence that the Forest Service either lacked the knowledge necessary to make such a decision or that it had ignored the conclusions of the available studies when committing the forest.

In other words, as long as the foresters had *considered* multiple use values, Plummer ruled, they did not need to *employ* them in their decision. Instead of being held to the highest example, the U.S. Forest Service— guardian of the country's most precious stands—was being held to the lowest possible standards. The right to choose the fate of Admiralty Island, even badly, remained in the hands of misguided agency men like Howard Johnson.

I had been skeptical of our chances but secretly hoped that I would be proved wrong—that Judge Plummer would prove sympathetic to our arguments. However, when the ruling was handed down, I was not surprised. Plummer had made it clear that he didn't buy our arguments, and we had anticipated losing. We moved immediately to appeal to the Ninth Circuit Court of Appeals.

THE APPEALS COURT was not due to consider our case until September 1972, and in the meantime, Peggy and I had much more of Alaska to explore. We had learned that flying was the best, sometimes the only, way to get where we wanted to go, and we couldn't always depend on agency planes to fly us around. So we were lucky in more ways than one to meet Jim Roush in 1969. He had been recommended by Sierra Club staffer Denny Wilcher, who had met the young pilot in Seattle. Jim had his own plane and was eager to see Alaska's wilds protected. He flew down to San Francisco to meet me and made a generous offer: he would fly Peggy and me wherever we needed to go in Alaska. In essence, Jim volunteered to be our aerial chauffeur.

I accepted gladly. I was beginning to map out the areas I wanted to see protected. Alaska's roads were limited and the country too vast for me to see these places without a plane. While the federal agencies had been helpful and one could also hire local pilots, the state's size and temperamental weather made coordination difficult. News of an impending storm would often force us to cancel flying plans at the last minute. With access to a private plane, we could change our itinerary and venture back to the original destination when the weather cleared.

Jim and I agreed to meet up that summer of 1969. Several days before the planned rendezvous in Fairbanks, however, we received word that Jim had been unexpectedly delayed. He and a friend had been canoeing in Canada's Northwest Territory when the temperature had dropped suddenly, heavy snow fell, and they became weathered in for several days. We connected in Juneau, finally, for the last leg of our journey. Clean-cut and bronzed, Jim flew us south to Seattle in his twin-engine Beechcraft; nicknamed the *Red Baron,* it could hold up to six people without luggage, four with bags and gear.

The next summer, 1970, our youngest daughter, Laurie, then fifteen, came along when Jim flew us up to Denali. That was the year of our first Alaskan river experience. Wayne Boden, the BLM's director of recreation in Alaska, had invited us to canoe the Delta River, which rises in the Tangle Lakes, just off the Denali Highway in the foothills of the Alaskan Range. Its clear, quiet waters flow north through the range itself, the joyous clear stream eventually widening into a silt-laden river, full of rapids until its take-out point on the Richardson Highway. We spent several days traveling down the river; the Delta whetted our appetite for river travel irrevocably. And Jim Roush became increasingly more important to our Alaskan odyssey.

We CONTINUED TO return to Alaska each summer, though our wilderness forays offered only brief respites from conservation politics. By the early 1970s, Alaska had become rife with division. The state was being divvied up, and everyone wanted a big piece of the pie. The state still had not chosen most of the lands it would hold under the statehood act. There was also the flaring issue of claims by the Alaskan Natives, who demanded compensation in return for the United States' acquisition of their traditional lands.

In this period of intense competition, conservationists asked: What lands would be protected? Would Alaska follow a path like that of the contiguous western states? Would it be left, like California, with only beautiful remnants of a once magnificent landscape? My own explorations had left me with the sense that no national park in the lower forty-eight was large enough to accommodate ever-growing visitor demand while ensuring a wilderness experience and maintaining the integrity of its habitat. In Alaska, though, such parks were still possible. There was no comparable untrammeled realm left on earth. To conservationists, Alaska represented our last and most critical opportunity for true wilderness preservation. To all Americans, Alaska represented a last frontier, the last region vast enough to satiate our hunger for adventure.

By the early 1970s, my interest in Alaska's conservation had grown into a devotion, then an obsession. My campaigns to preserve Mount Tamalpais and the redwoods had also been obsessions, but in Alaska, there was so vastly much more to cover, more boundaries to configure, more proposals to be drafted. I was no longer thinking in terms of tens of thousands of acres, but in terms of millions. And I felt at a disadvantage: in those other regions, I had an extensive ground knowledge of each area proposed for protection, but Alaska's scale precluded such an intimate understanding of its whole landscape.

Our summer journeys helped make up some of that ground. We continued to meet with members of the Forest Service, the NPS, the BLM, and the state. I also learned that a small group of conservationists, including Celia Hunter, Mark Hickock, and Richard Gordon, had formed a group called the Wilderness Council, which was mapping out and submitting proposals for state parks, wildlife refuges, and wilderness areas. They would soon become key players in conservation efforts, and I kept in touch with them.

The push for new national parks and wildlife refuges was critical. We couldn't trust the state or the Forest Service; both had proved they would sacrifice wilderness for short-term economic gain. The BLM had dedicated individuals, like Alaska director Burt Silcock, who were concerned about the fate of places like the Brooks Range and the Wrangell Mountains, but they felt that the Bureau had no real authority to protect the land, much less ensure its integrity for future generations.

The only agencies endowed with this protective power were the National Park Service and the U.S. Fish and Wildlife Service, and the NPS had wedged itself into a bureaucratic mind-set concerned more with the administration of parkland than acquiring and protecting more of it. The NPS said its people were stressed enough already; it didn't have the staff to administer a larger domain. I thought the agency was putting the cart before the horse. The only way they would get funding to hire more employees would be to take on more land.

Since my first trip to Alaska, I had been pressing National Park Service director George Hartzog to push for more land. Finally, in the summer of 1971, Hartzog had a change of heart. He called to ask Peggy and me to accompany him and Senator Alan Bible on a survey of proposed national parks in Alaska. Bible and Hartzog were friends. As chairman of both the Senate's Subcommittee on National Parks and the Interior Appropriations Committee, the Nevada senator could make or break a new park. It was critical to win his support for new parklands in Alaska.

Brought into office by Nevada mining interests, Bible began his political career as an ardent supporter of land development and business. He was also a states' rights advocate, wary of federal intervention—no doubt because two-thirds of his state was owned by the federal government. But he ended up as chairman of the National Parks Committee, a job seemingly antithetical to his orientation.

I had first encountered Bible on one of my early visits to Washington, D.C., as Sierra Club president. On these trips, I made it a point to call on our political allies in the Capitol, particularly the important chair of the Interior Committee, Senator Henry M. Jackson. Bible's office was a few doors down from Jackson's, and once, while walking down the hall, I passed his open door and heard him call out: "Hello, Mr. Sierra Club!"

I stepped into the doorway. Bible sat behind his desk, facing the hall. Middle-aged and of medium build, he had an open face and hair that had begun to thin. He was a new senator then from a state with a small population; his office was devoid of callers.

"You're always going to see Senator Jackson," he remarked. "Why don't you ever come and see me?"

From then on I did, later working with Bible and his staff during the campaigns for the GGNRA and Redwoods National Park. When our views were opposed, we agreed to disagree. This mutual respect often fueled our cooperation.

Now, while I looked forward to showing Bible the places in Alaska I had come to love, I was nervous, too, knowing that the trip had to be a success. We were scheduled to show Senator Bible four areas proposed for inclusion in the national park system: Gates of the Arctic and the adjacent large Noatak watershed (15 million acres in all), a 3.5-million-acre expansion of Mt. McKinley National Park, the Wrangell–Saint Elias region (16.5 million acres plus the contiguous Canadian Kluane Game Preserve), and Lake Clark (almost 4 million acres). Unfortunately, the demands of my medical practice kept me from attending the entire trip; Peggy and I were able to accompany the group only to the Gates of the Arctic and Mount McKinley before returning to San Francisco.

The group met in Fairbanks. The evening before our departure for the Brooks Range, Mrs. Bob Bartlett, the widow of Alaska's late senator, threw a party in Bible's honor, but Peggy's and my names were not on the guest list. The Champion suit had rendered the Sierra Club *persona non grata;* as a member of the old guard, Mrs. Bartlett no doubt did not want to see the Club's vice president mentioned in the next day's society pages. It was a difficult time to call oneself a conservationist in Alaska. Many locals considered the label akin to blasphemy.

The plane, a twin-engine Otter, took off from Fairbanks on a cloudy summer morning, headed for the proposed Gates of the Arctic National Park. For almost two hours, we flew north through overcast skies. No one spoke. From the back of the plane, I anxiously watched Senator Bible, seated in front of me. I knew this was our only chance to make a favorable impression; he had never been to Alaska before and wasn't coming back anytime soon. In my mind, the whole prospect could be dashed by clouds—just as fifteen years earlier Newton Drury and Arthur Johnson had stood on a fog-laden ridge of Mount Tamalpais, unaware of the panorama that lay just beyond their view, and saw nothing special about the place.

Suddenly, well north of the Yukon River, the clouds cleared and we looked down on a gorgeous Alaska landscape. As we cruised over the Alatna River, its jade waters and white sandbanks looked like a surreal tropical vision in arctic latitudes. Farther west, we passed over the colorful twisted fingers of the Arrigetch Peaks, where Bob Krumm had flown Peggy and me two summers earlier, and then flew close to snow-streaked Mount Igikpak. We descended over the mirrored surface of Walker Lake and then over the north fork of the Koyukuk River.

Senator Bible sat glued to the window. His stunned silence conveyed more than words. I knew he had never seen the likes of anything below us. Coming from Nevada's desert country, I don't think he could have imagined that such topography even existed. The land spoke for itself, and in my heart I knew he would favor establishing the park. We returned to Fairbanks via the pipeline route and the "Hickel Highway"—the winter road that had become a muddy scar on Alaska's northern visage.

The next day we boarded the train for Mt. McKinley National Park, and later the National Park Service flew us around the park borders. This time the weather cooperated from the start. Denali was in full view from the plane as I explained to Senator Bible that only the northern half of the mountain lay within the park's boundaries. The southern half, with its massive network of glaciers, rivers, and streams, was unprotected.

When Peggy and I left the group to return to San Francisco, we felt confident that Bible would support proposals for a Gates of the Arctic National Park and the expansion of Mt. McKinley National Park. The group would go on to tour the Lake Clark area, but later, when they tried to get to the Wrangell Mountains, the weather did not cooperate. Storms prevented them from flying. Bible never saw that region, and when legislation for its protection finally reached the Senate, Bible did not push for it as hard as he did for the Gates of the Arctic, the McKinley expansion, and Lake Clark.

A MONTH LATER, in September 1971, I was in Washington, D.C., for the Sierra Club board meeting and the Wilderness Conference. When I arrived, Stewart Brandborg, executive director of the Wilderness Society, approached me.

"We have to meet," he said, clearly in a state of distress.

He explained that while Peggy and I had been in Alaska, the Alaska Native Claims Settlement Act (ANCSA) had been moving through the Senate more rapidly than anyone had thought possible. The latest incarnation was sponsored by Senator Jackson but offered the Natives much more land and money than Jackson's previous bills. The year before, Jackson had sponsored a bill for 10 million acres and $100 million; now his figures totaled 40 million acres and $1 billion. (In fact, the Natives would receive a total of 44 million acres, the additional four million for sacred sites.)

Brandborg seemed desperate. "We've lost everything. ANCSA is going through, and there's no provision for parks or refuges or anything else."

Native claims had been an issue even before Seward's purchase of Alaska from Russia. Earlier proposals for small amounts of land and paltry sums of money had been quashed while Alaska was still a territory. Having failed to address the issue since 1867, Congress was now speeding through a lavishly generous bill. While I knew the bill was popular, I had also thought that Wayne Aspinall, Jackson's counterpart in the House, would stop it. The previous year, Jackson had sponsored a much more limited

Settlement Act, only to have it shot down in the House by Aspinall's Interior Committee. But this year the bill had passed the House with Aspinall as a sponsor.

Congress faced a different set of conditions in 1971 than it had ever before. For the first time, the Alaska Natives had developed a powerful lobby, the Alaska Federation of Natives. The AFN included representatives from every tribe in Alaska. Among the Native leaders were many young, energetic folk intent on bringing their people out of subsistence living and into economic parity with the rest of the country. While wishing to retain certain traditions, the new generation of leaders was frustrated with living in poverty. They wanted modern conveniences: telephones, televisions, snowmobiles.

With the Civil Rights movement in full swing, the Alaska Natives found sympathy from many progressives in the lower forty-eight. Liberals saw the act as the opportunity to redress more than a century of neglect. Some perhaps saw the Native Alaskan claims indirectly as a vehicle to alleviate their guilt over the cruel treatment of American Indians, driven out of their traditional homelands and herded onto reservations generations earlier.

The Alaska Native Claims Settlement Act wasn't just about giving the Natives their just due, however. In the rush to build a Trans-Alaska pipeline, the oil companies had met with resistance from Natives along the proposed route—particularly those in Stevens Village on the Yukon River—who did not want a pipeline to pass through their traditional lands. To quell a mounting conflict, Secretary of the Interior Stewart Udall previously had imposed a land freeze, preventing construction of the pipeline until the right-of-way issue was settled. Eager to clarify land rights and lift the freeze as quickly as possible, the oil companies joined the Natives in actively lobbying for compensation.

Suddenly, ANCSA wasn't just about fairness and equity; it was also about the potential of billions of dollars of oil revenue. While the push for Native claims would probably have found eventual success because of strong pro-Native sentiment, the speed and size of the impending settlement were undoubtedly due to the tremendous pressure exerted by oil interests. Together, liberals, Natives, and oil lobbyists formed one of the most unusual coalitions in American history.

I believed that Alaskan Natives deserved compensation. As the land's first human inhabitants, they had forged a harmonious balance with their habitat over thousands of years. They sustained this relationship despite exploitation by Russian and American settlers. Truthfully, though, my mind had been so occupied with park and refuge proposals that I had not followed the issue closely. Brandborg's announcement of a bill speeding through Congress took me completely by surprise.

The figures being talked about seemed almost staggering. The total Native population of Alaska numbered only fifty-one thousand. The bill's land figures translated to more than 780 acres for each Native. And the cash award would not go to individuals or to individual tribes per se. ANCSA called for the formation of twelve regional "corporations," often encompassing different tribes, to be run like any other business, with a board of directors dispensing profits to its members.

I was not happy about this concept. Merging tribes into corporations would only pressure the Natives to log, mine, and lease their traditional lands to developers. It seemed a gross perversion that, after rejecting several earlier attempts for just compensation to protect traditional ways of life, Congress would approve a solution that encouraged the Natives to conduct themselves as businessmen.

The state was being divvied up. What would be left as wilderness? Brandborg wanted to convene a small group knowledgeable about Alaska away from the Wilderness Conference to discuss what to do.

"Let me talk to Senator Jackson," I said.

Jackson was the chairman of the Senate Interior Committee. He was a friendly, broad-shouldered man of medium height. I had worked closely with him and come to trust him during my campaigns for a Redwood National Park.

With Jack Hession, the new Sierra Club conservation representative in Alaska, I walked over to Jackson's office that afternoon. Surrounded by staff and maps, the senator was very busy but took a few minutes to see us. I came right to the point.

"Scoop, last year you sponsored a bill to give the Alaska Natives 10 million acres and $100 million. This year you're sponsoring a bill for 44 million acres and $1 billion. How do you reconcile that with your principles?"

Jackson put his hand on my shoulder. "Ed, if I didn't, Kennedy was ready to sponsor one for 60 million acres. The way things are going in Congress right now, it would have gone through. What I'm offering is a compromise."

"Well, if you've got to do this, how about giving something to the rest of the people of the United States?"

Jackson knew exactly what I meant. "How much do you want?" he asked.

"One hundred fifty million acres."

"Aren't you asking for a lot?"

"I don't think so." I cited Alaska's statistics: 375 million acres, with 104 million acres guaranteed to the state, and now 44 million to the Natives.

"You want too much," he said. "Will 80 million acres satisfy you?"

"It won't satisfy me, but I'll take it."

"All right. I'll get Senator Bible to offer an amendment."

Although I did not know it at the time, 80 million was a number already much discussed. In fact, Representatives John Saylor and Morris Udall in the House had previously proposed an amendment with 80 million acres in land reserves. The Jackson-Bible amendment passed the Senate without difficulty. Since a similar proposal in the House had gained many votes, a conference committee of the two Houses approved Section 17-d(2), the National Interest Land amendment.

The Alaska Native Claims Settlement Act was signed December 17, 1971. As anticipated, ANCSA awarded 44 million acres and nearly $1 billion in compensation from the federal government, to be divided among twelve regional Native corporations. Natives would have seven years to select their lands, and if claims they made for lands immediately surrounding their townships conflicted with proposed state or federal selections, the Native claims would have priority. (As it turned out, the deadline would be postponed several times due to conflicting and unresolved claims.)

Section 17-d(2), covering the federal land reserves, directed the secretary of the interior to select up to 80 million acres of "unreserved" public land suitable for national parks, wildlife refuges, forests, wilderness, and wild and scenic rivers. Because Southeast Alaska was already under the purview of the Forest Service, however, and the 17-d(2) provision did not affect lands already designated as national forest, the fate of such wildernesses as Admiralty and West Chichagof islands remained open.

A deadline was set: the secretary of the interior would have two years, until December 1973, to make recommendations for the 17-d(2) lands. Congress then would have five more years, until 1978, to accept the proposed areas and delineate final boundaries.

It was a victory, yes. ANCSA opened the way to the largest land preservation measure ever. But the real work had yet to begin. Even if Interior's selections concurred with those of conservationists, they would remain recommendations only. It was up to Congress ultimately to decide the future of these lands, to bestow legal protection for posterity. In the meantime, I began to outline the Sierra Club's proposal for the 17-d(2) lands.

IN JULY 1970, Starker Leopold and Reginald Barrett, his research assistant at the University of California, Berkeley, had begun their study on Admiralty Island. As part of Champion's panel of experts, they were to research the effects of the proposed logging on the local wildlife. Since the experts agreed that Admiralty was the most important wilderness in Southeast Alaska, Leopold and Barrett chose to focus their research on the island rather than the other areas outlined in the Champion lease. Barrett would stay on Admiralty until the following July.

In fact, more than two years passed with no word of Leopold's results. In the summer of 1972, before our appeals case on Admiralty came up, I called Leopold several times, anxious to hear of progress of the research. I hoped their work might prove conclusive enough that Champion would pull out of the lease, thereby avoiding a trial. When I spoke to Leopold, his answers were vague, almost evasive. He had yet to reach any conclusive findings, he said; it was also true that his contract forbade him to divulge any results before his report had been completed. Leopold had accepted this condition, assured that the results of his completed study would be made public. It would be another six months before I learned the results of the team's research. In the meantime, we had no other option than to prepare for the appeal.

In September 1972, Angus MacBeth of the Center for Law in the Public Interest presented oral arguments before the Ninth Circuit Court of Appeals for the Sierra Club. MacBeth reiterated the fundamental flaws of the Champion lease and challenged the Forest Service's knowledge of the area as sufficient to draft a workable plan. He cited the agency's refusal to acknowledge any criterion outlined in the Multiple-Use Sustained-Yield Act of 1960 except logging, and noted that local economic benefit was not an acceptable criterion under the act.

MacBeth further argued that the logging would not fulfill a national need, but a foreign nation's need. He also argued that the Forest Service had failed to meet certain established ecological standards: that whereas the contract specified cuts in fifty-year rotations, experts agreed the trees would require 120 years to regenerate. Finally, he asserted that the agency's three-page, after-the-fact Environmental Impact Statement for the proposed mill at Katlian Bay was inadequate under the newly mandated National Environmental Protection Act.

In late January 1973, Leopold and Barrett at last made public the results of their research. The report, "Implications for Wildlife of the 1968 Juneau Timber Sale," was prefaced with a disclaimer saying that the findings did not necessarily reflect those of Champion. Leopold and Barrett concluded that "the 1968 timber sale contract between the U.S. Forest Service and U.S. Plywood–Champion Paper, Inc., seems to us to imply a level of timber removal in Southeast Alaska that is unrealistic by present-day standards of ecological acceptability." They recommended that no more than a third of the stands in any area be cut at one time, and that certain critical wildlife areas be preserved from any cutting whatsoever.

The first of the Sierra Club's arguments about the 1968 contract was confirmed. Hoping to avoid continued litigation, the Club asked Chief Forester John McGuire to reconsider the Champion contract in light of Leopold and Barrett's report. Initially, McGuire refused.

Two weeks after Leopold and Barrett's report became public, James Moorman, now the first executive director of the newly formed Sierra Club Legal Defense Fund, petitioned the appellate court to remand the case to the district court for reconsideration of the new evidence. The court agreed, ruling:

We conclude that the motion should be granted. . . . What is
here at stake is of such import as to call for the consideration of
the District Court. For . . . the purposes of this order, we accept
this interpretation with the caution that "due consideration" to us
requires that the values in question be informedly and rationally
in balance. The requirement can hardly be satisfied by a . . .
showing of knowledge of the consequences and a decision to
ignore them.

In December 1973, several members of the Sierra Club—including
Jim Moorman, Club staff representatives Brock Evans and Mike McCloskey,
forester Gordon Robinson, and myself—met with Chief Forester
McGuire, his staff, and the attorneys for the Forest Service. A Forest
Service attorney said he doubted that they could get out of the contract at
this point, but that they could "maneuver considerably" within its terms.

McGuire was not ready for serious change, however. He admitted
that, if he'd been in charge when the contract was drafted, he would have
altered a few conditions, such as raising the prices and slowing the construction of the mill. But he did not favor large-scale revision and thought
that the Forest Service had to proceed cautiously. At most, he would revise
the terms one at a time. He did not intend to renege on the contract.
Given McGuire's pace, I feared that Admiralty would be mostly cut by the
time the Forest Service had even begun to plod. We left the meeting
without resolution; the case would go back to trial. It would be another
two-year wait.

Jim Roush was unable to pilot us for our visit in the summer of 1973.
Peggy and I flew into Anchorage, where we met Jack Hession, who had
worked as the Sierra Club's conservation representative in Alaska for
several years. We flew a small commercial charter west to King Salmon,
where we hired a bush pilot named Jay Hammond to fly us down
the Alaska Peninsula and over the Aniakchak crater in his single-engine
prewar plane.

In addition to being a pilot and a master guide, Hammond until
recently had been a state senator. He was a Republican but was interested

in conservation and had opposed Governor Hickel's development policies. He had served in the state senate for several terms until Democratic redistricting the year before had all but ruined the chances of any Republican being reelected in his area. As we flew, he would point out off-road vehicle tracks over the tundra below.

He flew us over the wilderness of Katmai National Monument, over Becharof Lake and the upper part of the Alaska Peninsula, and southwest as far as the huge, impressive snow-splashed Aniakchak Crater. We passed over the town of Dillingham and the Wood River–Tikchik Lakes, their surfaces reflecting the morning's cumulus clouds. We left Hammond at Bethel, the limit of his territory. (Most of Alaska's bush pilots limited themselves to specific areas within which they could navigate expertly.) Though he would not have believed it possible then, Jay Hammond would become Alaska's governor in the fall of the next year.

That summer we initiated a series of meetings with the newly formed Native corporations to forge working relationships and to determine to what extent their claims would conflict with our proposals for the d(2) lands. In Dillingham we met with the heads of the Bristol Bay Corporation, a Native corporation based there. With more than five thousand members, Bristol Bay Corporation comprised some twenty-nine villages and represented about 8 percent of Alaska's Native population.

From Bethel, a second pilot flew us north to Kotzebue; from there, a third would take us to our meeting with the Arctic Slope Regional Corporation in Barrow. During the last leg of the journey, the weather turned against us. As we flew over the Noatak River, clouds were gathering to the north over the Brooks Range, whose gray-streaked peaks stood between us and the North Slope. We were unable to find any clear routes through the range. The pilot tried at least four different passes but all failed; they were too heavily clouded, and the plane could go no higher.

The Arctic Slope Regional Corporation had a reputation for being touchy about missed appointments, or we would have decided against another try. The pilot said he would make one last attempt. Peering out the windshield, I recognized the brown-and-white pattern of the new snow on the tundra below—we were back at the first pass we had attempted. The small plane was equipped with an alarm that would sound whenever the heaving winds pushed the nose up too high to continue forward safely. It sounded several times, and the plane began to shudder. Seated in back and unable to see out the front window, Peggy and Jack Hession were very frightened that we would crash. Then suddenly, all was quiet and we emerged over the flatland of the North Slope. I went to sleep. We reached Barrow safely and our meeting proceeded as scheduled.

That summer Jack and his wife, Mary Kaye, had invited us to kayak down the Alatna River. From previous air trips with the BLM and the NPS trip with Senator Bible, we had spotted the Alatna as one of the rivers we most wanted to see protected.

We flew to a small lake high in the Brooks Range. The weather was quietly drizzling; we set up our tents and settled in for a rainy night. The following morning, we packed our Klepper folding kayaks a quarter of a mile to the headwaters of the Alatna River in the heart of the proposed Gates of the Arctic National Park. We assembled the kayaks, stashed our gear, and pushed off. That first day, the Alatna fulfilled its magnificent promise. The sun soon emerged, and we glided silently down the Alatna's waters, a clear and brilliant turquoise. White sand banks bounded the river on both sides. To our west, Arrigetch Creek tumbled down the steep slopes of the Arrigetch Peaks into a broad, U-shaped valley. Later in the day, we saw black clouds in the northern distance, swelling around the summit ridges of the Brooks Range. We passed the first night quietly.

The second day, the clouds moved closer and the water grew increasingly turbid. That night we dined on the Alatna's sandy shores but at Jack's insistence camped on the highest ground of a small island four feet above the river's surface, anchoring our boats to a log beside our tents. During the night, I dreamed that rain began to fall heavily, that the river was rising and our tents were about to flood. The next morning, I stuck my boot outside the tent and hit water.

"Well, I'll be damned!" I exclaimed. The rain had indeed been falling during the night. The river had risen and now lapped at the edges of the tent. Our kayaks bobbed on the surface, tugging against their tow lines. The spot where we had eaten dinner was submerged under three feet of water. Had Jack not made us anchor the kayaks, they would have been carried away, stranding us.

Untying our kayaks, we resumed our journey. The Alatna was unrecognizable from just two days earlier. Its narrow stream had spread into a river of Mississippi-like proportions, brown and thick with mud. The sky turned clear again, but the shores were thick with mosquitoes, and the only endurable path was down the center of the river. As the day wore on, we ran short on water. Unable to drink from the turbid river, we had to fight our way up the rushes of a side stream to find clear water. For another two days we made our way down the Alatna, its level gradually subsiding, until we emerged at the outpost of Bettles, where our pilot met us for the flight back to Anchorage.

DURING THE TWO years Rogers Morton spent drafting the administration's proposals for the d(2) lands (as we had come to call them), I worked closely with Morton, President Nixon's second secretary of the interior. We had met a few years earlier when he first assumed the post; before then, I knew of Morton only as a Maryland congressman with a good conservation record. When he was nominated for secretary, the Club's executive committee gave Phil Berry, who followed me as president, permission to question the nomination; however, Phil went further and opposed it vigorously. So I was not too surprised when Morton refused my first two requests for a meeting. Since his role was so critical to the Sierra Club's issues, I continued to press for an appointment.

When his aide, Richard Curry, finally confirmed the meeting, I went in and found Morton seated alone at a desk in the annex of his spacious office—a large, quiet, middle-aged man, six and a half feet tall, looking rather lonely. He politely asked what I wanted. I told him I wanted nothing; I simply wanted to make his acquaintance.

"You must want something."

"No, nothing." I had met several of his predecessors, I added, and made it a point to meet each new secretary. I think he remained suspicious of my agenda, and when my allotted time ran out and I still hadn't asked for anything, he asked again, "What do you want?" Still I replied, "Nothing."

That "nothing" proved effective: from that day on, I was able to meet frequently with Morton. We became good friends and worked closely together. I accompanied him on two trips to Alaska, saw him in

Washington, D.C., and communicated regularly, usually via his assistant secretary for fish, wildlife, and parks, Nathaniel Reed. On our first Alaska trip in 1972, we flew into the wilds of the Wrangell–St. Elias Mountains in a sturdy amphibious Grumman Goose, World War II vintage. We landed at Glacier Creek to survey the enormous canyon made eons before by the Nizina Glacier and photographed the distant falls of the Nizina River flowing through it. We noted the area's great potential as a federally protected park—a vast wilderness that could be further enlarged by also preserving land on the other side of the border, Canada's proposed Kluane Wilderness.

In the summer of 1973 Morton invited me to meet with him and his staff at Anchorage's Westward Hotel, where they were making recommendations on (d)2 lands. As we perused maps of the areas, Morton would ask his staff for their opinions on different types of preservation. Which agency should be awarded which lands? How much land was necessary to protect habitat? Which areas deserved priority? After the staff members had volunteered their feedback, Morton would ask for mine. I'm sure my answers didn't surprise him: I advocated the least development and the fullest protection in each case.

Within President Nixon's cabinet, however, there had been a shift of power. Nixon had mandated that Secretary of Agriculture Earl Butz would have ultimate authority over all federal lands. Even though the national park and refuge systems are overseen by Interior, not Agriculture, Morton was to submit all his d(2) recommendations to Butz for final approval. And Butz wanted the U.S. Forest Service (which is under the purview of Agriculture) to have a large share of the d(2) lands, thereby extending its hold past Southeast Alaska and into the interior. The Forest Service was pressing for three areas in particular: the Charley River and the Lake Clark region, both of which we hoped would become national parklands, and the Porcupine River, a tributary of the Yukon and a potential national wildlife refuge.

When Morton asked if I thought the Forest Service should have these areas, my answer was a resounding no. Limited stands of white spruce grew along the banks of the Porcupine, and the other areas were practically devoid of sizable timber. Not only was I distrustful of the Forest Service's commitment to keeping these lands wild, but also I thought the selections inappropriate. I continued talking with Morton that September, after Assistant Secretary Nathaniel Reed went on his own tour of Alaska and provided additional recommendations.

THE ACTIONS WE took in the years 1971 to 1975 were crucial to carrying out the legislative campaigns of 1977 to 1980 for passage of the Alaska National Interest Lands Conservation Act—the congressional legislation that would confirm federal protection for the (d)2 lands. By 1973, the Sierra Club had between 250 and 300 volunteers from all over the United States working on Alaska issues. Because the Club's current volunteer structure was overburdened, for a time we recruited new volunteers from outside the Club's committees and chapters. Recruiting for a single campaign, a single issue—rather than for the advancement of the Club's whole platform—set a precedent for the organization.

Momentum was building throughout the Club for the Alaska campaign, with ever more person power, money, and publications being directed toward that single issue. Working out of the Club's Bush Street headquarters in San Francisco, we produced a newsletter called the *Alaska Report* (currently still in production). We sold poster-size prints of Alaskan landscapes, did slide-show tours, and produced a color film, *Alaska in the Balance,* which was later shown to members of Congress. Alaska represented the largest campaign the Club had ever waged.

I came to call Alaska "the campaign for which the Sierra Club was founded." In the late nineteenth century, the Sierra Nevada was an unspoiled wonderland, providing inspiration for John Muir and his colleagues. Despite Muir's efforts, though, the Hetch Hetchy Valley had been flooded and Yosemite Valley was now packed with cars. Eighty years later—in an era of intense resource exploitation and surging population, and perhaps as a reaction to those factors—conservation was making a strong impact on the national consciousness. In Alaska, we hoped to stay ahead of the curve.

The discovery of North Slope oil and the passage of ANCSA, calling for identification of the national interest lands, prompted Sierra Club Books (now under the stable direction of publishing professional Jon Beckmann) to expedite the publication in 1974 of *Alaska: The Great Land.*

This attractive Exhibit Format book was replete with color images, from such notable photographers as Wilbur Mills and Phillip Hyde, which encompassed the state's varied landscapes, dispelling the persisting myth of Alaska as a land of snowy darkness. The text was coauthored by journalist and Alaska state legislator Mike Miller and Peggy Wayburn. Miller wrote a section titled "Discovery and Development," tracing the early exploration and economic exploitation of the state. Peggy's section, "The Last True Wilderness," provided a thorough overview of Alaska's flora, fauna, and topography. My contribution was an epilogue: "The National Heritage: Looking to the Future," which served as a call to arms and outlined the Club's proposal for the national interest lands. I wrote:

> Alaska's pure wilderness—her unspoiled beauty, vast open spaces and sense of freedom provide refreshment to the human spirit. Unlike Alaska's economic resources, this intangible "commodity" is difficult to measure. But, in a world of increasing pressures, it is perhaps more valuable. Like oil, pure wilderness is becoming increasingly scarce. Like oil, once it is consumed, it is gone forever. In Alaska, we have our last—and finest supply.

With *Alaska: The Great Land,* we hoped to provide a compelling glimpse of a state very much in the national debate, but which many Americans had never seen.

Despite growing support for the Club's work in Anchorage, however, most Alaskans still saw the Sierra Club as a foreign intruder. A certain frontier mentality persisted; outsiders were distrusted. In fact, "outside" is how most Alaskans referred to the lower forty-eight states. Bumper stickers touted "Alaska for Alaskans" and "Yankee Go Home." Alaskans seemed to want to have it both ways—the privileges of belonging to the Union but complete freedom from control by the federal government. We knew that any proposal for federal preservation of d(2) lands would meet with resistance.

Nevertheless, while Interior was finalizing its d(2) recommendations, the Sierra Club was drafting its own proposals. On behalf of the Sierra Club and with the expert aid of Jack Hession and Richard Gordon of the Wilderness Council, I drafted a proposal totaling 106 million acres.

In September 1973, I met with Senator Henry Jackson, who agreed to introduce the Sierra Club's proposal for the d(2) lands. Jackson would also introduce the administration's recommendations, as committee chairs often did with legislation coming from the executive branch. Both bills were introduced "by request" of the authors. Although Jackson would not be sponsoring either bill, and "introducing" did not indicate as strong a level of support, the simultaneous introduction would give the Club's proposal equal weight with Secretary Morton's in the eyes of Congress.

By early October 1973, Morton had nearly finished Interior's recommendations for the (d)2 lands in Alaska. "You came out pretty good," he told me over the phone. A rough breakdown was as follows: 21–22 million acres for national parks, 21–22 million for Fish and Wildlife refuges, 10 million for the BLM, 18 million for the Forest Service, and another 1.5 million acres for Wild and Scenic Rivers. Morton added that his assistant, Larry Lynn, was in Alaska negotiating final adjustments with several of the Native corporations. By late October, Morton's figures would change—as they would continue to do right up until the December deadline.

In December 1973, at the end of the two years prescribed by ANCSA, Secretary Morton submitted his recommendations for Alaska lands deserving federal protection in some form. They totaled 83.4 million acres, 3.4 million more than the number mandated by Congress, but Morton said he could not in good conscience recommend less. For the most part, his proposals matched those of the Sierra Club, although we had asked for more land in each location and that no lands be transferred to the Forest Service.

The Alaska campaign now entered its legislative phase. That December, Jackson introduced both bills. He also agreed to write a letter urging Morton to keep all the proposed d(2) lands inviolate while Congress was considering the legislation. Morton was amenable to this idea and directed his assistants to try to safeguard our selections as far as possible against either state selection or Native claims until Congress had a chance to vote on the bill. By stalling the giveaway of land, Jackson and Morton created opportunities for future wilderness preservation.

Jackson claimed that a critical mass of senators was ready to follow his lead in supporting our bill to protect the maximum amount of land. At this point, he gave the impression that he supported the Sierra Club's position. In the House, our longtime ally Mo Udall, a member of the House Interior Committee, had agreed to introduce our bill. Although no hearings had been scheduled yet, the stage seemed set for action as 1974 began. But many more twists and turns in the road were still to come.

In 1974, WE brought our eldest daughter, Cynthia, with us on our summer journey to Alaska. Then in her midtwenties, Cynthia had been working hard both as the wilderness coordinator for the Sierra Club and as a paralegal assistant for the newly formed Legal Defense Fund. We thought she deserved a vacation and arranged for her to meet Jim Roush at his home in Seattle to fly north; Peggy and I would join them later in Juneau. Bad weather delayed Jim and Cynthia's departure, however, and it wasn't until several days later that we all connected in Juneau and flew on to Anchorage in the *Red Baron.*

A few days later Peggy and I were invited by another couple for dinner, and I suggested Jim take Cynthia to the Garden of Eden, one of our favorite restaurants in town. It was still light around eleven when Peggy and I returned to our room at the Kobuk Motel. As I leaned out the window of our stuffy motel room to catch the breeze, I saw Jim and Cynthia walking toward us side by side, smiling and clearly engrossed in conversation. Peggy joined me at the window and agreed they made a likely pair.

That summer we planned to make our first rafting expedition down an Alaskan river, the Chilakadrotna, in the heart of the proposed Lake Clark National Park, with Jack Hession again as our water guide. From Anchorage, Jim flew us to Lake Clark, where we hired a Cessna 180 on floats for the hop to Twin Lakes.

We camped overnight there, setting off in the rafts the next day under a glowing sun. Our rafts floated swiftly downstream through class two and three whitewater rapids. Ducks and shorebirds swarmed everywhere on the surface; salmon swam below. On the second day we passed out of the mountains and into the hills, where wildlife appeared as if on parade: a herd of bull caribou, beaver, porcupine, mink. We spotted several gray short-eared owls perched in the white spruces lining the shore. Overhead, flocks of wild geese disappeared into the horizon.

In the days that followed, the river spread as we wound out of the hills into the lowlands. Three days out we sighted a brown bear peering from the bushes at the water's edge and drifted in silence to within fifty feet before it saw us and scampered away. We passed the confluence where the Chilakadrotna empties into the Mulchatna River, the two streams braiding into a lattice of side streams and backwaters. Jack brought out his fishing pole, and we ate fried grayling for lunch. More brown bears appeared, lumbering along the shores. When we reached the take-out point after five days on the river, we explored around there, climbing through blueberry-studded tundra and woods before the Cessna appeared for our rendezvous.

The night we returned to Anchorage, I awoke in our motel room at 4:30 A.M., my mind buzzing with images of the Chilakadrotna. I was a total convert to river travel: flying overhead afforded panoramic views and access to vast spaces, but to run Alaska's rivers was to know her landscape intimately, its variations and vagaries. I could think of no greater thrill than to fly into the headwaters of a stream where snow still covered the tundra; to float by canoe, kayak, or raft past the changing shores: mountains and slopes giving way to broad expanses of tundra; to step on shore and hear the tundra crackle beneath my boots; to see caribou and brown bears close up. There is no better way to see this country than to travel quietly down her rivers.

Alaska's hypnotic beauty had entranced me all over again. We had crisscrossed the state several times by plane, and each time we set down to explore a new place, the Great Land unfolded in another magnificent display, an inexhaustible call to adventure. I opened my journal and wrote simply: "Lake Clark must be saved for the future!"

Several hours later, Peggy and I were in the *Red Baron* flying over Lake Clark, surveying the entire expanse proposed for protection. We passed over the Kuskokwim watershed, where both the state and the Forest Service wanted lands, though the trees looked too small to be coveted by the Forest Service. Touching down in Kotzebue for lunch, we ran into Jay Hammond, drumming up votes in his run for governor that November. Our Alaskan summer of 1974 ended shortly thereafter.

THE CHAMPION CASE opened for retrial in the fall of 1974 so that the district court could consider the new evidence provided by Starker Leopold's studies of Admiralty Island. Again the presiding judge was Raymond Plummer, who had amply demonstrated his hostility toward conservation goals.

On September 23, Jim Moorman called from Anchorage. "Plummer is dying of leukemia," he reported. Moorman described the judge as blind in one eye and unable to hear much of the proceedings; he also seemed "confused" and "hostile."

"He's rigged the proceedings in an impossible way." Moorman explained that Plummer would allow only the government to call witnesses from the U.S. Forest Service (thus excluding Leopold and Barrett) and that no previously withheld Forest Service testimony would be allowed into the record. Moorman sounded forlorn. He didn't think we had a chance. "Our best hope is for a reversal," he concluded.

Meanwhile, Alaska's soon-to-be governor, Jay Hammond, volunteered himself as a mediator in the case and was pushing for compromise. He suggested a smaller mill and a wilderness study for the island. But a smaller mill still implied logging. I didn't take him up on his offer.

Three weeks after Moorman's call, Assistant Secretary of the Interior Nathaniel Reed called Mike McCloskey and told him that Chief Forester McGuire had had a change of heart—he wanted to get out of the Champion contract. McGuire had told Reed that he wanted to move away from the Forest Service's emphasis on logging in Southeast Alaska but was getting strong resistance from his staff in Juneau. Reed reported that McGuire was willing to reduce the harvest terms of the contract to 5 billion board feet—about a 40 percent reduction.

Word had it that Bendetsen, the president of Champion, was difficult to deal with and was prepared to wait out the appeal process. Reed, however, said the government attorneys wanted to broker a deal with the Sierra Club. Personally, Reed wanted out of being the middle man. This surprised me, since I had never thought of him as an intermediary in the case, but apparently the administration had become involved.

McCloskey then asked Reed if McGuire would consider establishing a wilderness area on Admiralty, but McGuire still wasn't interested in wilderness, Reed replied. McCloskey asked my opinion.

"No deal," I said.

The case would continue until December 30, 1975, when Champion abruptly decided to pull out of its contract with the Forest Service. After five years of litigation, Champion's new president claimed that rising inflation had driven up construction costs of the proposed mill past the point of economic feasibility. Plummer closed the case, and the Forest Service was left without a client. But Admiralty's fate remained very much in jeopardy as long as the Forest Service controlled it with no other form of federal protection. We were still determined to gain wilderness status for it under the National Interest Lands legislation.

In January 1975 Rogers Morton announced that he would resign as secretary of the interior due to health problems. At a parting reception for him given by the National Parks Advisory Board, the secretary told the guests, "I've had a lot of fun in this job."

He appeared on the verge of tears. "But the thing I'm proudest of is the decisions I made in Alaska—and I want to thank Dr. Ed Wayburn for that more than anyone else." Although Morton did not know it, this was one of my proudest moments as well.

One day in the spring of 1975, I had dinner at the Washington, D.C., home of Nathaniel Reed, Morton's assistant secretary, with whom I formed a lasting friendship. At this time, in response to congressional hearings, both the administration and the Sierra Club were continuing to make adjustments to their d(2) proposals. When the subject turned to Admiralty, I expressed concern that two Native corporations had filed claims there: the Goldbelt Corporation (Juneau) and Shee Atika (Sitka) were both pressing for lands on western Admiralty. Champion wasn't opposing them, believing that the claims would only add acreage to their potential cut.

Reed agreed that Admiralty needed to be safeguarded against further giveaways and thought the corporations could be compensated with alternative lands. Reed said he also wanted to see Admiralty out of the Forest Service's hands. He was considering transforming the island into a wildlife refuge, as good an outcome as I could envision.

THAT JULY, PEGGY and I canoed across Admiralty Island, getting our first extensive on-the-ground look at the land we had been working for the previous six years to save. We flew into Alexander Lake and traversed the string of Hasselborg lakes that span Admiralty from its east side to the Tlingit township of Angoon on the west. From the air, the island was cloaked in vivid shades of green, its higher reaches increasingly treeless where the green tundra met splashes of white snow.

We canoed for a week. For the most part, the waterways were so closely spaced that one lake seemed almost to meet another, the narrow shores between lined with spruce and tundra. Our only major portage compelled me to heave the eighty-pound canoe up a half mile of unmaintained trail, steep and slippery with mud. The forest grew thick here; it was no wonder Champion had wanted to log these stands. As John Muir had feared for California's redwoods, the trees were "too good to be allowed to live."

On our next to last night, we camped at the Hasselborg River, fifteen to twenty feet above Mitchell Bay on a shoreline just out of reach of high tide. Below was the saltchuck, an intermediary zone that would be filled as the tide came in. We were entranced by the view across Mitchell Bay, its waters dotted with islands, each a tempting potential adventure. By the next morning, the tide had risen to meet our camp. Because we were due at Angoon for our rendezvous with the plane, we could stop only briefly at one of Mitchell Bay's islands for lunch, then we paddled on to Angoon.

The only settlement on Admiralty, Angoon stretches along two sides of a peninsula, with Mitchell Bay on one side and Chatham Strait on the other. In 1975 the Tlingit township was in dire need of economic rehabilitation. As Peggy and I walked the rutted mud streets, we saw that the buildings lining each side were mostly vacant or blighted with peeling paint and rotting sideboards. The Natives—now the Kootznoowoo Corporation under ANCSA—had no money to fix them.

The Angoon Tlingits had managed to retain much of their traditional culture and depended entirely upon a subsistence economy of fishing and hunting. Because they relied so heavily on the land for survival, the tribe recognized its interest in preserving Admiralty's forests and shores, even under economic pressure to develop them. The Forest Service logging contracts threatened their way of life, and the Angoon Tlingits wanted to see Admiralty protected as wilderness.

We met with several of the tribe's leaders, including the town's senior elder, Daniel Johnson, Ed Gamble, and Sterling Bolima, a chain-smoking half-Tlingit half-Filipino who proved to be an able congressional lobbyist.

The Angoon Tlingits opposed the claims of Goldbelt and Shee Atika for land around Mitchell Bay—claims they saw as a direct threat to their traditional lands. But they could not, they said, oppose the claim of the regional corporation Sealaska for 20,000 acres in central Admiralty. Sealaska had been left out of ANCSA because it had a previous compensation arrangement with the federal government. And even if Angoon leaders disagreed with Sealaska's selections, they would not air their differences publicly. ANCSA had the potential to carve deep rifts between the tribes, the leaders explained. To the extent possible, the Natives had to keep a unified front.

"They've done it again," a jaded Ed Gamble commented. "They've put a bottle of whiskey on the table and let us fight over it."

Peggy and I left Angoon satisfied that we had reached a level of accord with the town's leaders. This was not the case, however, with all of the Native corporations. Two months earlier I had met with the president of the Sealaska Corporation, John Borbridge. Borbridge, who carried himself with the pomp of an emperor, began our meeting by saying that whatever position he took, it didn't need defending. He considered the Natives, as Alaska's first human inhabitants, "the owners of the land." ANCSA had renewed his faith in the system. He supported Kootznoowoo's claims at Angoon, but as the regional corporation, Sealaska would continue to press for the subsurface rights to any village selection.

The implication was that Sealaska intended to mine the lands chosen by Kootznoowoo or other local corporations in its domain. When I suggested that stewardship, rather than ownership, might be a preferable model of protecting Alaska's wilds, Borbridge declared that the white man's moral conscience was irrelevant. "You're all latecomers," he admonished me. "We have been following principles for thousands of years. We're the owners of the land. You're dealing with the owners here."

T HE LATTER PART of our 1975 trip was an air tour of Alaska's proposed d(2) lands. On an overcast July morning, Peggy and I set out from Jack Calvin's home in Sitka for a trans-Alaska flight in Jim Roush's *Red Baron*. We knew we were in for difficult weather: the cloud ceiling was low and heavy, forcing us to fly in a channel just a few hundred feet off the ground. Below us wound the coastline of Calvin's beloved West Chichagof, its sinuous edges carving myriad bays between mountains rising thousands of feet high.

Expecting that we might have to turn around at any moment, we continued north, flying through intermittent clouds hovering over Glacier Bay, catching glimpses of its aquamarine waters dotted with ice floes. At Yakutat, we could see several areas where logging had already taken place, but a little farther north, in the Malaspina Glacier forelands, sizable trees were spreading along the new soil, landscape smothered by the glacier until just a few years earlier. Both the Forest Service and the Sealaska Regional Corporation had designs to log this area.

To the east, the clouds descended even farther as we cruised over Prince William Sound. Portage Pass, our gateway to the north, was reported closed, but Jim found a sliver of clear weather and darted through the mountaintops, still snowbound in high summer, to land at Merrill Field in Anchorage.

Refueling and continuing north, we encountered low cloud ceilings again over the Alaska Range. Jim threaded through Rainy Pass, and we emerged into the vast stretches of western Alaska. Passing first over the Kuskokwim River, then the Yukon, and finally the Koyukuk, the *Red Baron* continued to soar north and west. To the east, we caught a glimpse of the Great Kobuk arctic desert and its sand dunes. The country grew successively more hilly as we approached the Selawik network of lakes and the Baldwin Peninsula.

Six and a half hours after takeoff, we landed in Kotzebue—hard to recognize from the small, stagnant outpost it had been in the years before. Home to the regional Native corporation Northwest Alaska Native Association (NANA), the town was bustling. Construction was under way everywhere, including installation of the city's first sewer system. Downtown, a fifty-four-room luxury (by north Alaskan standards) hotel was being built, and dozens of new Native homes were in the works. Cars ran through the streets, small boats raced along the shoreline, and at the docks, a steady stream of barges unloaded equipment and supplies. We inquired for the Native leaders but were told they were all away on business.

The next morning was clear, and we awoke early in anticipation of continuing on to Point Lay or Wainwright to the north. Taking off, we skimmed the beach at Kivalina, the *Red Baron* hovering just a hundred feet off the sand, then meandered inland over the Delong Mountains.

We touched down next at Point Hope, a triangular sand spit ten miles wide and mostly covered by lagoons. Eskimos had lived on the point for two thousand years. It seemed a remarkable existence, isolated by both distance and weather. Though the sun shone overhead, a bitter wind nipped at our faces and ears. Winter was an unbearable thought. The sea here was eroding as much as eight feet of the spit each year, and the entire village was in the process of being relocated three miles eastward. Some houses had already gone under; elders remembered when they had stood on dry ground. An archeological dig, jointly funded by the National Park Service and ANCSA, was under way, retrieving remnants from the threatened houses. We watched as a team from the University of Alaska and a group of Natives examined the remains of the dwellings—most of them several hundred years old and many more than a thousand.

Compared to Kotzebue, little had changed at Point Hope. Chained sled dogs barked at the diggers. An Eskimo woman climbed down into an ice locker dug into the snow and hacked off a slab of whale meat, while her husband above lowered a bucket. The only changes visible at Point Hope were in the land itself, its slow surrender to the sea, its dissolving human traces.

The breeze picked up, whipping through our parkas. Overhead, wisps of fog began to veil the sky. To the north, a heavy cloud bank was building, and we knew we had to leave Point Hope soon or we would be stranded there. Point Lay and Wainwright would have to wait.

We were off again, this time heading east into the remaining sun, then south to recross the Delong Mountains. The Noatak River appeared below, a long, wide stream flowing through a broad valley. Tundra-covered plains stretched for miles without a tree in sight. Clouds continued to gather

252

from the north, the bank lowering with each passing minute. Following the Noatak's upper stream, we diverted toward the Arrigetch Peaks of the Brooks Range. Never had these mountains seemed so alluring, their sharp orange and gray granite edges swathed in storm clouds. Peggy and I shot roll after roll of film from the plane window, though we knew no photograph could ever capture the immensity of the landscape, its special light, or its beckoning lure.

An ominous dark gray curtain of clouds now hung over the eastern front. Passing through rain over the Alatna River, we turned south over Walker Lake and skirted the oncoming storm. A last look revealed the Brooks Range now engulfed by a dusky shroud of rain, and we turned toward Fairbanks to end our journey.

OUR EARLY HOPES for swift action on legislation for the Alaska national interest lands faded with the passage of time. Even though Senator Henry Jackson introduced Sierra Club proposals for the d(2) lands in both 1973 and 1975, and the Senate held hearings in 1975, neither our recommendations nor the administration's saw any debate. The Senate turned its attention elsewhere, and the issue all but died.

Nor did our bill move forward in the House. Ted Swem, who oversaw new land acquisitions for the NPS, reported that jurisdiction questions were preventing action. Interior chair Wayne Aspinall had been replaced by James Haley (D-Fla.), who did not seem eager to push the project along. He thought the proposals should be acted on first by the Public Lands Committee, where Don Young—Alaska's lone representative and a staunch states' rights advocate—would have considerable input. National Parks subcommittee chair Roy Taylor concurred with Haley. Taylor wanted the issues of national parks and wildlife refuges kept conjoined and would not push for his own committee to have first jurisdiction over the parks section of the bill. He too wanted the Public Lands Committee to review the proposal before making his own recommendations.

Thus the d(2) lands action was caught in a congressional stalemate. Essentially, no one wanted to take the first plunge. The issue involved tremendous acreage, familiarity with dozens of maps, and a plethora of details few legislators understood. Everyone anticipated that debate over

253

a bill, both in committee and on the floor of each house, would be cantankerous and time-consuming. Furthermore, unlike the issue of Native claims and the land freeze, there was no powerful coalition pushing for land preservation. Millions of dollars were not at stake—only millions of acres.

In the minds of Congress's leaders, the 1978 deadline still seemed far away; the issue of Alaska's parklands could always be postponed until the next session. For our part, conservationists continued to press for action in the Congress. We wanted to see debate on Section 17-d(2), but, like our representatives, felt there was plenty of time before the 1978 deadline would expire.

As 1975 drew to a close, we were also looking ahead to an election— one that held the possibility of new leadership in the White House and a clearer mandate from the executive branch for wilderness in Alaska.

CHAPTER EIGHT

CRISIS AND COMPROMISE

The Alaska National Interest Lands Conservation Act

❦

The American experience has been the confrontation
by old peoples and cultures of a world as new as if it had just risen
from the sea. That gave us our hope and our excitement,
and the hope and excitement can be passed on to newer Americans,
Americans who never saw any phase of the frontier.
But only if we keep the remainder of our wild as a reserve
and a promise—a sort of wilderness bank.

—Wallace Stegner, "Wilderness and the Geography of Hope"

In his 1976 campaign speeches, Democratic presidential candidate Jimmy Carter had raised the hopes of many conservationists, promising a strong Alaska Lands Bill. Even before he occupied the White House in January 1977, Carter told soon-to-be Secretary of the Interior Cecil Andrus that his first charge would be to rewrite Secretary Rogers Morton's Alaska bill. The new president wanted to push an even larger plan. His administration was receptive to conservation input but did not wish to contend with the multiple organizations interested in defining the d(2) lands. Hoping to streamline the process, Andrus requested that a single, unified conservationist coalition be established in Washington to advocate for Alaska lands.

We moved quickly into action. The Alaska Coalition was formed in October 1976, one month before Carter's election, and included representatives from all the major American environmental and wildlife organizations, including the Sierra Club, The Wilderness Society, the

Audubon Society, the Izaak Walton League, Defenders of Wildlife, the National Parks and Conservation Association, and Friends of the Earth. Regional organizations included the Alaska Conservation Society and the Alaska Wilderness Council as well as representatives from three Native corporations: the Northwest Arctic Native Association (NANA), Ruralcap, and the Calista Regional Corporation. In all, the coalition comprised several dozen members.

A three-day organizational meeting was scheduled in Washington to choose officers and assign tasks. Representing the Sierra Club were Jack Hession, the Club's Alaska conservation representative; executive director Mike McCloskey; Chuck Clusen, the associate director of the Club's Washington office; and myself. At first, most members looked to me to chair the coalition, but we soon realized that we would need someone based in Washington to oversee day-to-day developments. Chuck Clusen, still in his twenties, was elected chair. Jack Hession was given the arduous task of "cleaning up" HR 39—the Sierra Club's 1973 proposal for the d(2) lands—to the coalition's satisfaction. He would devote himself almost exclusively to the project for the next two months, ultimately producing a 150-page bill with a stunning amount of detail. Over the next several years, Hession, Clusen, and I spoke on the telephone nearly every day.

Dissension arose almost immediately between the concerns of environmentalists and those of the Natives in the coalition. Willie Goodwin of NANA wanted his organization to draft a separate bill, asserting that the Natives' priority was for the issue of subsistence fishing and hunting. Goodwin claimed that 90 percent of his forty-five hundred people relied on subsistence use for their survival, and he wanted access to all public lands. Several conservationists objected, fearing that even minimal subsistence hunting could irrevocably damage wildlife; they cited growing numbers of subsistence users, including whites who lived in the bush and who legally could not be excluded from the legislation on the basis of race.

Even conservationists were not wholly unified in their demands. The coalition's inaugural meeting was marked by heated debate over whether or not to include Forest Service lands in Southeast Alaska in its proposal. At first I balked at the idea. Until then, Southeast had not been included in

Secretary Morton's proposals because the earlier Native Claims Settlement Act authorized up to 80 million acres of "unreserved" public land to be set aside for protection, and Southeast was considered already "reserved" under the jurisdiction of the U.S. Forest Service. Its land lay within the Tongass and Chugach national forests, however inadequate that protection was. I feared that if we pushed for legislative protection for Southeast, the opposition in Congress would surely point out that our proposal went beyond the guidelines set by ANCSA, and this issue might take over the debate.

I was convinced by other members of the coalition, however, who argued that we might not get another opportunity to protect Southeast Alaska. The debate on Capitol Hill would be lengthy and tense; once Congress passed this bill, it would not likely return to the issue of Alaska's lands. The time was now or never. What of the fate of places like Admiralty and West Chichagof islands? Although people like Jack Calvin were working to establish wilderness areas in Southeast, the few dozen members of the Sitka Conservation Society couldn't do the work alone.

If Southeast were not included in the coalition's proposal, conditions under the Forest Service would not improve. Logging would continue unabated. After decades of policy that put timber cutting before protection, few of us were willing to blindly trust the agency. Rich Gordon, formerly of the Alaska Department of Fish and Wildlife, was especially persuasive in arguing for the need to include Southeast in the new legislation. As a result, the coalition recommended substantial wilderness areas in the region: 450,000 acres on West Chichagof and two wilderness monuments: nearly a million acres on Admiralty Island and 2 million acres on Misty Fjords, east of Ketchikan.

Although the Alaska Conservation Society strongly opposed some of the subsistence hunting provisions adopted by the coalition, to the group's credit, it did not continue to voice disagreement. We all knew from the outset that opinions within the coalition would differ, but once a bill was introduced it was of paramount importance that conservationists stand as a unified block. To me it was a lesson learned the hard way from the Redwood campaigns; if the opposition were allowed to divide and conquer, the bill would get nowhere.

THE CONGRESS THAT convened in January 1977 had a much different composition than that of 1976; it was one that held promise for conservationists. In a Senate reorganization, the Interior Committee became the Energy and Natural Resources Committee; Washington's Senator Jackson remained its chair. In December 1976, the Alaska Coalition had approached Jackson, asking him to introduce a Senate version of the revamped HR 39, as he had introduced our earlier Alaska lands legislation. But this time Jackson hedged; he wouldn't commit either way. He did say that if the bill were introduced, he would direct a special oversight committee to hold hearings in Washington, D.C., and in the field.

In the House, James Haley had retired, and Morris Udall, a longtime Sierra Club ally, became chair of the House Interior Committee. Udall had expressed interest in the coalition's bill early on, and as 1976 ended, Hession discussed revisions with the congressman's staff and prepared an accompanying map. On January 4, 1977, Udall introduced the new HR 39, calling for 115 million acres of federally protected lands. The bill had twenty-five sponsors, including the new chair of the House Subcommittee on National Parks, Phillip Burton. It was the first salvo in the congressional odyssey that would ultimately produce the Alaska National Interest Lands Conservation Act (ANILCA).

That same month I asked Burton to lead the Interior Committee hearings on the Alaska bill, but he said he was too occupied with his National Parks omnibus bill. Burton was fervent about this burgeoning proposal. "I don't know anything about parks," he told me over dinner at the House of Prime Rib. "But I'm going to get out more park bills than ever before."

Burton felt confident leaving the House Interior Committee hearings to his colleague Representative John Seiberling of Ohio, who Burton claimed would be sympathetic and thorough. Soon after, Udall appointed Seiberling chair of the Special Committee on Alaska and Oversight, a subcommittee of the Interior Committee. Udall also requested, on the coalition's behalf, that Secretary Andrus guard all possible d(2) lands from state selection until HR 39 had been considered. With a pro-conservation president and well-placed allies in Congress, HR 39 appeared poised for victory.

Also that January, the Sierra Club previewed its documentary film *Alaska: Land in the Balance* at the Club's new D.C. office. The film was well received; Seiberling was particularly enthusiastic. Two days later, Senator Jackson agreed to introduce HR 39 "by request," reiterating his desire to form a special oversight committee in the Senate and to hold field hearings.

The opposition—composed of the Alaska congressional delegation and the rest of the state's political establishment, along with oil, mining, logging, and other resource-extraction interests—went to work immediately on the weakest link in our chain, and from a political point of view the most coveted: the Natives. One night I received a call from Harold Sparck, a leader of the Calista Regional Corporation in Bethel. "We don't want wilderness around us," he said, clearly distressed. Wilderness was going to trap his people. He feared for their survival. He'd decided he didn't want HR 39.

It was such a strange thing to say, coming from someone whose people had flourished in the wild for thousands of years. I suspected that someone had been deliberately scaring Sparck. As we talked further it became clear that opponents of the bill had demonized the concept of wilderness. In an Associated Press news story concerning HR 39, opponents claimed that Natives would be imprisoned by vast, wild, and unenterable areas where they wouldn't be allowed to hunt or use snowmobiles. Sparck's village would become an isolated outpost, he feared. I reminded Sparck that wilderness was what had enabled his people to survive and reassured him that specific provisions guaranteeing the Natives' right to hunt and use snowmobiles were already in HR 39 or would be added. Even so, Sparck said that the Alaska Federation of Natives would draft its own bill for the d(2) lands; this threat went nowhere, however.

On January 31, 1977, Senators Jackson of Washington and Clifford Hansen of Wyoming introduced by request both former Secretary of the Interior Morton's proposal, S-499, and the Alaska Coalition's bill, labeled S-500, in the Senate. Secretary Andrus did not make any changes to his predecessor's proposal, saying he would wait until the Senate hearings to comment further. (The administration was supporting HR 39 in the House.) Jackson, while friendly, remained lukewarm about the coalition's bill and uncommitted to its passage. His guardedness was frustrating, and I didn't know how to push him into a firm commitment on the stronger Senate bill.

Seiberling's Alaska hearings began in April. The congressman from Ohio and his special House subcommittee took to their monumental task with gusto. In addition to hearings in Washington, the committee scheduled public hearings in five lower forty-eight cities: Atlanta, Chicago, Denver, San Francisco, and Seattle, as well as in practically every town and village in Alaska.

On April 21, the day before I was scheduled to testify, I left San Francisco to fly to Washington after staying up into the early hours drafting my remarks. At SFO, I boarded a nonstop DC-10 flight. Over Utah, a disturbing grinding sound erupted from the left side of the plane and passengers began to press their call buttons; the woman across from me turned white. The pilot came on the loudspeaker telling us the left engine had gone out; he would need to land at Salt Lake City and reroute the passengers to other planes. After a safe landing, I and about a third of the passengers were herded onto a DC-8 to Chicago. I grew anxious, not wanting to get stranded overnight; my testimony was scheduled for the morning. In Chicago, I was told the next flight for D.C. wouldn't leave for two and a half hours, but looking up at the departures board, I saw that another flight was leaving within a few minutes. I rushed across the terminal without a second to spare and caught it, arriving in Washington in time for a good night's sleep.

Alaska's Governor Hammond testified on the same day. The governorship had changed Hammond. When he had flown Peggy and me around in his bush plane, Hammond had professed strong conservation sentiments, and his track record as a state legislator demonstrated that he was as environmentally aware as one could hope for in Alaska. But as governor, Hammond found himself under tremendous pressure from oil, gas, timber, and mining interests and now claimed he was beholden to "all" of the state. Although he supported the conservation philosophy outlined in section d(2), he said, his testimony ran along the classic "outsider" lines.

"We Alaskans know our state best," he declared. "Federal jurisdiction is not what we Alaskans want." He invoked the catch phrase then in vogue:

"Alaska for Alaskans." Claiming that HR 39 would "fracture" his state, put up fences, and ultimately "dismember" its lands in the interest of federal control, he called for a new plan, dubbed the "Fifth System." This would create a new Alaska Land Use Planning Commission—a combination of state and federal representatives assigned to review all the state's unreserved lands and assign them a level of protection appropriate to their scenic and economic value.

Hammond pitched his idea as serving the average Alaskan. I knew, however, that the people who would really benefit from the state's pseudo-sovereignty over its lands were not lone Alaskans in the bush—independent miners, loggers, or fishermen. The damage done to landscapes and wildlife by such operators was relatively insignificant and not of concern to the Sierra Club. Those that really benefited from the state's lax regulations and zealous economic ambitions, and that truly endangered its wilderness values, were international corporations such as Humble Oil (a subsidiary of Exxon), ARCO, British Petroleum, Champion Paper, Ketchikan Pulp, and Alaska Lumber and Pulp. Most of those who profited greatly from Alaska's resources didn't live in Alaska.

In my own testimony, I had decided strategically to ask for everything, no matter how politically unfeasible. When my turn came, I testified in favor of preserving all the lands outlined in HR 39—115 million acres. No matter what we asked for, we would always get less. Compromise was best left to the politicians.

AFTER THE KICKOFF in D.C., the special committee went on the road for field hearings. The Sierra Club and other conservation groups had galvanized their ranks in preparation, and in both Atlanta and Chicago, the turnout was heavily in favor of the bill. In Denver, too, despite a strong mining lobby, support for the bill was strong. In early June, however, Seiberling canceled the hearing slated for San Francisco; my eldest daughter, Cynthia, who was organizing conservationist testimony in Seattle, called with the news. The committee was exhausted: it had already reviewed 810 witnesses and was missing key mark-up sessions in Congress. Members felt they could conduct only one more hearing outside Alaska, and they opted for Seattle at the expense of San Francisco.

This came as a grave disappointment. We had done a great deal of organizing and felt we would have produced a strong majority in favor of HR 39. Fortunately, Seiberling agreed to give equal weight to any written testimony as to testimony presented in person. Our witnesses wrote letters that the Club hand-delivered to Seiberling's committee when its members arrived in Seattle on June 20.

Of all of the cities in the lower forty-eight, we feared the most opposition in Seattle, the metropolis for a state dominated by logging and a longtime business base for many Alaskan corporations. The Seattle hearing was critical also because Washington was home to an emerging leader of the opposition, Congressman Lloyd Meeds. Meeds had prepared a substitute bill, which he had tried unsuccessfully to pass out of committee. Things went better than we anticipated, however. Cynthia had done a fantastic job gathering conservation support and called afterward to report that testimony in favor of HR 39 outweighed the opposition.

As the committee made an exhaustive tour of Alaska, it seemed that some issues would never be resolved. For example, Cecil Barnes of the Chugach Native Corporation felt that its two thousand people had been shortchanged by the Alaska Native Claims Settlement Act and was hoping to use the ANILCA to redress the situation. He wanted total control of the area around the Copper River, which flows through south-central Alaska between the peaks of the Chugach Mountains and into the Gulf of Alaska. The Sierra Club and the U.S. Fish and Wildlife Service both opposed Barnes; the area's fragile wetlands provided nesting grounds for several migratory bird species, and we hoped to see these lands awarded the highest degree of protection as a national wildlife refuge.

In Ketchikan, testimony was split: one-third in favor of the bill, two-thirds opposed. In Sitka, Alaska Lumber and Pulp offered a paid day off for any employee willing to testify against HR 39; only a few brave souls stood up to testify on its behalf. The company also sent hundreds of postcards with pre-typed testimony on the back, but these didn't impress Seiberling. The workers had only to sign their name, he noted, and under what pressure no one could say. In the end, three-fourths of the testimony was in opposition to HR 39. In Angoon, however, Alaska Natives Daniel and Vera Johnson testified in favor of establishing wilderness on Admiralty Island.

We fared better in the larger cities. The Sierra Club now had a solid base of support in Anchorage and Juneau, while the Alaska Conservation Society wielded considerable influence in Fairbanks. At least half of the testimony in these three cities supported the bill.

At the end of several months and several dozen hearings, after having listened to and read thousands of pages of testimony, an exhausted Seiberling and his committee returned to Washington in August 1977 to begin their mark-up of HR 39. Their efforts at the hearings had been outstanding.

THAT SUMMER OF 1977, we gained a valuable source of information within the administration when Cynthia Wilson, a former lobbyist for the Audubon Society, became Interior Secretary Andrus's assistant for Alaska. Chuck Clusen spent the day of August 24 briefing Wilson on the coalition's proposal. Wilson revealed that Andrus was compiling his own recommendations, which he expected to complete within a week. So far, he had selected 102.4 million acres, 20 million more than Morton had done. (Under ANCSA, the secretary of the Interior was charged with identifying lands to be reserved by the federal government, which became the basis of the administration's version of Alaska lands legislation.)

Wilson also said that Andrus was opposed to Hammond's "Fifth System." He believed that federal control was critical, a view shared by many in Congress. Within the week, however, Andrus's figure had dropped; his final recommendation emerged at 94 million acres.

Unlike Nixon's secretary for agriculture, Earl Butz, Andrus wanted to keep the Forest Service out of Alaska's interior. Of his selections, only 1.6 million acres was earmarked for Forest Service jurisdiction. The administration's stance made sense, since most of the state's timber grew along the coast. However, the Forest Service wasn't about to give up any of its claims without an exchange. The agency was demanding 45 million acres, nearly half of Andrus's proposed total.

Andrus held fast against assigning any further acreage in Alaska's interior to the Forest Service, but under pressure from the agency he refused to endorse HR 39's proposals for Southeast. Talk arose of the Forest Service acquiring the Copper River Basin and retaining Admiralty, West Chichagof, and Misty Fjords—areas we desired to see administered by the National Park Service.

After having fought for years to preserve Admiralty as wilderness, I now saw the possibility that it might be traded like a baseball card. Yet if the coalition insisted on keeping the Southeast lands in HR 39, the Forest Service might block the bill. Seiberling, who had worked with Andrus on Interior's selections, said he would be unwilling to go beyond Andrus's proposals. Our priority had to be getting the bill passed; we would hope to win back specific areas during debate.

That September, I argued before the Sierra Club board of directors that the campaign for Alaska was only one-third complete. We would need more money, more resources, more volunteers. The administration might make a good proposal, but without a successful lobbying campaign, Andrus's selections would never make it through Congress. Alaska was the largest campaign the Sierra Club had ever undertaken; other conservation groups were looking to us to take the lead, I reminded the board. The board voted to approve the additional support needed.

HR 39 WENT to the special oversight committee for mark-up by mid-October. Meanwhile, the coalition agreed it would continue to press for all lands but would endorse a compromise between HR 39's 115 million acres and Andrus's 94 million—aiming for about 104 to 105 million acres, with half that acreage designated as "instant wilderness" as soon as the legislation passed (as opposed to the usual process entailing years of study).

Early in November, Jack Hession called to report that the bill was moving slowly in the subcommittee. Members were only halfway through the process, reviewing slides and maps of Lake Clark, the seventh of fourteen proposed national park areas. Both the National Park Service and Fish and Wildlife had sent in task forces to help the overwhelmed representatives. Lloyd Meeds of Washington wanted to postpone the subcommittee's vote until January, and Alaska's lone congressman, Don Young, also was stalling for more time. The subcommittee seemed to be leaning toward an 800,000-acre wilderness on Admiralty, but remaining under the Forest Service. It looked doubtful that Lake Clark would make national park status, and there was talk of including it in 5 million acres being earmarked for the state.

On the Senate side, hearings were just getting under way. In December, Senator Jackson, chair of the Energy and Natural Resources Committee, held a special hearing on Alaska by invitation only. He wanted to hear from one or two representatives of each of the key stakeholders: the administration, the state of Alaska, agency chiefs, conservationists, business leaders, and Natives. The administration presented a good, though not ideal, package in its S-499 bill, and Secretary Andrus said he would be receptive to friendly amendments. Governor Hammond testified on behalf of the state. I testified on behalf of conservationists—much of my testimony a repeat of what I'd said before Seiberling's House committee the previous April.

The Senate committee reached no consensus at these hearings. Jackson announced that he would write his own bill; he was concerned about leaving out gas and oil lease rights in the proposed Noatak National Arctic Range. Committee member Lee Metcalf (D-Mont.) continued to press for HR 39, while Senator Frank Church (D-Ida.) pressed for the administration's bill.

Immediately upon returning to San Francisco I received a call from both Laurence Rockefellers, Sr. and Jr., who, with a group of other philanthropists and Natives, had formed a group called Americans for Alaska. The name was clearly a response to the states-righters' battle cry, "Alaska for Alaskans." The Rockefellers said it was imperative that I fly back to Washington to meet with Senator Jackson again. Jackson wanted to get a handle on the situation, they said, but was "concerned about environmental extremists" and worried about "locking up" oil and gas resources in the western Noatak region. The Rockefellers had arranged a private meeting with the senator, which would be attended as well by former Assistant Interior Secretary Nathaniel Reed. Exhausted and sorely needing to attend to my family and my medical practice, I had to decline. I thought I knew Jackson well enough: my attending the meeting or not would not change his plans.

From January to March 1978, Burton's National Parks subcommittee marked up the national parks portion of HR 39 before passing it on to the full House Interior Committee. The bill emerged from the full committee at just under 95 million acres. Two days later I met with a jubilant Phil Burton at the House of Prime Rib. He had been chair of the House National Parks Subcommittee for just fourteen months; the Redwood National Park Expansion bill had just passed, and Burton was making rapid strides toward completing his Parks Omnibus Bill. He clapped his hands together and asked, "When we finish this, what do we do next?" He also told me that HR 39's prospects in the House were very positive.

But four weeks later, California representative Pete McCloskey told me the House was still mired in bitter debate. Amendments were being offered in a hodge-podge way, muddling the discussion. At every turn, Representative Young tried to downplay the importance of wilderness, claiming that Alaskans weren't like other Americans: they needed to *use* their wild land. A compromise bill finally emerged onto the House floor on May 3.

That spring, the Sierra Club and the Alaska Coalition made a plea for volunteer lobbyists to help build momentum for our legislation. Fifty people answered the call, filling the Club's Washington office. They ranged widely in age and by home state; some had never lobbied before, but all were dedicated to preserving Alaska's lands. A few received monetary assistance, but most worked for free. Their enthusiasm lifted my heart. Within the Club ranks, fully a third of the staff as well as a large contingent of volunteers were now committed full time to the Alaska campaign. On May 5, Americans for Alaska ran a full-page ad in all the major newspapers in favor of HR 39. Two weeks later, the House passed the bill 277 to 31.

HR 39's counterpart in the Senate, S-500, enjoyed no such success. While proposals for the Kenai Peninsula, the Wrangells, and the Aniakchak crater remained intact, the Noatak Wildlife Refuge, Gates of the Arctic National Park, and Lake Clark all took substantial hits either in size or degree of protection in the Energy and Natural Resources Committee, diminishing the total federally protected acreage in the bill to just under 95 million acres. Jack Hession was now meeting regularly with senators to drum up support for strengthening amendments. A survey showed that the committee vote could go either way.

Beginning April 7, 1978, the Senate Energy and Natural Resources Committee held its hearings, which Senator Jackson had delayed until

Seiberling's House hearings were over. Mark-up by the committee was expected in mid-May. Jackson had said repeatedly that he would need only a few hearings—but when the process began he decided to weigh each part of the bill separately, much to my chagrin. Whether intentional or not, this amounted to a delaying tactic. Jackson would hold forty-four days of hearings in all. Also disturbing was that Jackson invited Alaska senators Gravel and Stevens to attend all the hearings, even though neither was on the Energy and Natural Resources Committee. The mercurial Gravel boycotted the hearing to protest that *any* bill was being considered.

Stevens, however, not only attended, but he dominated the discussions. Stevens was exactly the kind of opponent everyone feared: knowledgeable, clever, and driven. Our new champion on the committee, Senator John Durkin of New Hampshire, could not muster enough force to counter Stevens's energy and firsthand knowledge of the state. Jackson, for his part, tried to appear neutral, almost silent, although from his position as chair he could have directed the outcome of the proceedings.

When I and other members of the Alaska Coalition testified before the committee in late April, a vitriolic Stevens exploded at coalition member Douglas Scott, telling him he had "no right" to press for wilderness in Stevens's home state. Senator Durkin said he wanted to introduce a new bill, integrating some of the changes made by the House Interior Committee. Assistant Secretary of the Interior Robert Herbst tried to hold firm, saying that the department's bottom line would be 94 million acres. Stevens then threatened to filibuster any bill not to his satisfaction and stormed out of the hearings.

After our testimony, Jackson offered to meet with Chuck Clusen and me in private, saying, "I want to know more about the coalition's proposal." We were unsure how to respond. Jackson had introduced our bill in both its former and current incarnations. If anyone knew what it contained, it should have been he.

Mid-May, the original target set for mark-up by the Energy and Natural Resources Committee, came and went. The committee now claimed it would require until mid-June. On June 19, Jackson reasserted his pledge to get a bill out of committee, but he still was unclear about which bill—S-500 or a new bill he might write—would be used for mark-up. He wouldn't be able to control the debate once a bill reached the floor, he warned. Senator Gravel also was now threatening to filibuster. Senate majority leader Robert Byrd voiced displeasure that the bill would reach the floor late; there were others bills waiting, and he didn't want to let Gravel take over the Senate.

Cynthia Wilson, Secretary Andrus's assistant, reported that the administration was growing apprehensive about the approaching deadline set by the Native Claims Act. If the Senate couldn't decide on federal withdrawals and boundaries by December, the land freeze would end and all the acreage would revert back to unprotected public land. The only alternative to establishing congressional protection would be a proclamation by President Carter under the Antiquities Act of 1906. In addition to such an order, Andrus was considering withdrawing large tracts as allowed under the Bureau of Land Management's Federal Land Policy and Management Act, passed in 1976. Although we preferred to pass legislation, we agreed that this was a sensible fallback position.

In another intriguing development, the Canadian government in July authorized the withdrawal of 9.6 million acres in the Yukon Territory adjacent to the proposed Arctic National Wildlife Refuge. Studies had shown that 94 percent of the Porcupine caribou herd migrated across the range and across the international border. Just weeks before, Senator Jackson had submitted a proposal to the Energy and Natural Resources Committee for an eight-year oil and gas exploration study in the existing Arctic National Wildlife Range, to be funded jointly by the federal government and industry. Canada was making quicker headway in land and wildlife protection, it seemed, and without the benefit of a national environmental campaign.

PEGGY AND I traveled to Alaska in July 1978, as the Senate bill languished in Jackson's committee. We continued our exploration of the state's rivers that summer with a trip down the Alsek, which flows out of Canada into south-central Alaska. We were recommending that the Alsek watershed be included in an expanded Glacier Bay National Park and wanted to see it firsthand.

We also resumed our meetings with Native leaders to discuss their concerns about the d(2) lands. Many of the older Native leaders, understandably, were skeptical of any legislation offered by whites, fearing for their traditional ways. What would become of their rights to hunt, to fish, to travel in newly protected areas? We tried to assure them that preservation was the only insurance against eventual encroachment by industry and development on the lands they used for survival, and that their traditional rights would be included in each area we proposed.

The younger generation, however, was quite receptive to the idea of federal protection. Perhaps because they had never lived strictly by traditional means, they did not yearn to return to their ancestors' way of life. They were also more savvy about the realities of living in an industrialized world: they wanted both to learn the skills of their tribe and to have the white man's comforts. But with the latter, they recognized, also came development. Parks, refuges, and wilderness would provide buffers between the old ways and the new. Several of the younger leaders promised to distribute petitions in favor of HR 39.

By the end of July, Jack Hession had grown quite concerned about Senator Jackson, whose lack of leadership was clearly stalling the Senate committee proceedings. For the most part, the boundaries set by HR 39 were being respected, perhaps because the senators weren't familiar enough with Alaskan topography to argue the point. Mostly the debate bogged down over which federal agencies should be assigned which lands and what degree of protection each parcel should have. This encompassed questions of what activities would be allowed in each area: for example, mining, oil and gas exploration, hunting, camping, home-siting, and road construction.

Jackson's estimate for a bill to reach the Senate floor had been pushed back to September, four months behind his original schedule. Although the Alaska Coalition had four lobbyists working with Jackson's committee and its staff at this time, and seven assigned to the rest of the Senate, Jackson wanted to meet with me, Hession said. I couldn't get away from San Francisco, but I telephoned Jackson, asking him not to let Stevens continue to dominate the hearings. Jackson assured me that he was in control.

In August, Jackson's committee approved a three-year seismic study for oil and gas exploration in the Arctic National Wildlife Range. It also voted to allow oil and gas leasing in all refuges and mineral leasing in both refuges and parks. This was an alarming development, but Secretary Andrus issued a hard-line response: He would not support a bill allowing mining in refuges. The secretary also said he opposed Governor Hammond's Land Use Planning Commission, a concept still in debate. Nor would he support any wilderness reduction from HR 39.

The Senate committee was finally approaching mark-up, and the Alaska Coalition knew we had a choice. If we were willing to grant concessions, the bill would likely pass through quickly. Like Andrus, however, we chose to stick to our position.

In mid-August, Senator Jackson called in coalition chair Chuck Clusen and Jack Hession for a secret meeting, telling them he wanted "to work with the coalition." Again, Clusen found himself at a loss. We'd been trying to work with Jackson from the start: asking him to sponsor the legislation, speaking with him repeatedly, testifying before his subcommittee, working with his staff. We had grown impatient with Jackson and were starting to wonder if we would have to campaign against a weak Senate bill.

"I hope the coalition can back your ideas rather than buck them," Clusen told Jackson.

Meanwhile, majority leader Byrd told Jackson that if he didn't bring out a bill in the next several weeks, the issue would not reach the floor that session. No doubt in response, Jackson intensified the committee's schedule in the following weeks; instead of three times a week it met twice daily. But Jackson's support for a strong bill was weakening. Hession reported that a pattern had developed: as the committee examined each section of the bill in detail, areas proposed for preservation would be chopped, often significantly. First, committee staff would make recommendations, for the most part environmentally sound. Then Jackson would let Senator Stevens have his say. Stevens and Durkin would debate, with Stevens usually gaining the upper hand. Finally, the committee would vote, with the outcome inevitably weaker than the original staff recommendations. Jackson had become, at best, a mediator in his own committee.

Something had happened to the senator from Washington State—what it was I have never been able to explain to my own satisfaction. This was the man whom I had promoted for the John Muir Award, the Sierra

Club's highest honor, for his work in helping establish Redwoods National Park; the man most responsible for the 17-d(2) amendment creating the process for identifying national interest lands in Alaska; the man who had introduced our Sierra Club proposals for those lands—and he was becoming the biggest disappointment of my conservation career. Later I asked Jackson how he could have professed that the bill was a priority for him, yet allowed the hearings to ramble on at Stevens's discretion. Gone was the man who had been frank and direct. His response was all politician.

"I did what I thought was best for the country," he said.

A bad feeling now surrounded the bill. Work on it was draining the Energy and Natural Resources Committee, and Senator Byrd was afraid that Gravel and Stevens would filibuster once it reached the floor. Even Phil Burton, who would readily face insurmountable odds, was convinced that HR 39 would take too many hits in the Senate to survive. Of thirteen proposed national park areas in the bill passed by the House, twelve had been reduced either in size or degree of protection. Of the 54.3 million acres of proposed wildlife refuges, 20.7 million had been deleted. The total wilderness acreage in national parks and wildlife ranges had been slashed from 61.6 million to just 22.9 million.

At the Alaska Coalition, we decided that floor amendments were our only chance for an acceptable result in the Senate and began planning our amendment strategy. We wondered if Interior would rally behind such amendments or simply oppose the bill. At the end of August, I again spoke with a weary Jackson. He still pledged to get the bill to the floor, but didn't see how it could be debated before the Thanksgiving recess.

WHILE AN INDECISIVE Senate debated its future, Admiralty Island had become the subject of another conflict, this one centered on Native selections. In 1976, Juneau's Goldbelt and Sitka's Shee Atika corporations had filed claims for approximately 23,000 acres each in the Kathleen Lake region of the proposed wilderness. The Sierra Club and the Alaska Coalition strongly opposed these selections and repeatedly appealed to the Department of the Interior to deny them.

In November 1976, Sierra Club leaders met with representatives of the Shee Atika, Goldbelt, and Kootznoowoo corporations in San Francisco in hopes of reaching a settlement. The Kootznoowoo representatives, who also opposed the selections, said they intended to draft a proposal calling for Admiralty to become a national preserve that would allow subsistence hunting. Their lobbyist, Sterling Bolima, would later travel to Washington to push this plan. While Goldbelt and Shee Atika claimed they were willing to consider trading their Admiralty claims for equivalent timber acreage off the island, the conference ended with no resolution.

In May 1977, Jack Hession heard a rumor that the Kootznoowoo Corporation had changed its position and was now willing to support Shee Atika's and Goldbelt's selections at Ward Creek and Kathleen Lake. On my advice, Jack went to Angoon two weeks later but discovered that the rumors were false; the Natives at Angoon had yet to make a final decision. Goldbelt, however, threatened to oppose HR 39 if the Admiralty lands were not conveyed, and we expected Shee Atika would do the same; its attorney, Ed Weinberg, had said he would appeal to Secretary Andrus for their selections. We didn't want to lose the support of the Natives, who could provide critical lobbying and public relations for the Alaska lands bill. We resolved for now to continue negotiations aimed at finding equivalent land and timber values off Admiralty Island.

While Shee Atika remained committed to pursuing claims on Admiralty, Goldbelt did explore several options off the island with varying degrees of seriousness. In June 1978 it agreed to withdraw its selections on Admiralty in exchange for selections in the headwaters of the Situk River, located on the Yakutat Peninsula in the Gulf of Alaska. Ten years earlier these lands had been a part of the Forest Service–Champion contract.

Then followed a drawn-out, frustrating series of near misses with Goldbelt. The corporation vacillated continually in meetings with Sierra Club representatives; its negotiators seemed unsure of the company's position. They entered into negotiations with the Interior Department, only to back out of a deal at the last minute. The Situk selections were abandoned, and by September 1978 Goldbelt was demanding 30,000 acres on Hobart Bay, on the mainland across from Admiralty, as well as $8.5 million in cash from the federal government. The Interior Department countered with 20,000 acres and $2.75 million dollars. Ultimately, the Native and Interior positions were too disparate for compromise. The issue of Native selections on Admiralty remained unresolved as the lands bill made its slow way through the Senate.

In mid-September 1978, I was back in Washington for a meeting of the Sierra Club board of directors. At the Capitol, Senator Jackson said that he was receptive to the possibility of strengthening amendments, but he warned they would have to be in keeping with the "spirit" of the bill.

"I'm unhappy with the bill," I told him. If the coalition had been satisfied with the bill, we wouldn't be offering a slew of amendments.

"Then give me a list of the things that are bothering you."

We were talking in circles.

By the end of the month, Senator Stevens began pushing for the Senate bill to reach the floor. At first glance, this action on the part of our strongest opponent was surprising. But former assistant secretary of the Interior Nathaniel Reed had let it be known that Andrus and Carter again had discussed the possibility of combining an executive order and use of the Federal Land Policy and Management Act to freeze lands in Alaska. According to Andrus, Carter, still tentative, asked him, "Can we really do that?"

"You bet your life we can," Andrus replied.

"Let's do it," said the president.

Perhaps Stevens reasoned that if he did not usher through a weaker bill, the president and interior secretary would take stronger measures. Jackson now claimed the Senate bill would be filed by early October. The coalition continued to draft amendments.

On October 10, Stevens, now nervous about the committee's ability to get out a bill and forestall presidential action, called HR 39 champions Representative Mo Udall and Senator John Durkin to make a deal. Neither would do so. Stevens wanted Udall to introduce the Senate committee bill into the House. Udall refused. Whatever bill the Senate drafted, he said, would have to be at least as strong as HR 39 or the House wouldn't pass it.

Trying a different path in his maneuvering to weaken HR 39, Stevens then tried to tack his Senate bill onto Phil Burton's impending National Parks omnibus bill as an amendment. That effort—a typical Stevens tactic to supplant legislation he didn't like—also failed.

But Udall was willing to keep the dialogue going. The next day, Stevens, Jackson, Udall, and Seiberling tried to forge a compromise. They settled on 51 million acres of wilderness, a median between the House's 64 million acres and the Senate's 37 million. The fate of the Wrangells remained unclear, and wilderness for Admiralty looked doubtful. The following day, Senators Durkin and Gravel joined the discussions, as did Alaska congressman Don Young.

When Chuck Clusen tried to question Durkin about the negotiations, Durkin grew angry. The talks were secret, he said; he wasn't open to more lobbying. Even our allies had reached their breaking point. Clusen would learn bits of detail after the fact but was not allowed to participate in the confidential discussions. He called to say that he feared for the fate of Southeast Alaska.

On October 14, the House and Senate negotiators appeared close to putting out a package. Suddenly, Senator Gravel, who had been absent from that morning's discussions, entered the room and demanded that seven transportation corridors be put into the proposed federal lands. If not, he would filibuster. Jackson said he felt personally offended by Gravel's threat. The other attendees were beyond patience, and negotiations ceased then and there. Andrus responded to the rupture by saying the boundaries for his withdrawal would be completed by the first of November.

On October 15, 1978, Senator Jackson introduced the compromise bill on the Senate floor. Gravel immediately began to filibuster, and majority leader Byrd called off further action on the bill. At a press conference later that day, Jackson blamed Gravel for the negotiators' inability to come to terms, while a frustrated Durkin stepped to the microphone and noted that Gravel's actions would be appreciated by many Alaskans for exactly two months—until the administration withdrawals took effect.

Irritable and unyielding, Gravel stood like a sheer cliff, a totally unassailable obstacle to a solution. Although the version of the bill being negotiated was unacceptable by conservationist standards, he still refused to let it proceed. Unsurprisingly, he also rejected a proposal by the negotiators to postpone for another year the deadline set by ANCSA. Gravel was gambling on the improbability of the Senate passing a bill before the

December deadline in section 17-d(2)—and on his belief that President Carter wouldn't have the spine to invoke the Antiquities Act. "He doesn't have the guts," Gravel supposedly told the negotiating committee.

On the first point, Gravel wagered well. His delaying tactics worked: the full Senate would not debate the issue of Alaskan lands that year. On the second point, however, he was badly mistaken. In early December, President Carter designated 56 million acres as national monuments. Then Secretary Andrus established another 44 million acres as national wildlife refuges.

Rather than rely on these administrative decrees—part of which could lapse in two decades—Andrus and the Alaska Coalition still wanted a legislative solution that would provide permanent protection. Andrus made his withdrawals with a provision that allowed them to be altered if Congress acted by the end of its term, December 1980. If not, protection would be extended automatically for an additional twenty years. Congress, in effect, had been granted a postponement on the original ANCSA deadline of seven years. They now had another two. The debate would begin all over again.

THE YEAR 1979 marked a period of intensified effort on both sides of the Alaska land battle. Up to then, the opposition's tactics had amounted only to delay, while conservationists had organized and come out fighting. But as the ninety-fifth Congress opened, those who wanted to see Alaska's lands developed had both organizations and funds in place. The Committee for the Management of Alaska's Lands (CMAL) and the Real Alaska Coalition were the two principal groups fighting HR 39. The State of Alaska had earmarked $7 million for that campaign.

Fortunately, Carter and Andrus's withdrawals had provided a temporary safety net as conservationists went back to the drawing board on legislation. The Alaska Coalition helped House Interior Committee chair Mo Udall prepare a new bill, this one much stronger than the HR 39 passed the previous spring. From the onset, however, Udall declared a disappointing willingness to compromise. He claimed he'd felt out his committee and found less support than he'd hoped for. Representative Lamar Gudger of North Carolina offered a compromise bill, weaker than

HR 39, but it failed to muster enough support. Then Representative Jerry Huckaby of Louisiana, ardently pro-business and -development, proposed a bill even more watered down than Gudger's; it narrowly passed out of committee but went nowhere on the floor.

At this point, fearing that we could do much worse, the Alaska Coalition pressed for the reintroduction of HR 39 to the House. Lobbying efforts were beefed up, and the Sierra Club produced a five-hundred-thousand-piece mailing. Jack Hession and Barbara Blake, a young graduate of the University of California, Santa Cruz, began meeting daily with congressional aides. On March 23, one Sierra Club lobbyist made a round of the House and found 148 representatives willing to cosponsor the return of HR 39, as passed by the previous Congress. On March 28, in a display of bipartisan support, Republican congressman John Anderson of Illinois introduced the bill. By April 3, its cosponsors had increased to 151.

In addition to Hession and Blake, the Sierra Club had twenty lobbyists in Washington, as well as several regional representatives who flew into town specifically to work for HR 39. That spring, however, the talented and hard-working Chuck Clusen resigned from the Alaska Coalition to become conservation director at The Wilderness Society. I was disappointed to see him leave but recognized that his new position offered advancement. Douglas Scott, the Sierra Club's Northwest representative for conservation, who had been working with the coalition, replaced Clusen as chair. Other conservation groups had lobbyists in the capital as well.

These efforts culminated in an unprecedented campaign on every level. Lists were made of all the representatives: each received at least one call as the floor vote neared. At 5 A.M. (Pacific time) on May 16, the morning of the vote, I telephoned Representative Pete McCloskey of California, who was on the doubtful list. McCloskey was so impressed by the fact that I had risen so early to call, he pledged his support to the bill. The final vote was a landslide: HR 39 passed again, this time 360 to 63.

ON A SUNNY afternoon in May 1979, I gave away my eldest daughter, Cynthia, in marriage. The wedding took place in the garden of our home in Bolinas, on a bluff overlooking the Pacific. Breaking waves looked like white slivers against the serpentine shoreline. Far away rose the distant rounded humps of San Francisco, the strict lines of its row houses and granite towers softened by the haze of distance. Cynthia had gone with us to Alaska and fallen in love with Jim Roush—an unexpected consequence of our adventures. Their relationship had quietly blossomed, unbeknownst to either Peggy or me, until early 1979, when I had received a letter from Jim asking for my blessing. I gave it readily; Cynthia could not have found a finer husband. Jim had been a good friend for many years; now the pilot of the *Red Baron* was also our son-in-law.

This joyful event was a brief interlude in preparations for a looming fight in the Senate over the Alaska bill. By 1979, Senator Jackson's promises to get HR 39 through the Senate Energy and Natural Resources Committee echoed like a hollow refrain. During my trip to Washington that June, Jackson told me he was moving as fast as he could, but in fact he did virtually nothing in the months following HR 39's victory in the House. Meanwhile, Stevens, who chaired the Senate Interior Appropriations Subcommittee, refused to authorize any funds for the national monuments designated by President Carter. There wasn't even enough money for rangers to patrol against trespassers.

Finally, in October, Jackson's committee began to mark up a bill. By this time, Sierra Club lobbyist Barbara Blake had developed a close working relationship with Senator Paul Tsongas of Massachusetts, and Tsongas became the coalition's champion on the committee. Dissatisfied with the bill that finally passed out of committee on October 30, Tsongas committed himself to introducing strong amendments. Although the weaker Senate committee bill, S-9, bore no resemblance to the bill passed in the House, it was nonetheless renamed HR 39.

Although there was some debate on the Senate's HR 39, Congress recessed for the Christmas holiday before it came to a vote. Over the break, there was much talk among conservationists, who were beginning to feel discouraged after years of waging an unsuccessful campaign. Some felt that legislation must be passed at any cost—that the Andrus and Carter withdrawals left too much to chance. Who was to say that a pro-development Congress wouldn't reverse them twenty years down the line? Some were also afraid of the mounting opposition. The state of Alaska was in upheaval, with some residents threatening to secede from the Union.

Personally, I preferred banking on the withdrawals over a weak bill—at least the door would stay open for debate for another twenty years. Once a bill was passed, it would shut the door forever.

As it stood, we had a satisfactory House bill and an unsatisfactory Senate committee bill. Again, our best hope lay in strengthening amendments. On February 9, Senators Byrd, Jackson, Stevens, Gravel, and Tsongas held a meeting with the Senate parliamentarian and determined that the bill would be taken up by the full Senate by June. Stevens, who would be busy campaigning for reelection in the fall, wanted to avoid postponing debate on HR 39. Debate would not begin, however, until July 22.

Andrus did not wait until the eve of his departure to secure his withdrawals. In early February he told Congress that if it did not act in the next few weeks, he would use his authority to permanently withdraw some 40 million acres that had been temporarily protected under the Federal Land Policy and Management Act since 1978. On February 11, he acted on that promise, saying, "I'm glad the Senate is finally looking to scheduling the bill, but I am very concerned that the lateness of that date will lead to a stalemate in the closing days of the ninety-sixth Congress just as happened to its predecessor in 1978."

In early July 1980, Peggy and I returned to Admiralty Island. In Angoon, we found that funds from the Native Claims Act had produced tangible results. Many of the derelict dwellings had been repaired, and a string of new houses had been built on a hill above the main thoroughfare. The Tlingits still relied heavily on subsistence hunting and fishing but now had additional funds for equipment, schools, and medicine.

Other developments on the island were not as reassuring. It seemed almost certain that Admiralty would remain in the hands of the U.S. Forest Service. Although the coalition originally had pushed for a wilderness under NPS control, we had ceased to press the point to avoid further alienating either the Forest Service or Secretary Andrus.

We flew with forester K.J. Metcalf to Kathleen Lake, where it seemed the Shee Atika Corporation would be awarded 23,000 acres. Metcalf, who had managed the new Admiralty Island National Monument in the months since Carter's decree, would later leave the Forest Service because he could no longer stomach the agency's permissive logging policies. He also opposed Native selections in the region. Shee Atika had not been secretive about its intent to log; the corporation had demanded timber-rich land from the beginning. Metcalf would go on to buy the Angoon general store and continue to help organize for Admiralty's protection.

The lake itself was a jewel, tucked into one of the region's several large canyons. Tall hills bounded either side of the canyons, their upper reaches soaring into 5,000-foot coastal mountains whose summits remained streaked with snow all summer.

We rowed out on the lake in a boat left at the shore. Thick stands of Sitka spruce and hemlock surrounded us; a pale tundra carpet wove above the forest floor. We stayed the night in a primitive Forest Service log cabin, one of several scattered throughout the forest, and wondered how long the trees would remain standing.

I ARRIVED BACK in Washington the day before the debate to find the Senate hallways crammed with people. The Senate chamber itself was packed: the Sierra Club and other coalition members had called in volunteers to canvas senators. Every state was represented; there were several hundred people in all.

We divided into pairs, each pair taking a list of a few senators, and made our rounds. I was teamed with Marlon Perkins, the famous white-haired and mustached host of *Wild Kingdom*. Of the three names we had drawn, our first, Senator William Cohen of Maine, was undecided. While he favored the House bill, he explained, he was also a Republican and a freshman; he didn't want to cross Stevens, who had become the new minority whip. Our second name was development-minded California senator S. I. Hayakawa. Our talk with him was largely in vain, with Hayakawa calling Stevens's position "a rational stand." Finally we spoke to Senator John Warner of Virginia, who didn't need convincing: he had pledged firm support for the House version of HR 39. He was also a big fan of Perkins's show, asking him if he could find a bit part for Warner's new wife, the actress Elizabeth Taylor!

That night, July 21, the Alaska Coalition threw a party with a guest list reaching more than a thousand. Country musician John Denver performed. Our mood was expectant: so many individuals had come, often from great distances, to show their support. And yet we remained uncertain of what would transpire the next day. My own experience of making the rounds showed that the pledged votes were divided and many senators still undecided. While many tried to piece together the significance of the day's lobbying, there were no senators at the party and no one could predict the next day's outcome.

The next morning, I sat in the gallery above the Senate floor, watching the debate below. Senators Gary Hart of Colorado and John Chafee of Rhode Island introduced the first amendment, which called for the addition of several national wildlife refuges. Strategically, we wanted to begin on a strong note and thought the Hart-Chafee amendment was the most likely to succeed. Immediately Jackson, who felt the amendment ran counter to the spirit of his bill, stood up and moved to table it. That vote failed two to one, with seventeen Republicans voting against Jackson. A compromise amendment also failed by the same margin. The tide was moving in our favor.

Then Stevens lost his cool and stood up out of order; pointing his finger, he began accusing Hart and Chafee of "reneging on promises made to the state two years ago." Within a minute, he was livid. Half of what he said was incomprehensible, but among his exclamations was one clear threat: filibuster. If debate continued, Stevens would introduce eighteen amendments, each requiring a half hour of debate and a fifteen-minute vote.

His show was impressive, if bombastic. Although I believed he would do everything possible to carry out his threats, I also felt elated. It seemed certain that we now had the votes in the Senate to pass a good version of HR 39.

At this juncture Jackson, the floor manager, called the bill off the floor. Since he had become chair of the Interior Committee, Jackson had had a perfect track record; he had never lost a vote for a bill drafted by his committee but was now facing the possibility of his first failure. In the anteroom I approached him.

"Don't be 'Stonewall' Jackson," I urged him.

"I won't stonewall," he replied. "I've seen which way the wind blows, and I'm willing to compromise."

Jackson, Stevens, Hart, Chafee, Roth, and Tsongas were asked to devise a mutually acceptable compromise on the Senate's HR 39, and the group began to meet in secret. The hundreds of environmental supporters who had converged on Washington headed home, dejected. I returned to San Francisco several days later with little information. The euphoric sense of hope we'd felt now fizzled into nervousness, confusion, and above all, frustration. Two years earlier, Senator Gravel had single-handedly stifled the House–Senate compromise bill. Now another lone ranger, Stevens, had halted debate in the Senate. This arcane, flawed process tested my faith in the American legislative system.

By August, mostly due to Tsongas's willingness to compromise, the group reached an agreement. The new bill—introduced by Jackson, Roth, Hatfield, and Tsongas—included most of the geography we wanted, though some areas were decreased in size and a lot of administrative provisions added. Senator Stevens made a motion of cloture so that debate would be severely limited and to prevent Gravel, who again threatened to filibuster, from hijacking the proceedings. Without fanfare, the compromise bill—still called HR 39—passed the Senate on August 19, 1980.

Now: how to reconcile the Senate's HR 39 with the House version? We enlisted our House allies Udall, Seiberling, and Burton to influence their senatorial colleagues, but to little avail. Several senators flatly refused either to compromise or to hold a conference with the House. Even Seiberling's attempt to introduce a slightly weaker version of the House's HR 39 failed when Stevens got wind of it and bullied the Republican bloc.

An even bigger problem loomed, however. President Carter's chances for reelection were rapidly dwindling as anger mounted over the American hostages being held in Iran. There was also a very real threat of a Republican takeover of the Senate. And most senators were too preoccupied with the elections to accomplish anything significant in the last few weeks of the session.

On November 3, the eve of the election, I held an all-day meeting at my home in Bolinas. Present were Doug Scott, Jack Hession, Paul Lowe (chair of the Sierra Club's Alaska Chapter), and Pete Brabeck, representing the Southeast Alaska Conservation Council. Despite differences of opinion on some issues, we all knew we had to act fast and as a unified whole. The House's HR 39 would never make it past Stevens and the Senate Republican bloc. The only solution lay in quick passage of the Senate bill through the House. If we waited, it would only give the opposition more time to introduce weakening amendments. If the Republicans took control in January, as seemed certain, any chance for a strong bill in either house would be squashed.

On November 4, the GOP won not only the presidency but a landslide victory in Congress. For the first time, I recognized the absolute necessity of compromise. Five years of hard-nosed lobbying, campaigning, and testifying had amounted to several near misses. Carter and Andrus's withdrawals provided a temporary safety net, but they could be overturned by a later president or Congress, and we had little faith that the Reagan administration would prove more sympathetic than the current one.

The jig was finally up. Doug Scott returned to Washington to talk with Udall and Seiberling about the necessity of supporting a weaker bill. A week later on November 12, 1980, the Senate's version of HR 39 passed the House, and the president signed the new law a few weeks later.

THE ALASKA NATIONAL Interest Lands Conservation Act remains the largest piece of land conservation legislation in American history. It provides, in varying degrees, protection for 104 million acres of Alaska's lands and waters. Its geography stretches from the state's southernmost reaches to the Arctic Ocean and includes a plethora of landforms: mountains, glaciers, islands, forests, rivers, fjords, volcanic craters, and tundra. It set a benchmark for American conservation: in lobbying for its passage, conservationists had taken the unprecedented step of forming a single, unified coalition—an alliance that continues to provide a model for future environmental campaigns.

On December 2, 1980, I sat among the crowd in the East Room of the White House, witnessing the ANILCA signing ceremony in the company of many familiar faces. Lloyd Tupling, the Club' s first full-time representative, slipped into the chair next to me.

President Carter spoke first. Within weeks he would cede his office to Ronald Reagan, and our country would enter into a new political era, one that would pose great challenges for conservationists. Watching Carter speak was a bittersweet experience; his determination to issue presidential decrees had thrown ANILCA's opposition for a loop. While many Americans had lost faith in the president during the Iran hostage crisis, I was not among them. His policies had been questioned many times, but not his principles. He still stands out in my mind as one of this country's greatest presidents, perhaps in some respects too good a man for the job. At the end of his speech, the president received a long salvo of cheers.

Senator Jackson, and then Congressmen Udall and Seiberling, followed the president. All warmly praised the act and received enthusiastic applause. Then Senator Stevens spoke, railing to the end, promising to correct "problems" in the bill, such as the prohibition of mining in wildlife refuges. Finally Secretary Andrus came to the podium and rescued the mood with an upbeat speech.

After the ceremony, I walked through the Capitol halls with Phil Burton, who was working on passage of his latest parks bill, a proposal devoted to buying lots around Lake Tahoe to save its shores from rapid development. President Carter had pledged his support, but Burton would have to act fast. He combed his colleagues' offices, collecting signatures from representatives who had been absent from the Senate–House conference that day. We ran into Roy Greenaway, the top aide for California's Senator Cranston; both were depressed by the election results. I also talked with Senator Jackson, who advised me to move slowly with the new Republican majority.

The votes for ANILCA had been tallied; the president's signature gave it the indelible mark of law. What had taken form as a tenuous vision thirteen years earlier was now accomplished for posterity. Preserving Alaska's wilds had become my mission, at times eclipsing all other aspects of my life. I felt victory, satisfaction, even a certain sense of resolution.

And yet, I did not feel completion. The campaign for Alaska's lands had reached an important plateau, but not an end; I doubted it ever would. Issues of ANILCA's interpretation and enforcement would arise; there would be boundary disputes and outstanding Native selections to resolve. Conservation campaigns never really end. They cross certain milestones, but wild lands must always be defended against those who would encroach on their ecological integrity, mine their soils, log their forests, or drill their shores. To conserve is the *act* of preservation; the very name implies an ongoing process. I was reminded of the famous line, "Eternal vigilance is the price of liberty."

Although many imagined that, at seventy-four, I might hang up my cap after this milestone, I was not ready to do so. I decided to continue as chair of the Sierra Club's Alaska Task Force. I did not know where the next campaign would lead me or what form it would take. But then, I could not have anticipated how the fight to save Mount Tamalpais and the hills of western Marin County would unfold, or the redwoods campaign, or the battle for Alaska's lands. Who knew what wilds remained to be explored and defended, what adventures were still to come?

In THE YEARS since passage of ANILCA, I continued to keep a close eye on Alaska developments, tracking the precarious implementation of the landmark law under the hostile Reagan and Bush administrations, struggling against the ruthlessly pro-development agenda of the state's congressional delegation. And Peggy and I continued to visit Alaska on regular annual trips.

The battle for Admiralty Island had some irrevocably sad outcomes. Shee Atika leased its lands there to the Konkor Lumber Company, of which it was a part owner. The primeval forest around the cabin where we had stayed began to thin as the cuts began. The Sierra Club filed legal appeals throughout the 1980s to stop the clear-cuts but lost; federal courts ruled that the Natives had the right to do whatever they wanted with their private property. That land is now skinned—barren strips on an island otherwise dedicated to wilderness. It is impossible to convey the sadness of such a desecration.

Alaska's national parks increasingly became a battlefield. In the face of a powerful, hostile congressional delegation, national park managers became defensive and reluctant to enforce the law—doing so could jeopardize their careers. In Katmai National Park they were unable or unwilling to work for the welfare of the extraordinary brown bears. In Denali National Park, they had trouble preventing development by inholders and fending off new tourist and road developments. In Glacier

Bay National Park, commercial fishermen asserted alleged rights to pursue their occupation.

In Wrangell–St. Elias National Park, subsistence use pressures mounted formidably. Such hunting often involved the use of off-road vehicles, and their unrestrained impact damaged sensitive trails and hill-sides. This became a widespread and ongoing problem that continues today with rising use of off-road vehicles for recreation.

In the Tongass and Chugach National Forests, the Forest Service, to no one's surprise, bowed to the timber industry's relentless pressure for more cutting—often ignoring the advice of the agency's own scientists. We resorted to seeking legislation, and in November 1990, the Tongass Timber Reform Act passed and was signed by President Bush Sr.

The omission from ANILCA of permanent protection for the 1.5-million-acre coastal plain of the Arctic National Wildlife Refuge has led to the most contentious and heartrending battle for Alaska's environment that we have yet seen. When the Reagan-era Interior Department issued its study report in 1987, recommending that the plain be opened to oil exploration and development, our champions in Congress, such as Senator William Roth of Delaware, immediately introduced bills to designate the beleaguered region as wilderness. Alaska's congressional representatives, cheered on by the oil lobby, countered with their own development bills.

From then until today, Congress has remained a battleground between these two factions. The public has become engaged to a remarkable extent, and the coastal plain has become a true symbol of diminishing wildness in an ever more altered world.

Alaska lands benefited under the Clinton administration in the 1990s, but only temporarily. Several times the president vetoed budget and other measures that would have allowed the coastal plain of the Arctic National Wildlife Refuge to be exploited, its remote wildness and rich panoply of wildlife to be lost.

Under President Clinton, also, came a laudable push to protect road-less areas in national forests nationwide. Due to pressure from the Alaska delegation, initial drafts of this proposal prepared by the Forest Service did not include the Tongass National Forest. After a sustained outcry at public hearings and in the media, however, the final version of the plan did include the Tongass. However gratifying this was, the plan unfortunately was put into place too late in Clinton's tenure to take effect irrevocably before the George W. Bush administration stepped in. And this administration even now is laboring mightily to undo those protections against logging and road construction.

Permanent protection of many of Alaska's unparalleled, unique wildlands seems no closer today—but the vision of preserving them in perpetuity lives on, unquenchable and shining.

CHAPTER NINE

EXPANDING THE ARENA

The Global Environment

❧

*Human uses of planet earth must respect the
ecological constraints imposed by the natural environment.
Failure to respect them will mean more and more floods,
more severe and frequent drought . . . hurricanes and tornadoes . . .
essentially wiping out any economic gains.*

—Raymond Dasmann, *Called by the Wild*

OVER THE YEARS I've gradually extended my work in protecting natural areas around the United States to protecting natural areas all over the globe. I've learned that natural ecosystems do not stop at national political boundaries, nor do threats to those ecosystems and to environmental quality. I have become increasingly concerned about the persistent organic pollutants (POPs) that circle the planet in ever-greater amounts, about the worsening shortage of fresh water, about the dangers to native plants and wildlife posed by introduced species. More and more, I have been struck by the truth of John Muir's axiom: "When we try to pick out anything by itself, we find it hitched to everything else in the universe."

Thus, I have come to the inevitable conclusion that no matter how well we fare in our battles on a regional or national level within the United States, if we don't tackle environmental problems on a global scale—if we fail to achieve success around the planet—the war to protect our environment will be lost.

My international activities have taken place in two main arenas. One is my work with the principal international organizations set up through the United Nations, or the International Union for the Conservation of Nature (IUCN)—the chief international nongovernmental organization for conservation, now renamed the World Conservation Union. I have been active for many years in the IUCN and served on its Commission on National Parks and Protected Areas (CNPPA), also now renamed as the World Commission on Protected Areas (WCPA). I'm proud to have played a major role in the adoption of "wilderness" as a distinct category among the UN's land use designations. I've also worked extensively with the World Congress on National Parks and the independent World Wilderness Congress, which have convened periodically.

The other arena has been the Sierra Club's International Committee and International Program. In the late 1960s, during my second Club presidency, I helped shepherd the establishment of the International Program. The decision to initiate an international program with a staff director was a big step forward for the Club. Our desire to work with and influence the United Nations and its nascent environmental programs led us to employ an international staffer and, since the UN was headquartered in New York, to begin the program as a New York–based venture. Nicholas Robinson, a Club volunteer based in New York, was instrumental in this process. We hired Patricia Scharlin as the program's first director, a position she held from 1971 to 1985.

As in my American conservation campaigns, I've felt compelled to gain some personal experience—even if in a limited way—of the places where my concern focused. This goal has provided a gratifying focus for numerous trips abroad over the past several decades. I've now traveled to all six continents, purposefully observing and making notes on places of special interest—particularly the national parks of each country. And I have been struck by the differences, from one country to the next, in the status of national park lands. In England, for example, only 1 percent of national parkland is owned by the Crown, while 10 percent is owned by the National Trust—itself a public/private entity. All the rest is in private ownership but is restricted in use, with easements to allow public access.

I first traveled outside the United States in 1930—at that time, my love of nature and wild places had yet to develop into any real "environmental consciousness." When I graduated from Harvard Medical School in June of that year, I had six months free before beginning my internship in internal medicine at New York City's Columbia-Presbyterian Medical Center. Since I wanted to study pathology, I took advantage of this interval to go to Germany—in those days the undisputed leader in anatomical pathology, as it had been since the mid-nineteenth century—sailing on the Hamburg-America Steamship Line from New York to Hamburg and back. From the beginning to the end of the journey I refused to speak English, so I learned German in a fairly short period of time. After four months in the Institute of Pathology of the University of Berlin, I had mastered the language well enough that the professor, Herr Doktor Schurmann, asked me to teach part of an undergraduate course in pathology.

During those six months in Germany, I was able to make a three-week tour from my base in Berlin to Leipzig, Munich, Nuremberg, and Heidelberg, down the Rhine River, and back to Berlin. A highlight of that journey was having an opportunity to see, at the University of Heidelberg, the famous Heidelberg Man; the fossilized jawbone was kept in a locked drawer in a locked room. Although this trip focused on cities rather than on the countryside, I recall that the German rural landscape looked very well kept.

During World War II, I was stationed in England for two years—the first with a U.S. Air Force fighter squadron at the village of Martlesham Heath on the edge of the North Sea, and the second in London as chief of the Mass Chest X-ray Service of the U.S. Air Forces in Europe. Able to travel around England a good deal, I learned how land that had been occupied by humans for more than two thousand years, and completely altered from its natural condition, could still be cared for in a sustainable way. The English seemed to take better care of their lands than we Americans did of ours. This experience helped interest me in land stewardship and in looking more critically at land use and protection when I returned home to the West Coast.

During the 1960s and 1970s, Peggy and I made several trips to the Mediterranean Sea and the lands that surround it. The first was a seven-day Mediterranean cruise starting in Malta, with stops in Rome, Genoa, Nice, and Barcelona. These were mainly city visits, however, with scant opportunity to see parks and natural areas. In 1975 and 1979 we stopped in Europe on our way to Kenya to experience the great East African wildlife parks. The safari took us to the Masai Mara Nature Reserve and the Aberdare, Mt. Kenya, Nairobi, and Lake Nakura national parks, as well as the Mt. Kulal Biosphere Reserve. Although many reserves in Kenya are labeled "national parks," they are really reserves designed to allow visitors to experience the native wildlife—more along the lines of our wildlife refuges. The same is true of the Lake Manyara, Ngorongoro Crater, and Serengeti national parks in neighboring Tanzania.

ALL THESE TRAVELS helped shape my ideas about international conservation needs to some extent, but one journey most strikingly showed me the natural wonders outside my own country, and the need to safeguard them. In 1970 I led a Sierra Club trip to that showcase of evolution, the Galapagos Islands. Sailing from Panama City in a three-masted, gaff-rigged schooner, the *Te Vega,* we reached the islands in five days; on the return voyage we sailed on to Costa Rica. On the voyage, the beauty and fascination of the sea took over our souls; we were its pliant creatures. The weather was tropical and serene.

On reaching the enchanted realm, we spent fifteen days roaming from island to island, wandering around on shore as if in a dream world. Each island is different, each a small bit of desert perfection. The wildlife was intoxicating, unlike anything I had seen before: blue-footed boobies so tame you could step on them, or they would step on your feet. We could stroke the iguanas and swim among the seals, which seemed to enjoy our company.

As so many others have realized, we were in a place of incomparable and unique beauty, which must be preserved. Once home, we gave encouragement and support to the Darwin Institute and other agencies that have worked to preserve this amazing place—which is now an Ecuadorian national park. But in the last thirty years, visitation has increased many-fold, affecting the environment greatly; one wonders how fully the islands' natural values can be retained.

The early 1970s also saw my first forays into the politics of global environmentalism. In 1972, Executive Director Mike McCloskey and I were the Sierra Club's representatives to the First International Conference on the Human Environment, sponsored by the United Nations in Stockholm. At this memorable event I was first exposed to a global perspective on environmental concerns; the following account can be considered representative of many other such meetings I would attend later.

My first impression was of a six-ring circus—and it was: three major committees and a plenary session going on simultaneously, each attended by as many as 114 national delegates. In addition, there was the Miljo Forum for nongovernmental organizations (NGOs), with its own speeches and sideshows, some extra events like the Population Institute lectures, and more.

A United Nations forum is enormously complex. The variety of languages spoken underscores the wide-ranging problems of technology, development, and varying degrees of national affluence that come into play. The UN Secretariat has its own allegiances and patois. Five kinds of NGOs attended the conference: the "old-line" UN agencies that had been around for twenty-five years, financed by private funds and not previously involved with environmental issues; groups representing business interests; scientific groups associated with the UN and/or the IUCN; and finally environmental groups. At the conference, we learned to lobby in this milieu.

At the start of the conference, I was dismayed to read the proposed recommendations of the preparatory committees. We had welcomed this event as the first international forum recognizing the importance of the environment, but it was obvious that during the preceding month, the preparatory committees had deviated from this principal topic into issues of social and socioeconomic justice—topics for which many other fora existed. On the plus side, I was encouraged to see that Arctic issues, in which I had a particular interest because of my Alaska advocacy, were included in the discussions.

The various NGOs held briefings of one to one and a half hours every morning, as well as meetings among themselves every afternoon. The economist Barbara Ward Jackson guided these brilliantly. There was a great deal of talk about maintaining national sovereignty, about redistributing wealth, and about improving the environment while maximizing development. The emphasis seemed to be on the science of ecology and how it could be used to further economic goals. Mike and I tried to counter this by articulating a broader preservation philosophy. The idea of a nongovernmental organization advocating for the environment was largely an American, and more recently a European, phenomenon. The movement was not yet under way in undeveloped nations—but it was needed.

The debates in Committee Two—on Natural Resources, Environment, and Development—often ran very long. Several factors were responsible: the wide range of ideas in any large group meeting for the first time, lack of knowledge on the part of some delegates, conflicting attitudes on the respective value of undeveloped versus developed land, and issues of national sovereignty. Beyond that were the difficulties inherent in translating several spoken and written languages, with English, French, German, Spanish, and Chinese—in various dialects—all being used.

The conference went on for ten very full days. As the days passed and the committees made slow progress—sometimes working until 1:30 A.M. — I began to feel hopeful and gradually encouraged. Out of the welter of debate and friction, final recommendations began to emerge, and often they were improved as they changed. I remember, for example, the recommendation on international bodies of water: Romania offered a series of amendments that broadened the mechanisms and changed the emphasis from economic to environmental—altering the whole thrust of that recommendation.

Some of the small nations had representatives of high quality, notably Kenya. The head of Kenya's three-man delegation was most impressive in the plenary session, and we came to rely on the Kenyans for help with our Sierra Club resolutions. The Club had prepared three resolutions for the conference. We first took them to Russell Train, who was leading the U.S. delegation. Train, who had chaired the Council on Environmental Quality in the first Nixon administration and served as undersecretary of the interior in the second, advised us, "The United States has no clout at this conference. Anything the U.S. proposes will be defeated—go to one of the Third World delegations."

Throughout the conference, in fact, we felt a good deal of undercover and even open hostility to everything American. The U.S. was attacked, insulted, and outvoted in meetings, and as a result kept a low profile. The federal government did send every environmental official it could—sixty delegates and alternates in all—devoting an enormous amount of talent and energy to the event. And as the delegation chair, Russell Train did an excellent job.

So we took his advice and went to the delegation from Kenya. They agreed to introduce our resolutions and were successful in getting them passed.

Mike and I also entrusted Perez Olindo, director of the Kenyan National Park Service and a member of Kenya's delegation, with the task of keeping out of the final conference report certain recommendations to national governments that were bad for the environment—such as a recommendation on forestry that promoted economic development over protection and a recommendation on wildlife that encouraged hunting-based tourism. These items were not in the final report that went to the plenary session.

At the end of the conference, several hundred recommendations were made for international action. Most important, nations now recognized the necessity of dealing with environmental problems and agreed to work together. Concrete results of the event included the official establishment of the United Nations Environmental Program. The action plan for creating UNEP specified:

a) A governing council of 54 members, reporting to the United Nations General Assembly, through the Economic and Social Affairs Council (ECOSOC);

b) an executive director with a small staff to correlate and direct activities, alone and with existing agencies such as the Food and Agricultural Organization (FAO) and the IUCN;

c) provision of funding, beginning at the rate of $20 million a year for five years; and

d) a potential Declaration for the Human Environment.

The Sierra Club supported Kenya's bid to have UNEP based in Nairobi instead of in Geneva, Switzerland.

I came away from the Stockholm Conference on the Human Environment convinced that the Sierra Club could play a greater role in environmental affairs internationally. What we were already doing in the United States (and to an increasing extent in Canada) needed doing all over the world. I hoped that our new International Program office could serve as a two-way conduit of environmental information and action with the UN and other agencies. Shortly after the Stockholm conference, Mike McCloskey, Pat Scharlin (staff director of the Club's program), and I met with Gerardo Budowski, Frank Nicholls, and Ray Dasmann of the IUCN—a meeting that formed the basis of future cooperation.

BECAUSE SO MANY of my efforts in America concerned the establishment and protection of national parks, my involvement in global environmental work naturally came to focus on national parks and protected areas. In September 1972, my global education was furthered by attending the Second World Congress on National Parks, held at Grand Teton National Park in Jackson Hole, Wyoming. These decadal international conferences on national parks were first sponsored by the U.S. National Park Service and later by the IUCN. Attendees included representatives from the parks agencies of other nations, as well as other government staffers, and from a variety of NGOs. The first Parks Congress had taken place in Seattle in 1962.

The Wyoming event was a type of gathering more familiar to me than the Stockholm Conference. At a symposium on Interpretation and Education in National Parks conducted by Professor Mohandas Kassis of Egypt, the president of IUCN, I learned how many countries longed to adapt for their own use the original American concept of national parks. Participating were representatives from Ghana, Tanzania, the Philippines, Thailand, Sweden, and Great Britain, besides the United States. A discussion on Alaska lands—although a minor sidelight for the conference—was of special interest to me. The discussion singled out the Alatna River region as a top-priority choice for a national park, and the conference issued a recommendation that Congress pass legislation or provide for a land exchange. No action resulted from this until the Carter administration withdrawals, though the region is now part of Gates of the Arctic National Park.

A decade later, in 1982, I participated in the third Parks Congress, held in Indonesia. In connection with this journey, Peggy and I took time to visit several parks on the islands of Bali and Java. Native people live in or on the edge of these parks, and use the trees for firewood. By U.S. criteria, few would be considered national parks. A dramatic sidelight of that trip was a hiking accident on the Bromo Volcano in southern Java (yes, the source of the name Bromo-Seltzer), in which Peggy broke her ankle. She had to be carried out by foot, Jeep, and airplane to medical facilities in Surabaya.

The program for the Fourth World Congress on National Parks, held in Caracas, Venezuela, in February 1992, addressed the place of protected areas in the world, discrepancies between the wealthy north and the poverty-stricken Southern Hemisphere, extraction of resources, the need for international environmental efforts, and the role of sustainable development in maintaining society.

At this meeting I presented a paper titled "The Role of a Non-Governmental Organization in Preserving National Parks and Protected Areas." It described the rise of conservation organizations—particularly national advocacy organizations such as the Sierra Club among them, recounting what we had accomplished in the past hundred years and what we hoped to be able to do in the future. I stressed our international interests and extended an invitation to all the NGOs represented at the congress to turn to us for help. I hoped to share the benefits of our century of experience in fighting the adverse effects of development.

This talk aroused the interest of two officials of the Comite Nacional Pro Defensa de la Fauna y Flora de Chile (CODEFF). Dr. Miguel Stutzin and Hernan Verscheure met with me to discuss ways in which our two organizations could cooperate for betterment of Chile's environment.

My efforts at this congress, I realize in retrospect, focused on pointing out what was missing from its program: the congress largely failed to address threats to endangered protected areas or the dangers of proliferating human population. Concerning the latter, I offered an "intervention" to Adrian Phillips, chair of the recommendations committee, asking that the congress advise world governments to educate their people on the dangers of rampant population growth, and noting that human numbers already exceeded the earth's carrying capacity for sustaining a quality environment. Addressing the plenary session on the Caracas Declaration, which would summarize the conference's deliberations and aims, I outlined the dangers posed by overpopulation to protected areas in particular and to human life in general. I asked that the declaration contain a statement calling on governments to institute education and stabilization measures addressing overpopulation. Such language was approved by the plenary session, but I never saw it in the final declaration.

ON A BROADER LEVEL, an ideal forum for the Sierra Club's involvement in global environmental issues proved to be the International Union for the Conservation of Nature (IUCN)—now known as the World Conservation Union. Officially launched in 1948 under the joint auspices of the United Nations Economic and Social Council (UNESCO) and the French government, the organization grew and evolved steadily. General assemblies were held every three to four years. I participated in four of these: in Madrid (1984); San Jose, Costa Rica (1988); Perth, Australia (1990); and Montreal (1996). Among my goals was always to turn the delegates' attention more strongly toward environmental protection.

At the 1984 assembly in Madrid, I succeeded in getting IUCN to consider designating wilderness as a separate category in the UN's system of classifying protected lands. In subsequent assemblies, Mike McCloskey and I teamed up to promote recognition of wilderness, and our efforts finally succeeded in 1990.

The Costa Rica gathering began in January 1988 with a meeting of the Commission on National Parks and Protected Areas, my primary focus. At that meeting I offered the Sierra Club's aid to IUCN in increasing media promotion of national parks and other protected areas and in broadening public support. The General Assembly began a few days later with numerous workshops and symposia; sustainable development in Central America was a strong theme. As at other events, I tried to move IUCN away from exclusively emphasizing the scientific aspects of conservation and onto the path of advocacy. I kept urging the council and secretariat to include advocacy for environmental protection—especially for maintaining protected areas—as a major topic, to balance its emphasis on science. It is gratifying to me that, in the last decade, IUCN has become noticeably more advocacy oriented.

This gathering offered the chance for another side trip: a flight to Corcovado National Park, Costa Rica's large, magnificent tropical rainforest park. On our flight in, we observed much devastation—mountainsides devoid of forest and overgrazed, eroded grasslands slashed by raw, red roads. Patches of land cleared by squatters turned streams into torrents of mud. The park itself provided an astounding contrast; here a canopy of trees of all sizes—flowering trees, native palms, and varied hardwoods—spread out over lush ground cover. Flying back over the Pacific coast and the mountains, we witnessed in reverse the dramatic transition from natural landscape to devastation.

After our stay in Costa Rica, the McCloskeys and Peggy and I had the opportunity to travel on to Peru, where we visited several national parks as well as Peruvian NGOs. We saw parks in three distinctly different environments, beginning with Huascaran National Park in the Andes, at 13,000 feet, where we were driven along high, tiny roads to encounter huge El Capitan–like cliffs lining narrow canyons. We enjoyed fantastic views, cloud-obscured in the higher reaches of the Cordillera Blanca. Our botanist guides pointed out the region's unique vegetation communities, though we also noted many exotics (introduced species), including monoculture pine and eucalyptus forests and a great deal of broom.

Next we journeyed to Cuzco and the Inca ruins of famed Macchu Picchu. As all accounts led us to expect, it is an incredible place, memorably integrating natural splendor with human culture. To complete our tour, we descended to the coast to visit Paracas National Park (Reserve) and the adjacent Ballestas Islands, which are comparable to our own Farallon Islands a few miles outside San Francisco's Golden Gate—but much larger. This reserve protects seabird habitat on its 800,000 acres of land and water. Regrettably, nearly two-thirds of the reserve was slated for elimination to accommodate the scallop fisheries, which had expanded significantly during the El Niño year of 1982–83. We feared it would take tremendous will power on the government's part to safeguard this unique reserve—the only marine park in the nation.

Back in Lima, we met with leaders of various Peruvian conservation organizations, including ECCO (Asociacíon de Ecologia y Conservacíon Cetaceas Grupo), the Peruvian Society for Environmental Law, and others whose names I noted only as acronyms: ANCON, FPCN, and SPDA.

In 1988 and 1990, Peggy and I made journeys to Australia and New Zealand. On the first trip we spent most of our time in New Zealand on the south island, where we tramped the famed Routeburn Track that runs through Fiordland and Mt. Aspiring national parks. We drove and walked through the spectacular Westland and Nelson Lakes national parks, and we took an air tour that displayed Mt. Cook National Park in all its glory. During ten days in Queensland, Australia, we were fortunate to enjoy several days at the Great Barrier Reef, a magnificent marine national park encompassing some 3 million acres. We also visited national parks at Daintree River, Barron Falls, the Atherton Tablelands, and Cape Tribulation, where the rain forests grow from the mountains to the seacoast.

Our 1990 trip was a prelude to the IUCN assembly in Perth. On the way there, we explored the protected lands of New Zealand's north island with Bruce Jeffreys, east coast regional coordinator of the country's Department of Conservation and a friend since our trip to Bali. Bruce explained how the New Zealand conservation system worked: with national parks, protected forests, and historical parks under his department, and commercial forests under a separate Department of the Environment. After the general assembly in Perth, we spent a week in the extensive park-lands of Tasmania.

We were impressed by the wealth of protected lands in this part of the world, but it made sense: Australia and New Zealand became developed nations at a time when the principles of conservation had already been established in the United States, and they absorbed its lessons. They also had democratic governments that could work with conservation groups to foster protection, and a high percentage of outdoor enthusiasts among their people.

MY TRAVELS ABROAD had begun in Europe, and half a century later, my conservation work would take me back there with a new perspective on the Old World.

During my many years of close involvement with the IUCN's important Commission on National Parks and Protected Areas (CNPPA),

I attended significant regional conferences in Italy and Czechoslovakia (as well as one in Canada). In May 1989, Peggy and I attended the regional meeting of CNPPA in Florence. Among our objectives on this trip were to see and to evaluate specific national parks and protected areas in Italy.

Our visits included three days in Stelvio National Park in the Alps, just over the border from Austria and Switzerland. This scenically and biologically outstanding area seemed eminently worthy of national park status. We spent another three days in Abruzzi National Park, in Italy's Apennine Mountains, as guests of the Italian Forest Service. On this latter visit, we learned much about the agency and how it administers its land—for example, that it manages a critical "natural area" in the middle of Abruzzi National Park, less than three hours from Rome. We actually saw two grizzly bears there, part of a tiny population of the same species that inhabits North America.

National parks in Italy are a far cry from those in the United States, however. The federal government owns comparatively little land and administers just five national parks under two different jurisdictions. Selective logging is allowed in the Italian parks—as are grazing and mining, by permit—and tourism is encouraged.

In addition to the national parks, many reserved areas are designated and administered by the regions, provinces, and local communities. We visited several of these "nature parks" in the Alps and the Dolomites. From the scenic and biological point of view they were outstanding, but they had even less protection than the national parks. Grazing is prevalent, and tourism, with emphasis on skiing, is promoted. There are roads everywhere, including up the steepest, most precipitous gradients. Villages occupy perpendicular slopes on hillsides, often within the borders of a national park or other protected area.

At the end of a most pleasant and instructive month in Italy, I commented in my journal,

> There is the pressure of too many humans, too many vehicles,
> too much tourism everywhere. Cities are most obviously affected;
> the countryside is still kept rural. But the fields are all in use.
> The overwhelming problem is "what happens next?"

Everywhere the villages and cities clamor for more tourist trade. In Europe they are afraid of the dropping birth rate, that there are never enough people coming into the job market. But they don't want immigrants, especially of another race. . . .

What of the quality of life—with standing room only? Our amenities are disappearing, even as we try to protect areas. Pollution grows apace, smog; water in the canals of Venice and Amsterdam is filthy. How to get more cars on the roads? Superhighways, viaducts, and tunnels have defaced the hills and mountains in Italy. All the cities are hazardous to drive through.

The CNPPA Conference in Czechoslovakia took place in May and June of 1990, at the Hotel Horal in the middle of the Krkonose Mountains National Park. The conference reviewed actions taken by different member countries during the past year, and continued preparations for the upcoming IUCN General Assembly later that year in Perth. Visible from our conference center were several massive clear-cuts, as bad as any I've seen anywhere—justified as salvage logging of trees that had succumbed to acid rain.

On a field trip we visited several forest areas that were all monoculture Norwegian spruce, planted after a concerted logging program in the park, rather than native species or a healthy ecological mix. Conference participants all felt that much more work was needed to make Krkonose worthy of the title "national park." Conservation organizations in Czechoslovakia, we learned, were restricted in their activities to research on flora and fauna.

After the conference, Peggy and I enjoyed five days of sightseeing in historic Prague—still beautiful despite serious neglect during forty years of Communist rule. Restoration work was proceeding on several buildings, but very slowly and haltingly. Outside Prague we visited a Czech nature reserve with botanist Jarmilla Kubikova. Here a hundred acres were protected, an ecotone underlain with limestone and reflecting vegetation from as far west as Spain, as far north and east as Siberia.

On our own, although we felt a bit intimidated, we drove through the Czech and Polish countryside to Krakow, Poland, for a meeting with the Polish Ecological Club and to give interviews with the Polish print, radio, and TV media. The Ecological Club was trying to stimulate ecotourism to aid Poland's economy.

In the early 1980s I became involved with the World Wilderness Congress. The brainchild of Ian Player of South Africa, this was another periodic series of international conferences that began totally independently of the IUCN. To plan and conduct the first congress, in Johannesburg in 1977, Player hired a young man named Vance Martin, who has since assumed the principal role in the effort. At first, IUCN leadership would have nothing to do with this "rogue" effort that popped up outside its aegis. This attitude has softened over time, and today IUCN is a sponsor.

In 1983, Sierra Club president Denny Shaffer asked me to attend the third World Wilderness Congress near Inverness, Scotland. By now I was firmly convinced of the value of regular national and international gatherings to bring together policymakers and land preservation advocates, so that all might be inspired toward braver efforts and better coordination worldwide. Shaffer wanted me to assess whether the Club should abandon this congress or alternatively play a stronger role in it, so we could more effectively advance our concerns.

I was impressed by the possibilities that the congress presented for future action. With a cosponsor from South Africa, forester Bill Bainbridge, I proposed a resolution that wilderness be included as a separate category in the UN land classification system. Until then, the category of wilderness had been astonishingly absent. This was my first attempt to promote the idea on an international level; I wanted to establish a precedent the UN might eventually follow.

When this resolution was passed in Scotland, I took it next to the 1984 General Assembly of the IUCN in Madrid. I realized that it took time for new ideas to begin flowing through a large body of people representing many nations and interests; but I was encouraged that the assembly was at least willing to consider it. Four years later, in 1988, at the IUCN's General Assembly in Costa Rica, wilderness as a category was approved. And at the 1990 assembly, the designation of wilderness was finally included in Category I, under "strict protection."

The full CNPPA list of categories, adopted by the IUCN in 1992, was as follows:

I. Strict protection
   Ia. Strict Nature Reserve
   Ib. Wilderness Area
II. Ecosystem conservation and recreation
    (National Park)
III. Conservation of natural features
     (National Monument)
IV. Conservation through active management
    (Habitat/Species Management Area)
V. Landscape/seascape conservation and recreation
   (Protected Landscape/Seascape)
VI. Sustainable use of natural ecosystems
    (Managed Resource Protected Area)

The fourth World Wilderness Congress, held in 1987 in Estes Park and Denver, Colorado, was the one on which I had the most influence. As a member of the executive committee planning this major international event, I was involved for two years preceding the conference in detailed correspondence and several preparatory meetings in Fort Collins, Colorado. Notable proceedings of that conference included proposing the establishment of a World Conservation Bank, the first call for new conservation finance mechanisms, which eventually led to the $1.1 billion Global Environment Facility of the World Bank; the first World Wilderness Inventory, prepared for the WWC by the Sierra Club; continuing to advocate inclusion of wilderness as a separate classification under the World Conservation Union (IUCN) Categories of Protected Areas; and the first proposal for a World Conservation Corps, or Service, as an avenue for effective, public environmental action.

The Fifth World Wilderness Congress took place in Tromso, Norway, in the fall of 1993. Conflicting themes of wilderness exploitation and protection were a feature of many discussions here, and there was considerable emphasis on development. In a discussion of the Norwegian government's decision to resume hunting of Minke whales, for example, experts who favored the International Whaling Commission's ban on such hunting were excluded. But Norwegian proponents of whale hunting, who stressed the "legality" of their position, were present in overwhelming proportion.

Another contentious issue was the right to self-determination of native peoples, including the Lapps (or Sami) tribe of northern Norway and Sweden, indigenous inhabitants of Greenland, the Eskimos of northern Canada, and Natives in Alaska. Conservationists tended to fear that honoring self-determination claims by Natives would lead to destructive industrial development. Unfortunately, there was little opportunity for discussion of these controversial issues. Overall, I found the fifth Congress less well organized and integrated than the fourth. In Colorado, participants were housed together and physically well connected. In Norway, delegates stayed farther apart and came together less intensively.

WHILE MUCH OF my international travel has been in connection with organized conferences, I've also tried to fulfill personal travel goals. In December 1992 and January 1993, Peggy and I—along with our daughter Cynthia, her husband Jim, and their two children—took an extraordinary journey to the southernmost continent. We first enjoyed nearly four weeks traveling the length of Chile's varied landscape, visiting its superb national parks and stately native forests. But we also toured formerly forested areas, noting how the land had been degraded. Widespread monoculture plantations of exotic species, such as Monterey pine and eucalyptus, occupied land that previously had supported native forests, and in many areas, the destruction of globally significant native forests was extreme.

In Puerto Montt, we saw mountains of wood chips awaiting shipment to Japan, as well as huge quantities of lumber destined for the same fate. A bill providing for the restoration of native forests was being debated in Chile's parliament during our visit, indicating that at least some officials recognized that their worth as primeval forests was far greater than their monetary value as chips. Peggy and I also met with representatives of CONAF (Corporación Nacional Forestal), the Chilean agency that was endeavoring to monitor forest activities.

YOUR LAND AND MINE

From Chile, we joined a trip sponsored by Stanford University and embarked on the ship *World Discoverer,* bound for Antarctica. We sailed from Punta Arenas to the Falkland Islands, South Georgia, Elephant Island, and from there to the South Orkneys and South Shetlands before reaching the Antarctic continent. Our return took us through Drake's Passage in the Antarctic Ocean and around Cape Horn to Puerto Williams.

Our tour group numbered 130 passengers—the upper limit, I felt, for even brief visitation without excessive impact on Antarctica and the fragile subantarctic islands. (On South Georgia and the Falklands, where we spent much of our time, there had been considerable tourism already and our added imprint there did not concern me.) The trip left me believing that Antarctic cruises should be carefully limited in the future. Even in 1993, visits to this remote and sensitive ecosystem were becoming markedly more frequent, and their cumulative impact was sure to be profound. I soon joined the Antarctic and Southern Ocean Coalition (ASOC), organized to protect these marine environments, and served as a director of one of its constituent groups, the Antarctica Project, for half a dozen years.

The Antarctic is one of many arenas where the Sierra Club's international committee and program have been active. Until 1985 the international program remained based in New York. That year it was transferred to Washington, D.C., so that it could concentrate on what the Sierra Club does best—working with Congress and the executive agencies of the U.S. government. At this juncture we hired Larry Williams, who nurtured and led the program for the next thirteen years; he was succeeded by Stephen Mills, who holds the post as of this writing.

I have served on the Club's International Committee for most of the last thirty years and as its chair for seven years. While I chaired the committee, the need to work closely with NGOs in other countries became strikingly evident. Since the separate establishment of Sierra Club Canada in 1969, the Club steadfastly has declined to charter chapters in other foreign countries, instead choosing to work closely with like-minded NGOs and interested individuals abroad. It has been the International Committee's role to oversee that cooperation, with support from the International Program staff in Washington.

Throughout this time I have repeatedly urged the Club's board of directors to enlarge the international staff, to upgrade the status of the committee, and to provide funding for international campaigns. The board often has been reluctant, understandably concerned about allocating our limited funds and about whether more emphasis on international crusades would cut into our domestic efforts. I haven't pushed all-out; those who hope to guide organizations have to stay at their forefront but not too far ahead.

Other than supporting the international program and staff, my principal activities with the committee have focused on winning greater recognition within the Sierra Club of the importance of staying involved in the global arena, promoting much more active cooperation with environmental NGOs in other countries (including training and financial assistance), and expanding our efforts to establish and protect national parks around the planet.

The Club's international work is ongoing and ever growing. Progress seems slow, but the scope is enormous. Currently the Club's priority programs focus on global population control issues; human rights and the environment (including working on behalf of activists fighting pollution and irresponsible development, who are often persecuted for their efforts); and responsible trade practices that protect the world's natural heritage and our children's future. I'm proud to remain part of this work.

EPILOGUE

OF WHAT WILL WE DREAM?

❦

Ah, but a man's reach should exceed his grasp,
Or, what's a heaven for?

—Robert Browning

WHEN I BEGAN my conservation career, after the Second World War, most people considered the natural world a resource to be exploited for human benefit. Aside from its aesthetic value to poets and painters, nature was not perceived to hold any intrinsic value. Humans, in the view of modern, developed societies, were absolute masters of the earth. The land, the air, and the water were ours to use as we saw fit.

A populist conservation movement, a philosophy of wilderness, or even the term *conservationist,* as we now use it, did not exist. Many of those who sought to preserve natural landscapes were businessmen and professors; some were employed in mining companies, chemical firms, or real estate. They were often prominent in their fields, usually moderate in their politics. Such qualities were respected by the government leaders and custodial agencies who called on these men for advice. Most early preservationists served as friendly counselors in a spirit of cooperation; they did not confront or provoke. Such tactics would have been useless, since there wasn't enough public support to demand an audience for opposing views. Prewar wilderness advocates didn't register on the political spectrum. They were tolerated because their efforts did not disturb the power players of the time—and because they were friendly with the power players.

"Nature enthusiasts" was the usual name given to those interested in wild places. We were hikers and climbers, birdwatchers and skiers, our appreciation of nature linked to specific outdoor activities. Nature was something to be *enthusiastic* about, a hobby. Humankind's connection to our environment was not considered significant enough to warrant a spiritual relationship, let alone an ideology. Only a handful of true iconoclasts, such as Henry David Thoreau, George Perkins Marsh, and especially John Muir, insisted on a more profound relationship with wild nature.'

When the conservation movement bloomed in the 1950s and '60s, it was out of necessity. The emerging ideology of wilderness and the growing ranks of organizations were, at root, reactions and defenses against a sudden onslaught of human encroachment. The postwar boom that brought buildings, dams, roads, resource exploitation, and surging population required a response.

The Sierra Club was at the heart of this response, and its growth has been nothing short of extraordinary. Although I played a pivotal role in expanding the organization, its success continues to amaze me. In 1939 I joined a club of 3,000 volunteers. In 1952, the year I call the "turning of the hinge," the Club made several decisions—to grow, to grow nationally, and to hire a professional staff—that would change its nature forever. As of this writing, its rolls number more than 750,000, with members in all fifty states. Although it continues to rely on its dedicated volunteers, the organization employs 500 staffers, while its legal offshoot, Earthjustice, has eight offices and a staff of 150.

Despite its large size, the Club has not lost sight of the need for local action. Each of its sixty-five chapters concentrates on local issues as well as supports national campaigns. As I read the volunteer and staff reports from all over the nation, I feel pride in the effectiveness of the work.

My OWN IDEAS and goals have evolved along with the conservation movement. When I joined the Sierra Club, I was a nature enthusiast looking for adventure in the mountains. Later I became interested in preserving scenic beauty. But as I explored and learned about the open lands around San Francisco and the remaining wilderness throughout our nation, I came to realize that the key challenge was not to save postcard views and roadside tree corridors, but to protect natural ecological boundaries.

Nature does not recognize manmade boundaries. It has its own, etched by mountains and streams and shaped by winds. Rain falling west of the Continental Divide runs into the Pacific; rain falling east runs into the Caribbean Sea or the Atlantic. The water does not care how many states it must traverse to reach its destination. Watersheds, the areas drained between ridges, are the essential units of land protection. In the 1960s I learned that we need to protect not only watersheds but also larger *habitats*. Habitat comprises the land with its native plants and animals, as well as its air and water. Sustaining habitat requires an integrated vision of natural processes. Scenic magnificence is far from the only criterion in land conservation, perhaps not even the most important. Native vegetation and natural disasters, however messy and unpicturesque, fulfill functions in the natural order. Our best defense is to protect areas as large and intact as possible.

But even if the integrity of wild places has been violated, we can't give up on them. Although reclaiming lost wilderness is difficult and requires great patience, it is possible. For instance, there have been efforts to revive the salmon population in the Golden Gate National Recreation Area's Redwood Creek. I remember walking in Muir Woods in the 1930s and '40s, watching salmon two and three feet long swim upstream. Salmon are migratory fishes, very particular about where they spawn. They require a certain temperature and a certain mixture of sand and gravel. As in many places, overgrazing and logging destroyed the river banks and spawning beds. For many years sightings were rare, but thanks to restoration work, salmon are starting to repopulate Redwood Creek.

Two of the places closest to my heart—the GGNRA and Point Reyes—are not even truly wild. They bear human traces: roads and trails, visitor centers and oyster farms, as well as other evidence of development before the land became protected for the public. But these places are wild enough to maintain an elk reserve and a waterfowl sanctuary, and wild enough for humans to roam. For those who walk their trails—even for those no longer able to—these parks offer a sense of freedom and the solace of wildness.

IN ENVIRONMENTAL ADVOCACY, first comes a vision, then an obsession to do the job so that the vision will endure. In pursuing my obsession, I have followed a few rules to advantage:

- Choose your targets and don't be diverted. Always consider long-range as well as short-term objectives. With the constant onslaught on wilderness today, it is easy to get sidetracked into any number of issues. Clarity of purpose is critical.
- Never let anger take over. Certainly there have been occasions when my opposition's acts and words have aroused my wrath, but I've tried not to let negative reactions divert me from my goals.
- Keep the land from being chopped up. Whether the issue is a planned subdivision or clear-cut logging, the watershed must be protected. I learned this lesson during my early attempts to create a national park in California's redwoods, when the integrity of watersheds was neglected.
- Early compromise is the downfall of any conservation campaign. Proponents of the either/or philosophy argue that it can lead to a speedier resolution. But early compromise can kill a park or wilderness designation, either before legislation gets to the Capitol or after inadequate borders are put in place. Ask for less than your goal at the start and you will end up with even less. Ask for what you want and most likely you will still end up with less than the optimum, but it will be closer to the mark. Compromise may be inevitable but must be tolerated with reluctance.
- Environmental organizations must present a unified front whenever possible. Internal disputes will arise but are best kept behind the scenes. There is no easier excuse for Congress to avoid action than the opportunity to say: *If you guys can't make up your minds, how are we supposed to?*
- Finally, once you have taken hold of a project, follow through. Campaigns may reach climaxes, but they do not end.

I continue to be deeply involved with the fates of Redwood National Park and of open space in western and southern Marin County. And I am actively working to counteract ongoing attempts by developers, legislators, and administrations to undermine the Alaska National Interest Lands Conservation Act. As of this writing, we have just beaten back another push in Congress to authorize oil drilling in the Alaska National Wildlife

Refuge—but its proponents will not stay quiet for long. What seems safely protected may not always be so. Judges can overrule, Congress can repeal and amend, presidents can revoke, and the public, in fear and desperation, may demand measures harmful to the environment. Environmentalists are not aggressors; we are defenders, and so we must always be on guard.

At age ninety-six, I am concerned about the natural world not for myself; I am concerned about what will be left for my children and theirs. Collectively, we have very little time to change the way we live before habitable conditions on this planet disappear. Some researchers say we are already beyond the point of redemption. Perhaps this task should not fall so heavily on the present generation, who have inherited less of the earth than any previous generation and who are no more guilty than those who came before them. But I do believe this generation will be the last to have this choice—and it will require nothing less than a complete change in the way we live.

Environmentalists talk about *carrying capacity:* the ability of a community to sustain itself indefinitely using only the resources of a given space. Earlier societies coexisted with the land, and some cultures consciously valued spareness, deliberately not taking more than they needed. But even in ancient times, cultures that overpopulated and overexploited their resources paid the price: the Tigris and Euphrates rivers were once the lifeblood of booming civilizations; that land is now reduced to desert. The once-lauded cedars of Lebanon in ancient Israel are found only in history books. In the United States, and especially in California, we have reached a critical juncture.

Most of us agree that we must change the way we live on this planet, and that there are too many humans in the world. But we lack commitment to making the difficult changes needed for real solutions. Politicians avoid the issue of population control, fearful of its potentially racist overtones. But this issue must somehow be confronted: the ability of humans to reproduce is infinite, while our resources are not.

Some changes are in process: efforts at recycling, reducing toxic emissions, and reducing smog. These are minute, however, compared to what must be done in the coming decades. There are enormous obstacles to change, not least our own greed and ignorance. Most of us no longer live in close connection to the land; our survival is no longer tied to its fertility. And making money has become our dominant value: we care more about housing values than about the land our lives still depend on.

Environmentalists are often mocked for being overly sensitive. We must stand firm when derided as "hysterical" and resolute against charges of extremism. But the most malicious accusation, and the hardest to rebut, may be the claim that conservationists care more about a few birds and trees than we do about people. It is ironic that we can be characterized as emotionally fraught on the one hand, yet stolid and uncompassionate on the other. All these claims, however, miss a fundamental truth about environmentalists. We, too, act out of self-interest. Conservation is as much concerned with preserving human habitat as with the habitat of other species.

The health of our planet rests not only in its multitude of species but also in its inherent balance. Our species' survival is not aided by exterminating other species. We cannot improve upon the natural design, and yet time and again we justify our destruction of wild lands and natural systems on the basis of *need*. We have come to believe that we need certain things to lead a comfortable existence—a sports utility vehicle, a larger house, wider freeways—just as we *need* to clear-cut forests, mine mountains, and drill coastlines for new sources of oil.

We must learn modesty and coexistence. Human comfort is not the only important value on earth. And all too often, we underestimate the harmful effects of our actions on the natural world. Human impact is not just where we put our feet; our influence reaches into the very atmosphere and beyond. Holes in the ozone layer over the South Pole have existed for years and now occur over the North Pole as well. Scientists have discovered toxins—carbon dioxide, carbon monoxide, and DDT—in Antarctic ice samples. DDT has even been detected in the muscle tissue of polar bears. Humans do not live in these places, yet we have intruded from afar. I suggest that, rather than spill over into every available space, we, as a species, need to keep ourselves at bay. There are places on this earth where environments are so finely balanced, ecosystems so fragile, that humans should not trespass at all.

The past decade saw six of the hottest years on record. As global warming continues, scientists predict that plant species in the Northern Hemisphere will shift north, as will the migrations of birds. Some species may simply disappear: California's coastal redwood, *Sequoia sempervirens,* whose name means "forever green," may prove otherwise. But even if a particular species becomes extinct, it still is important that its former habitat remain unaltered by humans, kept intact for whatever nature intends to replace it.

THE FURTHER I have looked, the more value in wilderness I have seen. For wilderness does not merely add to the human condition. In essence, wild places represent possibility, what Wallace Stegner called "the geography of hope." Our curiosity about the unknown has inspired humans to wonder and to wander. We are drawn to the unfamiliar and the uncharted. What will happen to our spirit when every terrain has been mapped, purchased, and divided? What will be the value of our freedom if there is no difference between here and there? To where will we escape? Where will we roam? Wilderness is not a luxury; it is a necessity. An ocean horizon, a primeval forest, a mountain pass, an icy fjord—each waits, luring us forward with its call to adventure. Without wilderness, there is no adventure. And if not of adventure, of what will we dream?

The earth will continue to spin around the sun for millions of years. The moon will rise at night and fade with the breaking day. Clouds will gather, burst, and drop rain, and humans may perhaps continue to exist for as long as our planet does. But even if we manage to outlast our dwindling resources, will we be satisfied merely to subsist, propelling ourselves from one concrete mass to another?

Conservation is not merely a matter of keeping the planet alive or insuring the perpetuation of Homo sapiens. Conservation addresses our need as humans to perpetuate tolerable conditions on earth. We act out of what we consider to be our own long-term interest. And in protecting wild lands we seek not mere survival, but our hope, our solace, our inspiration, and our joy.

INDEX

INDEX